BARRON'S ART HANDBOOKS

THE RENAISSANCE

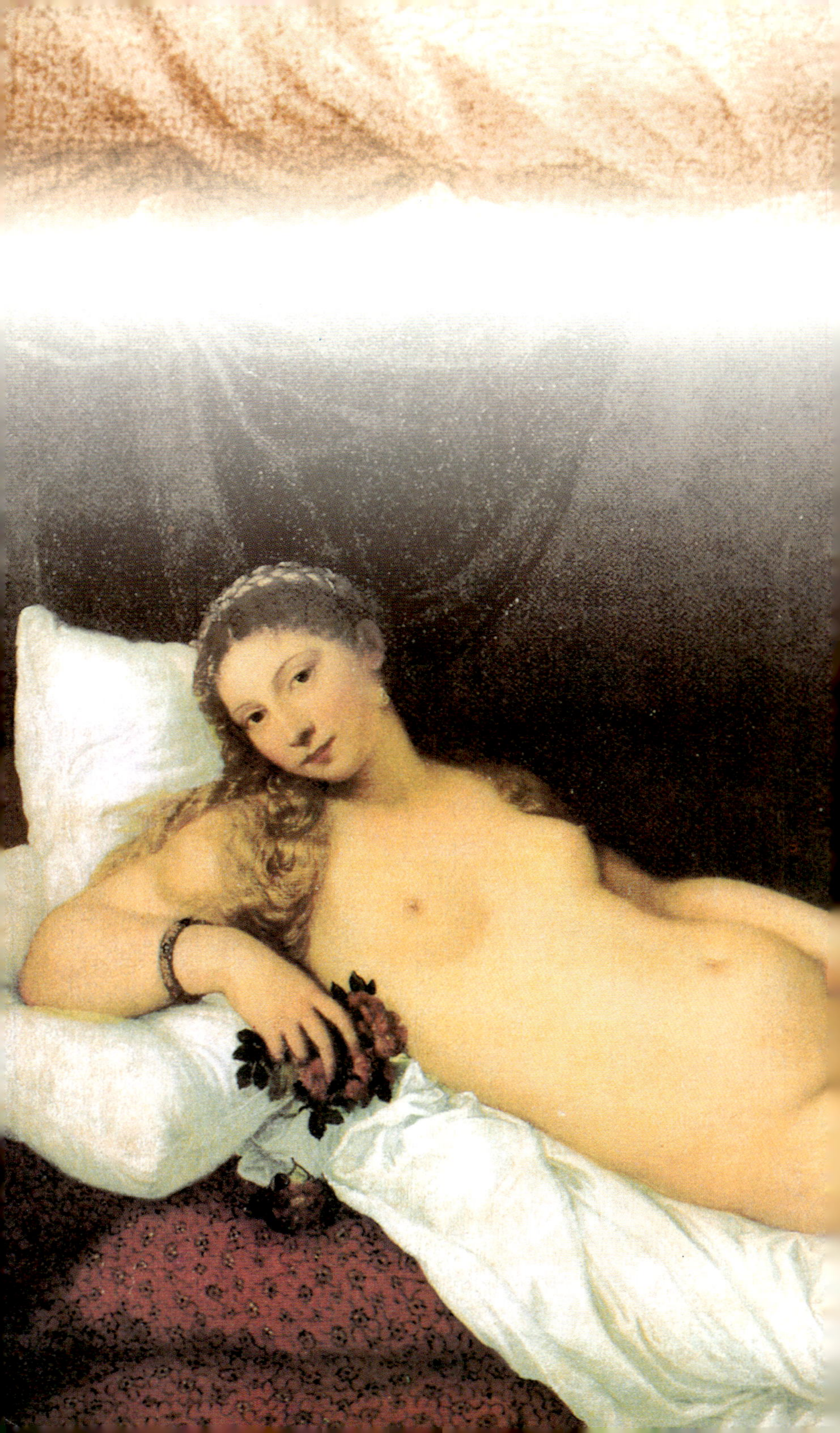

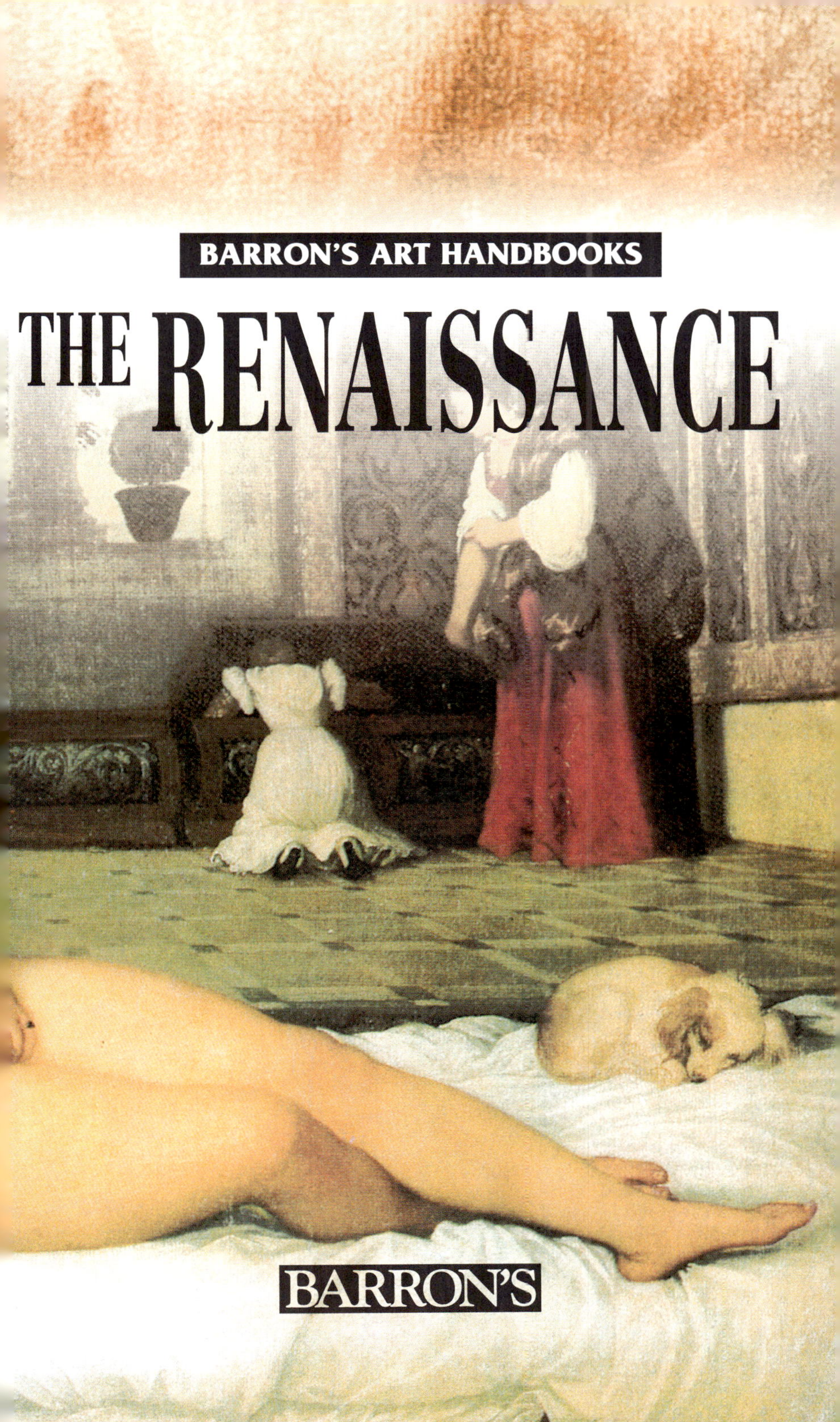
BARRON'S ART HANDBOOKS
THE RENAISSANCE
BARRON'S

CONTENTS

INTRODUCTION

The fifteenth century marks the end of the Middle Ages and the beginning of the Modern Age. Throughout Europe, culturally it represented the progressive abandonment of scholastic thinking, the birth of scientific reasoning, and the development of a culture that was more secular, critical, and interested in the individual.

Literary Humanism

The spirit of the Renaissance began to manifest itself through the literary humanism of Petrarch (1304–1374), Boccacio (1313–1375), and their many followers—men of letters who abandoned theology and medieval learning to study more closely Greek and Roman literature, which were considered humanist arts. Little by little, man and nature came to occupy the center of the cultural movement that today we call the Renaissance.

In the Florence of Lorenzo de' Medici, and under his direct patronage, the Platonic Academy was founded, presided over by Marsilio Ficino (1433–1499). The humanists were fervent admirers of Plato, discussing his ideas and translating his work. Great personalities, such as Pico della Mirandola (1464–1494), contributed to a greater knowledge of the ancient world and offered a new ideal of humanity. *The Divine Comedy* by Dante Alighieri (1265–1321) is the poetic expression of everything that was believed in the Middle Ages concerning God, the universe, and man. The humanist ideal shaped during the fifteenth century is defined in the work *Cortegiano,* written in 1514 by Baltasar Castiglione (1478–1529). A friend of Raphael, Castiglione describes the court of Gidobaldo de Montefeltro, Duke of Urbino, and explains the art of being the complete courtier. He presents a portrait of the Renaissance man as being a humanist interested in all aspects of culture: literature, art, music, and the natural sciences.

Until well into the fourteenth century, society in the Middle Ages had valued human individuality very little. The individual's work was considered a contribution to the common cause, in order to attain the supernatural destiny of the great Christian family after death. In contrast, the Renaissance man aspired to reaffirm his individuality, because he felt himself to be the center and measure of all things. It is the triumph of individualism that led human work to be valued and from which sprang great writers, painters, sculptors, architects, businessmen, scientists, and navigators, all of whom were admired by society and gave a hitherto unknown impulse to all human activities. A *pride in being human* appeared, as well as an enormous thirst for power, the cult of wealth, and the gradual disappearance of a transcendent meaning of life.

The Artists of the *Quattrocento*

In the intellectual world, with its base in humanistic thought, the social and professional value

Filippo Brunelleschi. Dome of the Cathedral of Florence, *Santa Maria dei Fiori (1417–1446). Arguably the first architectural project of the Renaissance, the construction of the dome represented the solution to serious technical problems. Its grandiose nature required a new system of construction to be invented so that it closes in on itself as it rises.*

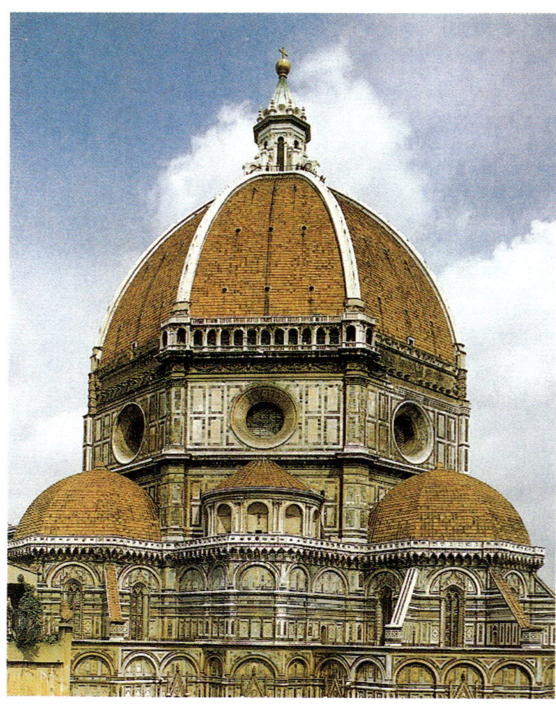

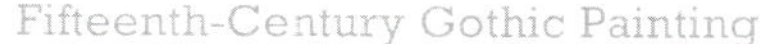

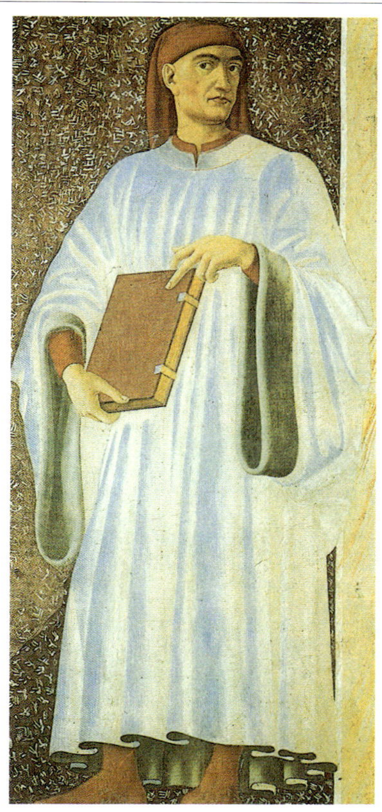

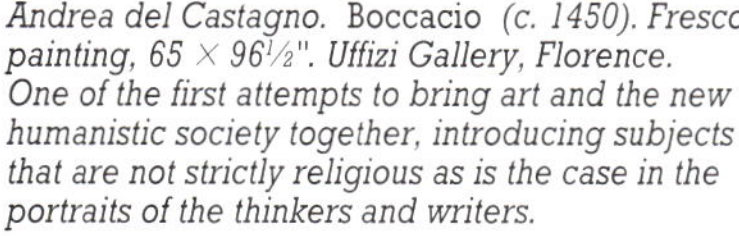

Andrea del Castagno. Boccacio *(c. 1450). Fresco painting, 65 × 96½". Uffizi Gallery, Florence. One of the first attempts to bring art and the new humanistic society together, introducing subjects that are not strictly religious as is the case in the portraits of the thinkers and writers.*

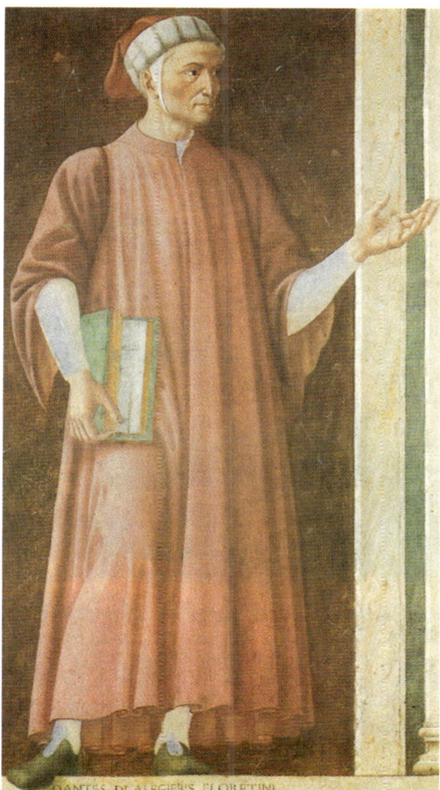

Andrea del Castagno. Dante *(c. 1450). Fresco painting, 65 × 96½". Uffizi Gallery, Florence. This work outlines the principal dilemma of the Renaissance, that is, in the realm of space, the desire to cross the terrain of the picture incorporating it into reality, as with the foot and the hand that stand out from the frame and introduce themselves into the reality.*

of art evolved slowly. The painters, sculptors, and architects of the *Quattrocento* (who were generally from modest backgrounds) were considered simple craftsmen. Neither natural talent nor genius gave the artist the right to work, but rather an apprenticeship (sometimes very long) acquired in the workshop of a master who, in accordance with the demands of the guild of craftsmen of the city, decided when the apprentice had reached the level of training to be a master. The demands of the guilds were not suspended until 1571 (and then only in Florence). The concept we have today of the artist is very different from that of the multiskilled artisan of fifteenth-century Italy.

The Multiskilled Artist of the *Quattrocento*

The work produced by the artistic workshops of the Italian cities of the first Renaissance was highly conditioned by the diversity of the commissions they received. These could consist of anything from a work of architecture to the design of gold and silver, or from an altarpiece to a multicolored statue. The varied nature of the artisans' work obliged the artist of the *Quattrocento* to master different techniques and to be multifaceted, as the artists of the Middle Ages had been. For example, the artist had to be architect, painter, sculptor, and goldsmith. Architecture was considered to be the most important skill, as it incorporated the other plastic arts and was, in turn, the most obvious manifestation of the new culture, which attempted to recover the constructive elements of classical antiquity. Brunelleschi, Michelozzo, and Alberti, for example, were sculptors of the *Quattrocento* who inclined toward architecture, in the same way that in the sixteenth century, two painters

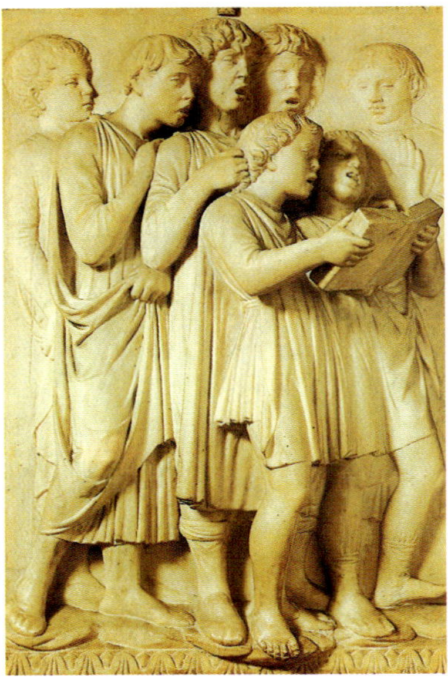

Luca della Robbia. Panel from the Cantoria *(1431–1438). Relief in marble, 41" × 42⅛". Cathedral Museum, Florence. It forms part of a series of works for the completion of the cathedral, which marked the beginning of the Renaissance. It is characterized by strong reference to classical tradition and deep understanding of the laws of perspective.*

such as Bramante and Raphael applied themselves with true genius to architectural creation. Michelangelo, essentially a sculptor and an architect, created one of the unmatched works of universal painting.

Nevertheless, architecture in the *Quattrocento* was never a well-defined profession, unlike painting, sculpture, and the other artistic professions, in that architects lacked a professional guild to look after their interests and attend to the needs of apprentices. The three great architects who "invented" the architecture of the Renaissance, Filippo Brunelleschi (1377–1446), Michelozzo di Bartolomeo (1396–1492), and Leon Battista Alberti (1404–1472), the first theorist of Renaissance architecture, each worked individually to develop their ideas and establish the foundations of the coming centuries.

Patrons

Another change produced by the humanist culture of the first Renaissance, to the detriment of what is traditionally called scholastic culture (based on theology), was the growing value placed on art by intellectuals and the ruling classes. From the beginning of the fifteenth century, these people began to take pride in their artisans, who were capable of filling the interiors of their great mansions and churches with artistic beauty (a beauty that was increasingly related to realism) and could adorn their powerful city-states with beautiful buildings and monuments.

And although the artist, from a professional point of view, continued to be viewed as a craftsman, the desire of the ruling classes to use the services of the best architects, painters, and sculptors improved the social position of these craftsmen. Finally, humanism, related to the arts, had two effects:

First, the multidisciplinary training of the craftsmen gave way to a certain degree of specialization, which was necessary in order to achieve the perfection that the ruling classes demanded of each work, whether in painting, sculpture, or architecture.

Secondly, in order to guarantee the services of the best artisans, a great nobleman would become his patron, being almost paternal in his protection. The price for this paternalism was a long list of demands, some of which even threatened the dignity of the artist. The patrons demanded from their craftsmen a wide range of work, not only as far as their artistic specialties were concerned but also in terms of the intrinsic importance of their specialties. Great artists were employed as conservators of antique collections, as painters of furniture and murals, as woodcarvers or architects, and at the same time they were asked to create new weapons, to design the costumes for an opera or a ballet, or to plan court parties. This was the case with Paolo Uccello, Filippo Lippi, Ghirlandaio, and Botticelli, under the patronage of the Medici family in Florence. In Urbino, Piero della Francesca worked under the protection of Federico II of Montefeltro; in Ferrara, the Este family were patrons of Cosimo Tura and Francesco del Cossa. Segismundo Malatesta de Rimini (1417–1468), the Gonzaga family of Mantua, and the Popes of Rome were also great patrons who encouraged the arts.

Proof of the level of appreciation for art and artists that existed in the republics of Renaissance Italy is given by the above-mentioned Baldassare Castiglione when, in *The Book of the Courtier,* he recommends that to complete their artistic and musical training, courtiers should learn the art of drawing.

An Empirical Understanding of the World

During the Middle Ages, the artistic qualities of the representation of the figure were never considered to be of fundamental importance. Medieval art was basically an artistic expression of a code of conduct in which the only important aspect was the meaning, rather than formal elements of the way the message was conveyed. This was due to spiritual idealism rather than realistic idealism.

Renaissance art, on the other hand, gave particular importance to the artistic values of the

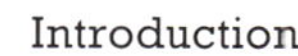

Donatello. Saint George *(1415–1417). Marble sculpture, 82 1/3" high. Bargello Museum, Florence. Donatello is probably the most important artist of the Italian* Quattrocento. *In his sculpture he aspired to emulate the models of ancient statuary. In* Saint George, *the* schiatto *bas-relief of the base of the statue is notable. This is a technique that achieves a spatial effect through the superimposition of very fine layers.*

representation of the figure, although thematically it continued to be linked to Catholic morality and dogma.

The method of painting and sculpting no longer related to a spiritual idealism, but rather to specific laws, closely related to the empirical sciences of the fifteenth century: mathematics, geometry, optics, perspective, mechanics, anatomy, and the theory of light and color.

For the artists of the *Quattrocento,* the arts were sciences, and hence were a way to understand reality and explain it artistically. The artist drew closer to the natural world and acquired empirical knowledge, from which he could deduce rational laws that allowed him to master drawing, shape, and color. Proportion was a question of geometry, space was a problem of perspective, and the shapes of the human body no longer corresponded to an idealistic and intuitive vision but rather to an extensive knowledge of the body's anatomy.

Sculptors

The artistic humanism of the *Quattrocento* manifested itself in sculpture more emphatically and with fewer concessions to Gothic art than in painting. In his reliefs in the Baptistry in Florence, Andrea Pisano (1290–1348) was already demonstrating a surprising assimilation of the classical aesthetic in work of purely Gothic spirit. Likewise, Lorenzo de Bertoluccio, better known as Lorenzo Ghiberti (1378–1455) and Brunelleschi, whom we have already mentioned, still demonstrated a Gothic spirit, despite the fact that the classically inclined realism of their figures had progressed far beyond Pisano.

The artist Jacopo della Quercia (1374 or 1375–1438) from Siena was already an innovative sculptor, both in his figures, which were closer to nature, and also in his ideas concerning composition, which was notable for the force of its expression and doubtless had an influence on Michelangelo.

Nanni di Banco (c. 1382–1421) a sculptor of magnificent classical elegance, Donatello (Donato di Niccolo di Betto Bardi) (1386–1466), and Lucca della Robbia (1400–1482) were already, in formal terms, Renaissance sculptors.

The Florentines Agostino di Duccio (1418–1481) and Andrea di Cione, known as *Verrocchio* (1435–1488) can complete this list of the great exponents of Italian sculpture of the *Quattrocento* without whom the Renaissance would not have had the same impact on all the figurative arts. It is important to mention that despite the fact that the subject of this guide centers on painting, during the Renaissance painting developed around formal concepts very similar to those proposed by the sculptors.

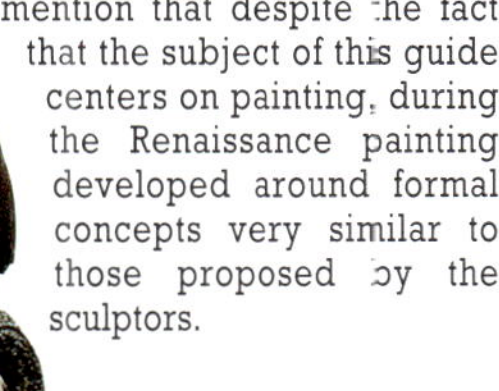

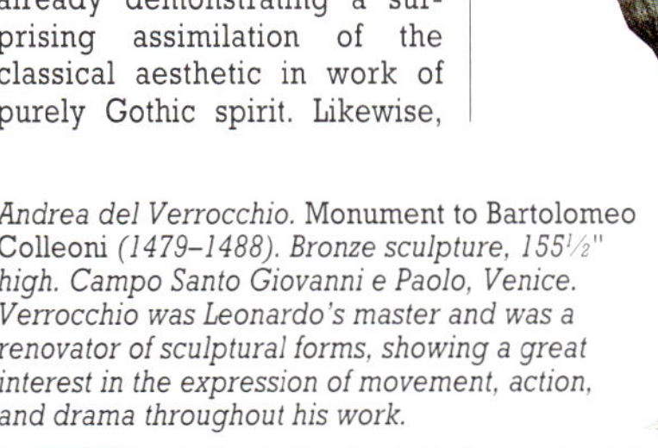

Andrea del Verrocchio. Monument to Bartolomeo Colleoni *(1479–1488). Bronze sculpture, 155½" high. Campo Santo Giovanni e Paolo, Venice. Verrocchio was Leonardo's master and was a renovator of sculptural forms, showing a great interest in the expression of movement, action, and drama throughout his work.*

GOTHIC PAINTING AT THE BEGINNING OF THE FIFTEENTH CENTURY

While Gothic architecture and sculpture did not take root in the area of Tuscany and central Italy, due largely to the strong presence there of ancient art, the last painting that can still be considered Gothic reached a veritable high point in Florence at the beginning of the fifteenth century.

Late or International Gothic

In Europe, in the last third of the fourteenth century and the beginning of the fifteenth century, the taste for beauty grew. The cause was a refinement of a newly emerging bourgeoisie that demanded artistic products that before had been the exclusive patrimony of the nobility and the church. Gothic art (not just painting) underlined the importance of decoration and the embellishment of sinuous lines. Late or international Gothic painting, in which the Gothic mentality was preserved, arose from painting in which formal goals were clearly in evidence, leading to the natural realism of the Renaissance.

Late or International Gothic in Florence at the Beginning of the Fifteenth Century

The elegance and luxury that characterized International Gothic painting in the courts of Europe inevitably satisfied the desire for magnificence of noble Florentine ladies and also of the church, which saw in painting an efficient way to express and transmit its idealism and mysticism, as well as the splendor of its rituals.

The Uffizi Gallery in Florence holds the most significant paintings of International Gothic (with many works by anonymous artists) whose influence can be felt even in those painters of the *Quattrocento* who decisively opted for the new, naturalist ways of Florentine humanism. Within the context of late Florentine Gothic, and the Uffizi collection, three artists are most representative of the incorporation of the sense of naturalism.

Gherardo Starnina

Little is known about the life of this painter, who worked in Italy (Florence) and Spain (Valencia and Toledo) during the final years of the fourteenth century and the early years of the fifteenth. It is known that in 1387 he was inscribed in the Guild of Saint Luke in Florence, and that between 1398 and 1401 he created paintings and frescoes in Valencia and in the cathedral of Toledo. When he returned to Florence (around 1409), he worked in the chapel of San

Gherardo Starnina. The Thebais *(end of fourteenth century). Tempera on panel, 146½ × 97¼". Uffizi Gallery, Florence. A follower of the academic and allegorical movement, Gherardo Starnina is a painter whose work is still little known but who was a great influence in Florence in the second half of the fifteenth century.*

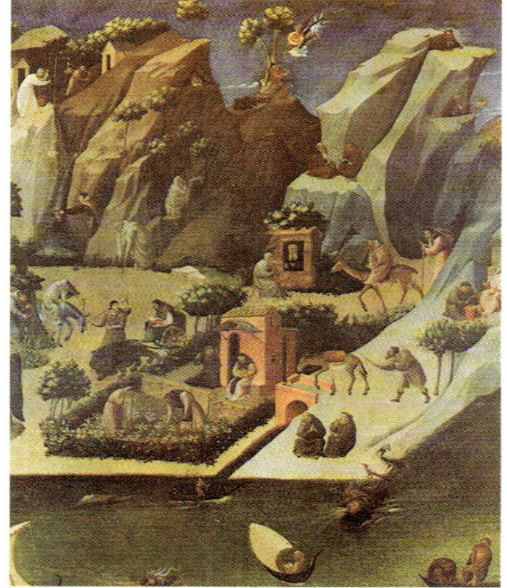

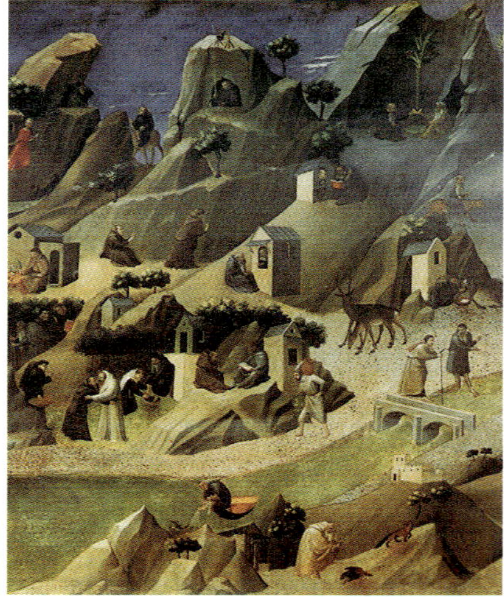

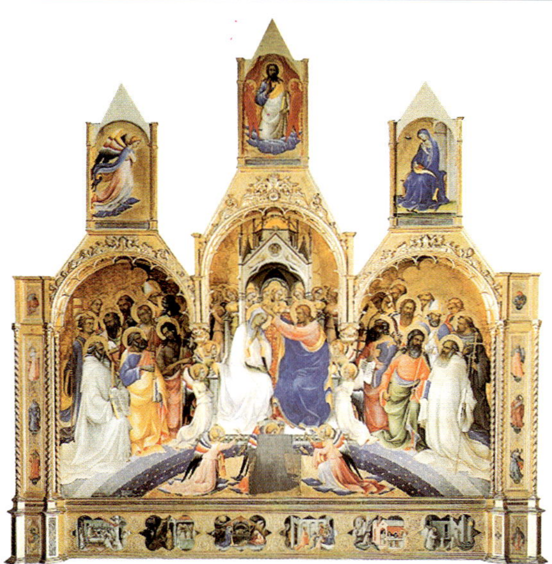

Lorenzo Monaco. Coronation of the Virgin *(1413). Painting on panels, 101⅕ × 146½". Uffizi Gallery, Florence. Without abandoning the tradition of Giotto, Lorenzo Monaco introduced in his works of mystical character more popular elements, appropriate to his monastic life.*

Esteban in Empoli, near Florence. A *triptych of the charterhouse of the Gates of Heaven* (Museum of Valencia) is attributed to him, although with little basis.

The Uffizi Gallery has a painting entitled *The Thebais,* which has traditionally been attributed to Starnina, although recently serious doubts have arisen over its authority, since it is believed that the painting dates from post-1420, whereas Starnina died around 1413. The painting, from the Florentine school, shows an unusual Theban landscape peopled by monks and anchorites. From a perspective of the evolution of painting to naturalist tastes, one should appreciate the minute realistic detail with which the figures have been treated, and the details of the complex location.

Lorenzo Monaco

This monk from Siena (c.1370–1423) was trained in the Gothic school of painting but was able to incorporate into his work the formal grace of the naturalist tendencies of Late European Gothic, which was beginning to appear in the plastic arts in the final years of the fourteenth century. His coloring, doubtless inherited from the miniaturists who worked in the scriptorium of the convent of Santa Maria degli Angeli, uses chiaroscuro not as much to convey relief as to achieve an austere mysticism, together with a certain drama. The gestures and dark tones of some of the figures give a dramatic feeling to a style of painting that, perhaps unconsciously, includes an incipient humanism.

The Coronation of the Virgin with Saints and Angels of 1414 and the *Adoration of the Magi* (both of which are in the Uffizi Gallery) are his most notable works. The predella of the altarpiece of the coronation shows scenes with characters represented in a deliberately realistic environment.

Gentile da Fabriano

Gentile de Niccolò de Giovanni de Massio (c. 1370–1427), known as Gentile da Fabriano, is the most important representative of Florentine International Gothic. Born in Fabriano, a city in the province of Ancona, Italy, he was trained in the artisans' workshops of Siena, Orvieto, and Perusa, which instilled in him a love of miniatures and of detail in gold. He was successful in translating this detail into his large-scale works, turning them into depictions of a subjective reality that is extraordinarily luminous and entirely idealized. His masterpiece, the altarpiece of the *Adoration of the Magi* (Uffizi Gallery) of 1423, is characterized by the extraordinary richness of the figures, which form an endless procession to the feet of the holy family. Despite its size (118 × 111") it maintains all the characteristics of a miniature. A magnificent work of art, it is notably influenced by Oriental taste, as shown in the clothes, the harnesses of the horses, and even the fantastical city that crowns the landscape through which the fabulous entourage of the Magi travels.

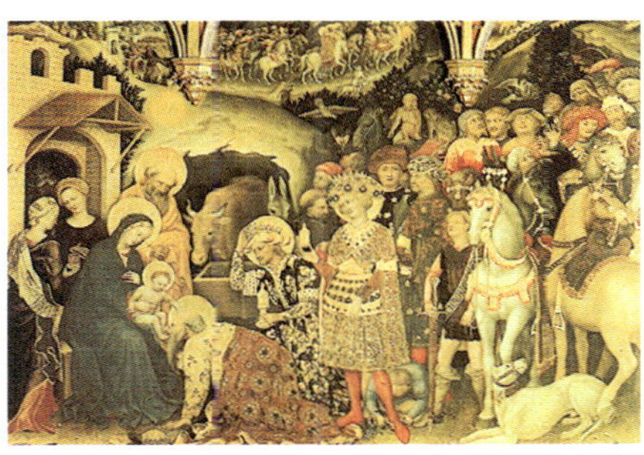

Gentile da Fabriano. Adoration of the Magi *(1423). Painting on panels, 118 × 111". Uffizi Gallery, Florence.*

FROM GOTHIC IDEALISM TO RENAISSANCE NATURALISM

FRA ANGELICO

The great example of human naturalism that Giotto gave in the fifteenth century with his frescoes in Padua and Assisi was continued in the Italian painting of the *Quattrocento,* with the appearance and affirmation of classical naturalism. The aesthetic change, which represented a move from the idealism of Gothic painting to the naturalism of Renaissance painting, was marked by the work of artists of greatly differing character. Consequently, their contributions to the change came as responses to aesthetic concepts that also differed widely, although their common goal was to achieve naturalism in representation. The Dominican Fra Giovanni da Fiesole, known as Fra Angelico, is without a doubt the *Quattrocento* painter who most clearly straddles the two tendencies.

The Painting and Work of Fra Angelico

In order to understand and value the work of Fra Angelico, one cannot disassociate his deep religiousness from his ideas concerning the aims of the art of painting. Fra Angelico did not paint (nor did he wish to) the temporality and individuality of beauty arising from human anatomy. For Fra Angelico beauty in art is a reflection of the ideal, transcendent beauty that can be seen in humans and in things. In this sense, his painting is linked to Gothic idealism. For him it is more important to reflect the beauty of what is good and pleasant than to approach reality through naturalism.

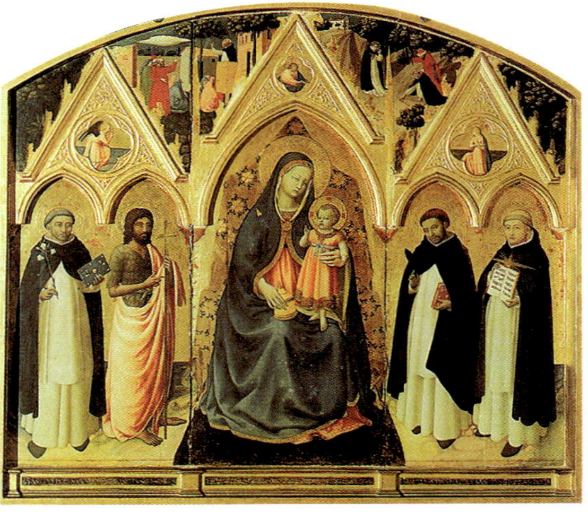

Fra Angelico. Triptych of Saint Peter the Martyr *(1425–1428). Tempera on panel, 66⅛ × 54 ". St. Mark's Museum, Florence. The career of Fra Angelico begins in Florence in 1417, and becomes more active from 1423 with his entry into the convent of San Domenico of Fiesole. This triptych is his earliest surviving work.*

Naturalist Aspects of the Work of Fra Angelico

Already in the *Triptych of Saint Peter the Martyr* of 1425–1428 (St. Mark's Museum, Florence) despite the Gothic idealism that inspired its creation, one can appreciate a certain naturalism in the restrained treatment of the forms, something entirely original in comparison with court Gothic. This naturalism is a reminder of the influence of the work of Giotto and the Tuscan Masaccio, one of his contemporaries, which can be seen in the side panel (the expulsion of Adam and Eve from Paradise) of *The Annunciation* (1430–1435) in the Prado, a key work in the history of painting. In this work the Gothic spiritualism of the Siena school shapes the figures of the Virgin and the angel. But these Gothic figures are bounded by a Renaissance portico, to whose left the figures of Adam and Eve as they abandon Eden (a garden that is very conventional and minutely detailed, so that it seems to have come from a Pompeiian painting) respond to a completely naturalistic form of human figuration. Such naturalism is in marked counterpoint to the idealism of the characters that, in a manner of speaking, belong to the celestial world.

This dichotomy is present throughout the painting of Fra Angelico, at times with a predominance of Gothic idealism, at times with naturalism predominating, and these two tendencies seem to enter into contradiction with the general spirit of the work under consideration. In *The Coronation of the Virgin* of 1430 (Uffizi Gallery) and *Last Judgment* (1433–1435) a panel in the St. Mark's Museum, for example, perspective and composition,

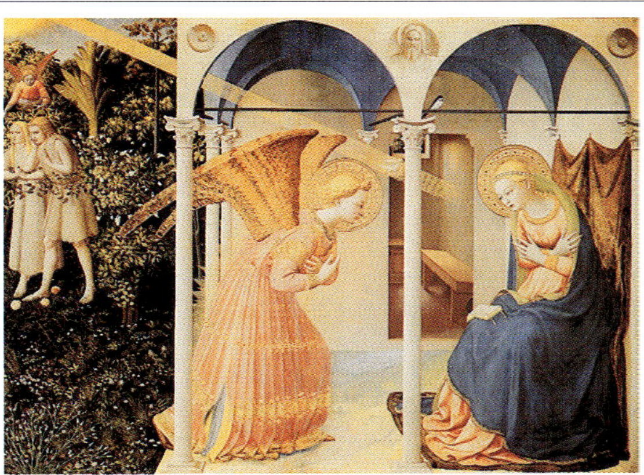

Fra Angelico. The Annunciation *(1430–1435). Tempera on panel, $76\frac{3}{8} \times 76\frac{3}{8}$". The Prado, Madrid. Originally painted for the Church of San Domenico of Fiesole, it is one of the works that arose from the collaboration of the friar with the miniaturist Zanobi Strozzi, who joined the convent in 1430. This joint work inspired Fra Angelico to further develop Florentine naturalism.*

which give a Renaissance flavor to some fragments of the work, contradict the general treatment of the work as a whole, which is in the Gothic tradition. In *The Linaiuoli Altarpiece* of 1433 (St. Mark's Museum), in *The Annunciation* in the Church of San Domenico of Cortona (1433–1434), and in the *Triptych of Perusa* (1437), Fra Angelico reveals his taste for perspective and space, with figures that have a clearly volumetric nature.

A special mention must be made of the frescoes of St. Mark's in Florence (from 1437) and those he painted for the chapel of Nicholas V in the Vatican, between 1447 and 1450. The ones in St. Mark's have an intimate character, devoid of any proselytizing or indoctrinating function. They represent a form of painting that is entirely free of superficiality and that was painted not to be admired but rather to preserve the internal fervor of the friars. *Noli me tangere,* a painting that is spatial in concept, despite its formal conventionality, *Holy Conversation, The Coronation of the Virgin,* and *The Annunciation* are scenes that reveal a concept of composition and space that is linked to a Renaissance perspective.

The frescoes in the Vatican, which he painted for Pope Nicholas V, show episodes in the life of Saint Lawrence and Saint Stephen, and do not demand the artist's usual mysticism and ingenuity, but rather his capacity for historical evocation. Here he creates majestic architecture in which he places naturalistic human groups.

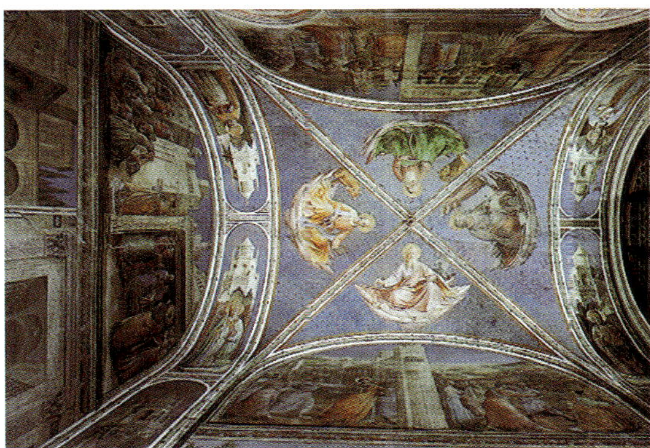

Fra Angelico. Scenes from the Lives of Saint Lawrence and Saint Stephen *(1447–1450). Fresco. Chapel of Nicholas V. The Vatican, Rome.*

THE ARTIST'S LIFE

The life of Fra Angelico is not one of a religious painter but rather of a religious man who painted and who, according to Vasari, never picked up his paintbrushes without having dedicated himself to prayer. It is a life that was divided between his obligations as a Dominican friar and his work as an artist.

1397. Guido di Pietre is born in Vicchio, a village in Tuscany.

1407. He enters the Dominican convent of Fiesole, taking the name Fra Giovanni de Fiesole.

1417. It is known that in this year Fra Giovanni, known as Fra Angelico, features as an independent painter of Florence.

1423. He is ordained as a priest and increases his artistic activity in the convent of San Domenico of Fiesole.

1437. In Florence he paints the mural decorations of the cells of St. Mark's convent.

1447–1450. He lives in Rome, where he is ordered by Pope Nicholas V to decorate his chapel.

1455. He dies in Rome.

THE BIRTH OF RENAISSANCE PAINTING (I)

THE FORMAL REVOLUTION OF MASACCIO

The evolution of painting toward naturalism, from late Gothic on, is due to the summation (and later assimilation) of aesthetic concepts introduced by greatly differing artists of the *Cinquecento:* Masaccio, Paolo Uccello, Filippo Lippi, Andrea del Castagno, Ghirlandaio, and many others, who were the pioneers of the birth of what would become the great painting of the fifteenth century.

The Painting and Work of Masaccio

Tommasso di Giovanni di Simone Guidi, known as Masaccio, was the first painter of the *Quattrocento* who unreservedly embraced naturalism to achieve a three-dimensional, volumetric painting that sprang from the real world, away from the artificiality of golden backgrounds. The forms no longer required linear outlines, and became the translation of visual sensations through a language of perspective, light, and color.

The short life of Masaccio (1401–1428) possibly terminated the anticipated dawn of the great painting of the *Cinquecento.* What we know of his artistic output occupies only the final three years of his life.

The first Masaccio is closely linked to Masolino (1383–1447), a notable master of late Gothic with whom he collaborated. From their collaboration arose such significant works as the panel *Virgin and Child with Saint Anne and Five Angels* (Santa Ana Meteraza) of 1424–1425 (Uffizi Gallery) in which Masaccio's naturalist style can be seen in the central figures, which are compact and modeled with excellent chiaroscuro. The figures of *Crucifixion* of 1426 (National Museum of Capodimonte, Naples) painted on gold, show the same characteristics.

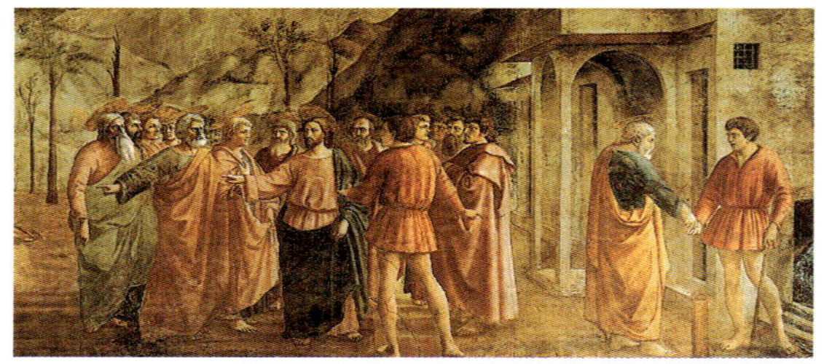

Masaccio. The Tribute Money *(1427). Fresco painting, 235½ × 100⅜". Brancacci Chapel, Santa Maria del Carmine, Florence. The story of the miracle of the coin in the fish's mouth occupies a marginal position in the painting, which suggests that beyond the story of the gospel the painting conceals a more everyday meaning. The paying of the tribute represents the recently instituted obligation of all citizens to pay taxes to the registry of the city of Florence from 1427.*

But it is the predella panel of the altarpiece for the church of Santa Maria del Carmine in Pisa (a polyptych that is now dispersed among different institutions) in which Masaccio's painting makes the definitive leap to a Renaissance aesthetic. The work in question is *Adoration of the Magi,* in which light and color achieve a volumetric, clearly naturalistic feel. The three characters adoring the child are real beings, deprived even of the traditional halo of sainthood, and wearing the typical clothing of Florentine gentlemen of the fifteenth century. Exoticism and sophistication have disappeared entirely from this small work, as a consequence of Masaccio's desire for naturalism, and for the representation of reality, which led him to a total renovation of painting.

Masaccio. Adoration of the Magi *(1426). Paint on panel, 24 × 8¼". Predella of the altarpiece of the church of Santa Maria del Carmine in Pisa. National Museums, Berlin. This painting forms part of a larger altarpiece that is now dispersed among various museums. Despite the correct form of perspective and the humanist nature of the work, it still shows characteristics of the Gothic past in its use of gold.*

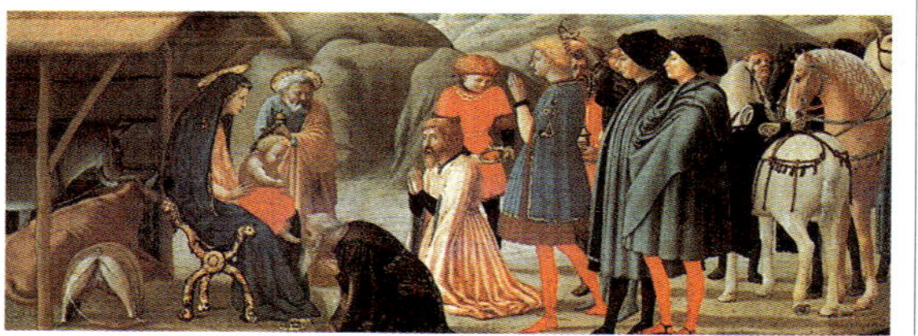

Masaccio and Perspective

Masaccio was deeply interested in perspective, the science of drawing that he mastered with genuine virtuosity, as is shown in

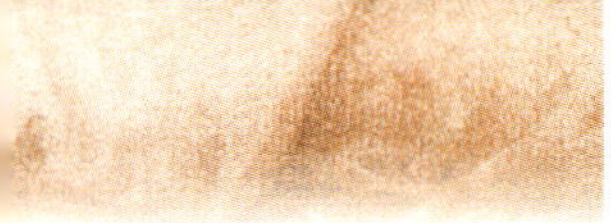

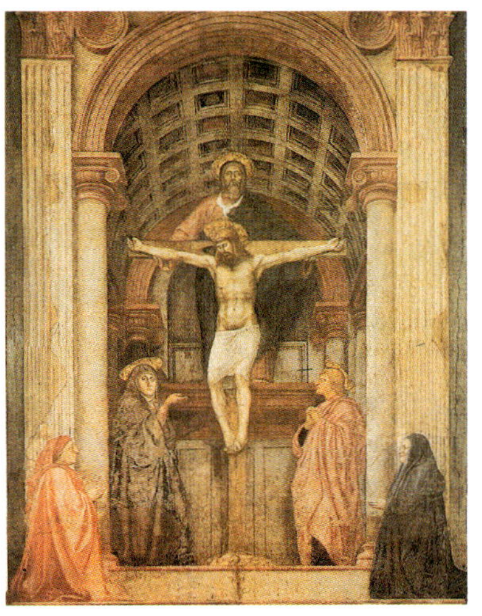

Masaccio. The Trinity *(1427). Fresco painting, 124¾ × 262½". Santa Maria Novella, Florence. Next to the representation of the trinity appear the donors of the work, who achieve divine dimensions. Below, death is represented by a skeleton accompanied by the warning "I was once what you are now, and what I am now you will one day be."*

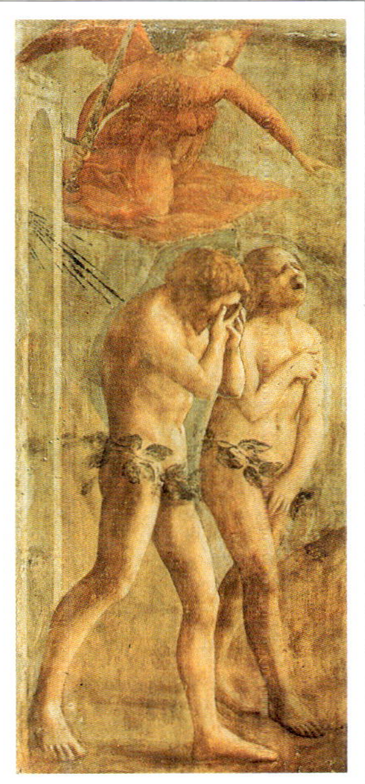

Masaccio. The Expulsion from Paradise (1427). *Fresco painting, 34⅝ × 81⅞". Brancacci Chapel, Santa Maria del Carmine, Florence.*

The Trinity, a fresco in Santa Maria Novella, Florence (1427), and a key work in the development of perspective. The work is a simulated piece of architecture. A painted chapel with a coffered barrel vault ceiling opens out into the central nave of the church by means of an arch flanked by thick pilasters and a rich entablature.

The Frescoes of the Brancacci Chapel

The master works of Masaccio are the frescoes that he painted between 1426 and 1428 for the walls of the Brancacci chapel, Santa Maria del Carmine, Florence, some of them in collaboration with Masolino. The most notable is the one that shows the evangelical scene *The Tribute Money* (Matthew 17, 23). It is a narration that offers different time frames within the same compositional space. In the center is Jesus, surrounded by his disciples, instructing Peter on what he should do to get the money that will allow him to pay the tribute demanded by the tax collector of Cafarnaum. The apostle, with a gesture, points to the left to a scene in which he fulfills his master's order, when he finds the coin in the mouth of a fish. To the right, in a third narrative time frame, Peter pays the tribute before entering Cafarnaum. The expectant immobility of the apostles, who surround the extraordinarily noble figure of Jesus, give the figures a remarkably majestic, statuelike quality. This work was admired by Michelangelo and Raphael.

The same chapel contains other notable scenes: *Saint Peter Baptizing, Saint Peter and Saint John Healing with their Shadows, The Raising of Tabitha, Raising the Son of Theophilus* (Masolino-Masaccio), *Saint Peter in the Cathedral of Antioch,* and *Distribution of the Goods of the Church.* The most surprising fragment in the series is *The Expulsion from Paradise.* It was the first time in the history of art that a biblical scene had been represented as a human drama. The expressions of Adam and Eve show their despair and reveal all the profound drama of humankind.

THE ARTIST'S LIFE

1401. Born in San Giovanni Valdarno (Florence) on December 21.

1417–1422. He arrives in Florence. Nothing is known of him until he enters the guild of doctors and pharmacists.

1423. He begins his collaboration with Masolino and according to Vasari makes a journey to Rome.

1424. He enters the guild of San Lucas of Florence.

1425–1426. Many of the chronological dates of his life are uncertain. It is possible that between 1425 and 1427 he paints the fresco of *The Trinity* in Santa Maria Novella, Florence. In 1426 he paints the famous predella of the altarpiece of the church of Santa Maria del Carmine in Pisa.

1427–1428. He paints the frescoes of the Brancacci Chapel, Santa Maria del Carmine, Florence.

1428. He moves to Rome to work with Masolino and dies there, reportedly poisoned.

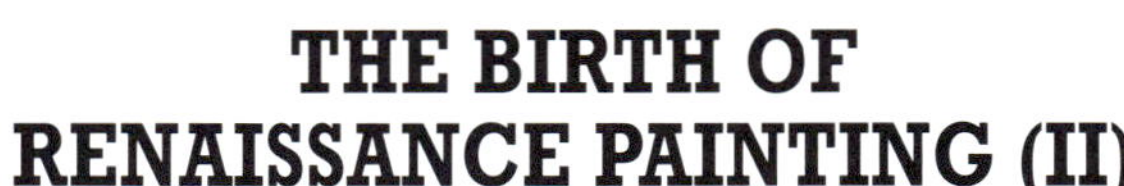

THE BIRTH OF RENAISSANCE PAINTING (II)

VOLUME AND LINEARITY IN *QUATTROCENTO* NATURALISM

In the search for volumetric qualities in pictorial figuration, the Florentine Paolo Uccello played a decisive part and was the most significant of the fifteenth-century constructivists. At the other end of the spectrum is the painting of Filippo Lippi, a manifestation of Renaissance naturalism that was still able to maintain the elegance of International Gothic linearity.

The Painting and Work of Paolo Uccello

Paolo Uccello trained alongside various sculptors; he collaborated with Ghiberti on the great door of the Baptistry of Florence, and he was a pupil of Donatello. This explains why his painting is dominated by a sense of volume. This tendency and his obsession with perspective made Paolo Uccello more of a "mathematical" painter than an emotive one.

There are not many works that can be attributed to him with absolute certainty. It is thought that the Gothic-like work entitled *Tabernacle of Lippi and Maccia* (1416) is one of the works of his youth. It could also be argued that he contributed to *The Story of Genesis* in the old cloisters of Santa Maria Novella, with some small-scale portraits that show a marked taste for volume. His sculptor's vision of form shows itself in *The condottiero Giovanni Acuto* (or Sir John Hawkwood) of 1436 in the Santa Maria dei Fiori Cathedral in Florence. It is a painted monument that is drawn with a perspective from two points of view, one for the base and another for the equestrian grouping. His enthusiasm for perspective can also be seen in *The Nativity of the Virgin Mary* and *The Presentation of Mary at the Temple* (1440), murals in the Prato Cathedral in Tuscany, and in his ingenious version of the legend of Saint George and the Dragon, of 1460 (National Gallery, London) a minor work with the air of a *divertimento* of

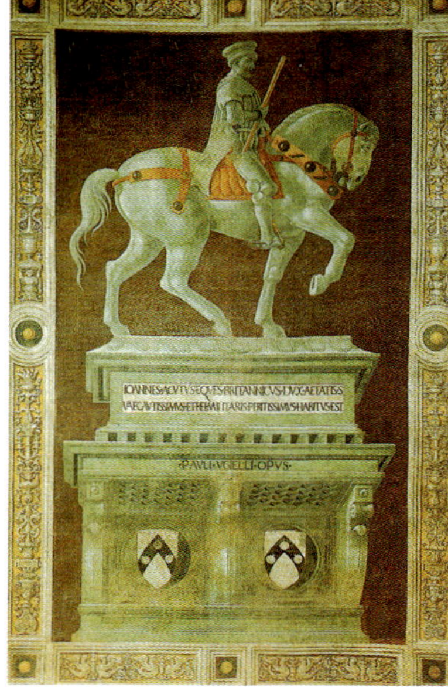

Paolo Uccello. The condottiero Giovanni Acuto (or Equestrian Portrait of Sir John Hawkwood) (1436). *Fresco painting on canvas, $202\frac{3}{4} \times 322\frac{7}{8}$". Cathedral of Santa Maria dei Fiori, Florence. This painting by Uccello is an exercise in perspective in which the artist experiments by using different vanishing points in the same work.*

THE ARTIST'S LIFE

1396 or 1397. Paolo de Dono is born in Pratovecchio. He is known as Uccello.

1407. He is a young apprentice at the workshop of the sculptor Ghiberti.

1425. He works for Ghiberti in Florence.

1425–1430. He works on the mosaics in San Marco in Venice.

1436. In Florence he paints the monument to Giovanni Acuto, the Condottiero, known in English as Sir John Hawkwood.

1451–1457. The years spanning the creation of the panels of *The Battle of San Romano.*

1465–1469. He creates his last works.

1475. He dies in Florence, poor and unknown, with the only consolation of having been able to dedicate himself to perspective.

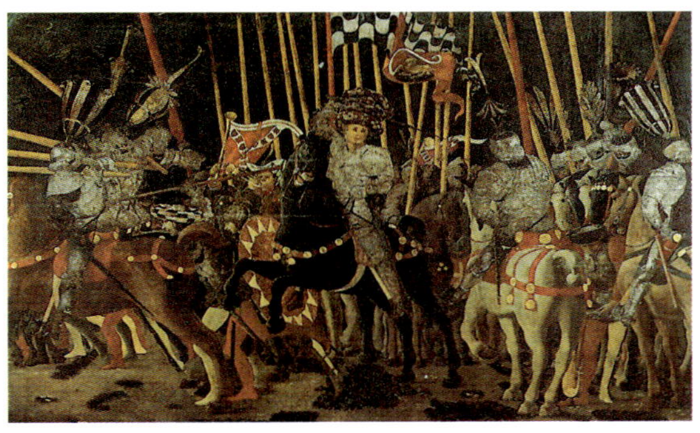

Paolo Uccello. The Battle of San Romano. *Panel (1451–1457). Tempera on panel, 124¾ × 71⅝". The Louvre, Paris.*

perspective. However the most important works by Paolo Uccello are the panels that he painted between 1451 and 1457 with scenes from *The Battle of San Romano,* for the alcove of Lorenzo the Magnificent in the Palazzo Medici-Ricordi but that are now divided between the National Gallery and the Uffizi Gallery. Carefully thought-out figures form a multicolored group of horses and knights, which are visually linked by enormous lances and banners. They are notable for their meticulously detailed material qualities, which gave the panels a brilliance that time has faded, destroying the metallic applications that covered the weapons and that were doubtless very important in the aesthetic impact of the work.

Among his last works can be highlighted the altarpiece called *The Miracle of the Host* in the Corpus Domini Church in Urbino.

The Painting and Work of Filippo Lippi

The work of this exceptional representative of *Quattrocento* painting is exclusively religious, as befits a Carmelite friar, and is characterized above all by the elegance and even sensuality of its figures. In the works of his prime, Lippi's style links with the lyricism of Botticelli, being predominantly linear and with a gentle, luminescent atmosphere and effective use of tone. Light and the rhythms of the lines are the artistic elements that dominate in his work.

Between 1430 and 1432 Lippi's works abandon the ideas of Masaccio to adopt more linear and dynamic forms, as is evident in the painting *The Virgin of Humility* of 1430-1432 (Castillo Sforzesco, Milan) and more so in the great beauty of *Annunciation* (Alte Pinakothek, Munich), and above all in the painting *Coronation of the Virgin* (Uffizi Gallery) painted between 1441 and 1447. More intimate are the Madonnas and Child, which are full of poetry: *Madonna Adoring the Divine Child,* Uffizi Gallery (thought to be a portrait of Lucrezia Buti) and *Madonna and Child* show the iconography of the Renaissance *madonnas.*

Filippo Lippi. Coronation of the Virgin *(1441–1447). Tempera on panel, 113 × 78¾". Uffizi Gallery, Florence. The work of Filippo Lippi was obscured and criticized because of his licentious life. Furthermore, in Florence the tendency represented by Masaccio had triumphed over the more sensual and scientific painting of Lippi.*

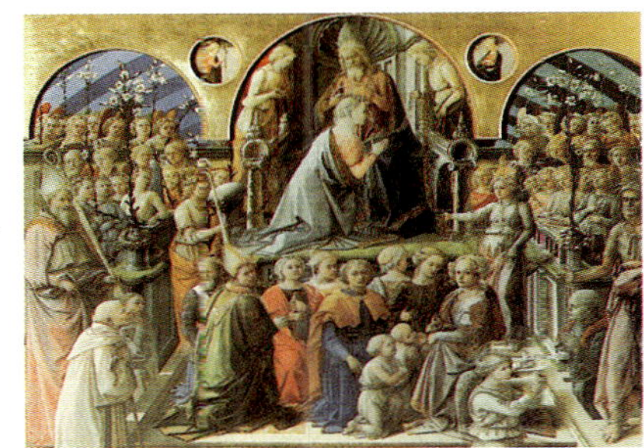

THE ARTIST'S LIFE

1406–1409. Born in Florence, the son of a butcher. He was orphaned at the age of seven, and educated at the Carmine convent, where he met Masaccio.

1421. He enters the Order of Carmen.

1430. At around the age of 25 he becomes the painter of the convent.

1432. At about this time he goes to Padua, returning to Florence in 1437.

1450. He is named the chaplain of the convent of Santa Margerita of Arezzo. At the age of 50 he seduces the novice Lucrezia Buti, by whom he has a son, Filippino, a painter like his father. It is said that thanks to the intervention of Cosimo de' Medici the couple were freed from their vows and allowed to marry.

1469. Filippo Lippi dies in Spoletto, a city in Umbria, where he had painted the murals in the apse of the cathedral.

THE BIRTH OF RENAISSANCE PAINTING (III)

MATERIALITY AND NARRATIVE IN TWO PAINTERS OF THE *QUATTROCENTO*

In his determination to achieve a form of painting whose visual effects were comparable to those of sculpture, the work of Andrea del Castagno is especially interesting. He was an artist whose violent and passionate character was reflected in his painting, which suggests the materiality of multicolored stone. The narrative tendency of the *Quattrocento* was best exemplified by the work of Ghirlandaio.

Andrea del Castagno. His Painting and His Work

The style of Andrea del Castagno takes the volumetric quality of the work of Masaccio and pushes it to its limits. His characters are as robust and as solid as sculptures and convey intense internal drama.

His first works, such as the decoration of the mural of the chapel of San Tarasio (1442) in the church of San Zacario of Venice, or in *The Hanged* on the facade of the palace of Podesta in Florence (pre-1442) combine the formal energy of Masaccio and the geometry of Paolo Uccello, as well as the coloring of his contemporary Domenico Veneziano (1400–1461). The material quality of his painting reaches its pinnacle in the scenes of *The Passion of Christ* (1448) in the refectory of Sant'Apollonia in Florence. In *The Last Supper* his style tends to a roughness of form that gives grandeur and drama.

One of the works of the *Quattrocento* that best reveals the Renaissance spirit is his work for the Gallery of Famous Men and Women in the Villa Carducci. Painted by Andrea del Castagno in approximately 1450, it is a series of idealized portraits (though painted in a naturalistic style) that are now in the Uffizi Gallery. Soldiers, poets, sibyls,

Andrea del Castagno. Pippo Spano, *Gallery of Famous Men and Women, Villa Carducci, Soffiano (c. 1450). Fresco painting, 65 × 96½", Uffizi Gallery, Florence. The series of "Famous Men and Women" is an expression of the humanist spirit that reigned in Florence. It is a mixture of portraits of contemporaries of the artist and of great poets, sibyls, and queens.*

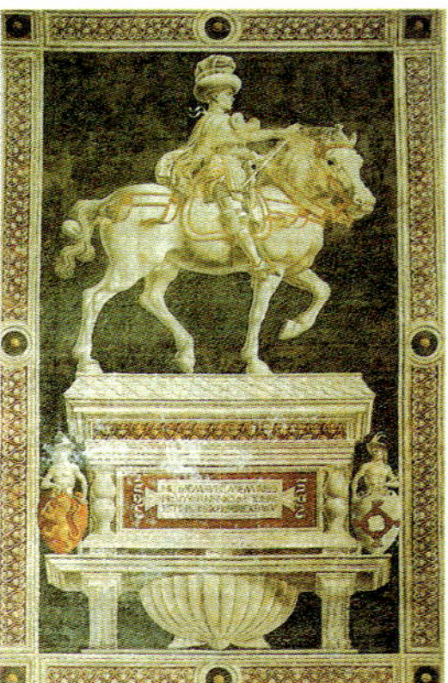

Andrea del Castagno. Niccoló da Tolentino *(1456). Fresco painting, 201½ × 328". Cathedral of Santa Maria dei Fiori, Florence. Standing opposite its partner, the fresco by Paolo Uccello in the Cathedral of Florence, the painting by Castagno is less serene but more realistic, and is perhaps anecdotal in its preoccupation with luxurious details and the muscles of the horse.*

THE ARTIST'S LIFE

1423. Born in San Martino in Corella. Soon his family moves to Castagno, from which he takes his name. It is said that while he was still a child Bernardo de' Medici made him an apprentice in the workshop of Paolo Uccello.

1442. In Venice he paints the murals of the church of San Zacario.

1448. Back in Florence he paints the frescoes of Sant' Apollonia.

1450. He paints the series of "Famous Men and Women."

1454–1456. He paints for the church of the Annuziata (Saint Jerome) and for the cathedral of Florence (Niccoló da Tolentino)

1457. He dies in Florence, victim of the plague.

and queens are portrayed as statues with powerful bodies, proclaiming human vainglory. Another example of Renaissance humanism attributed to the same artist is the equestrian figure of Niccoló da Tolentino (1456) in the Cathedral of Santa Maria dei Fiori in Florence, a painting that forms a pair with the one that Paolo Uccello painted in honor of Giovanni Acuto (Sir John Hawkwood) many years before.

The Descriptive Realism of Domenico Ghirlandaio

The tendency toward narrative painting that in fifteenth-century Florence pursued the applause of a *dilettante* public, found its most impressive representative in Domenico de Tommaso Bigordi, known as Ghirlandaio. He was a master of pictorial techniques and placed his art at the service of the elegance of forms, which were still molded, but not as much as those of Andrea del Castagno. The idea of volume that Ghirlandaio applied corresponded to a "pleasant" art that freed his characters from all tense or exaggerated drama, although as with Andrea del Castagno he enjoyed solving complicated problems of foreshortening, perspective, and movement. These characteristics can be appreciated in the youthful work *Vision and Burial of Santa Fina* in the collegiate church of San Gimignano, *The Last Supper* (1480) a fresco in the convent of Ognisanti and, masterfully, in two series of murals. One series is in the *Tornabuoni Chapel* in Santa Maria Novella, including the *Birth of the Virgin* (c. 1485). The other is in the *Sassetti Chapel* in the Santa Trinitá Church, to which *The Funeral of Saint Frances* belongs.

Ghirlandaio. Adoration of the Magi (1487). Oil on panel, 67⅜" in diameter. Uffizi Gallery, Florence.

Ghirlandaio was a magnificent portraitist, a genre in which he shows his great artistic skills. The portrait of *Francesco Sassetti and his Young Son Teodoro* (Metropolitan Museum, New York) and his well-known oil on panel *An Old Man and a Boy* in the Louvre, which can be dated between 1480 and 1490, are beautiful examples of the unarguable Flemish influence, a school with which he became familiar with Hugo van der Goes.

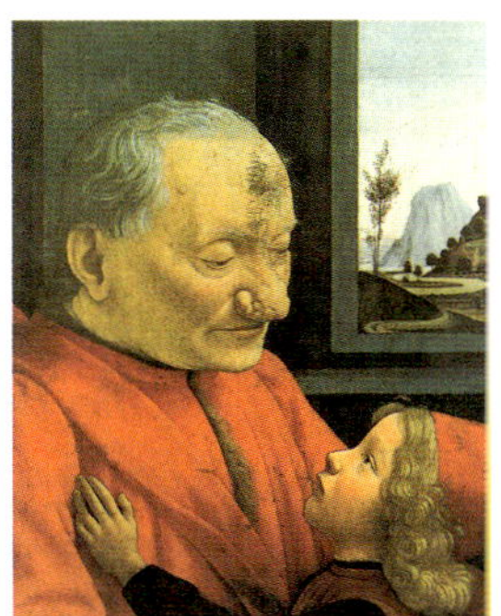

The Flemish influence is also in evidence in the *Adoration of the Magi* of 1487 (Uffizi Gallery) a painting that shows the painter's interest for detail and anecdote. Similar characteristics appear in *Virgin on the Throne with Saints* (Uffizi Gallery) an altarpiece from his final period (1480–1487) and an example of the refined technique of the artist who, according to Vasari, was the most distinguished of his period.

Ghirlandaio. An Old Man and a Boy (1480–1490). Oil on panel, 18⅛ × 24⅜". The Louvre, Paris. Although the artist was accustomed to carrying out his skillful portraits with live models, the portrait of the old man who is sick with rhinitis may have been made from an engraving after his death. This would explain the interest in the landscape with a river through the window, which iconographically alludes to the passage from life to death, as well as referring to classical mythology and the river that had to be crossed to reach Hades.

THE ARTIST'S LIFE

1449. Born in Florence. He becomes an apprentice and student in the workshop of the painter Alessio Baldovinetti.

1480. He begins to make a name for himself in Florence. He receives one of his most important commissions: to paint the frescoes of the Ognisanti convent.

1485. The merchant Giovanni Tornabuoni commissions him to paint the frescoes of the chapel of the chorus of Santa Maria Novella (the Tornabuoni chapel) for 2,200 gold escudos.

1480–1489. Years in which the two previously mentioned portraits can be placed. With the altarpiece *The Virgin Enthroned* of 1480 and *The Adoration of the Magi* of 1487 they represent the pinnacle of his painting.

1494. He dies in Florence.

A STEP TOWARD THE HIGH RENAISSANCE (I)

FLORENTINE SCULPTORS WHO INNOVATED PAINTING: POLLAIOLO, VERROCCHIO, LORENZO DI CREDI

The multifaceted training of the Renaissance artist explains the commitment of the great sculptors to painting and the wealth of sculptural work by artists who were essentially painters, notably the Pollaiolo brothers, Andrea del Verrocchio, and Lorenzo di Credi.

Antonio and Piero Pollaiolo

Antonio del Iacobo Beci was born in Florence around 1431, becoming known as Antonio Pollaiolo because his father was the owner of a poultry shop in the city. His brother Piero, nine years younger (born in 1441), was a sculptor and painter like Antonio and worked very closely with him, so that sometimes it is difficult to say for certain which parts of their joint works belong to each artist. Nevertheless, it is Antonio, beyond question, who achieved a greater mastery of the art of color, bringing to his painting the vitality of the human body in movement; a movement that the artist considered to be the supreme value of painting. He can be considered the forerunner of the same exaltation and vitality in the expression of the human body that reached its highest artistic representation with Michelangelo.

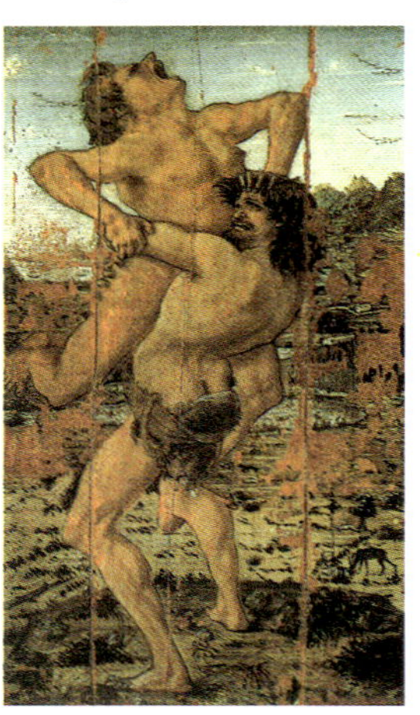

Antonio Pollaiolo. Hercules and Antaeus *(c. 1475). Tempera on panel, 4¾ × 7⅛" and 3½ × 40⅝". Uffizi Gallery, Florence. The Pollaiolo brothers renewed Florentine painting by developing influences from sculptors such as Donatello and following the teaching of the painter Andrea del Castagno.*

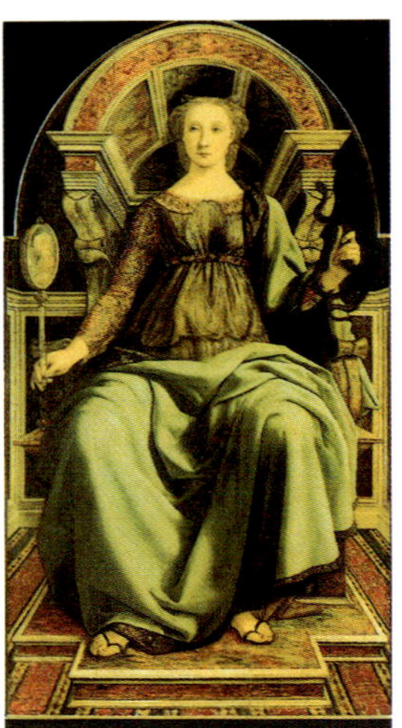

Piero Pollaiolo. Prudence *(1469). Tempera on panel, 30⅜ × 61¾". Uffizi Gallery, Florence. Whereas Antonio retains a classical feeling due to his use of form, Piero is led by intellectual desire. The series "The Virtues," of which this painting forms a part, is a good example.*

As far as his pictorial work is concerned, the most significant pieces in the Pollaiolo style are perhaps his *Tobias and the Angel* (c. 1459) in the Pinacoteca in Turin, *Dancing Nudes* (1470), one of the frescoes in the Villa Gallina in Arcetri, Florence, *Hercules and Antaeus* (c. 1475) in the Uffizi Gallery, and especially *The Martyrdom of Saint Sebastian* (c. 1475) in the National Gallery, London. It is a composition that is notable for the grandeur of its landscape and the dynamism of the poses of the bodies of the archers who are martyring the saint. While this painting is attributed to Antonio, it was one that he painted together with his brother Piero. Also noteworthy is Piero's tempera painting *The Virtues,* painted in 1469 for the tribunal of Merchants of Venice, which is now in the Uffizi Gallery.

Antonio Pollaiolo died in Rome in 1498 and wanted to be buried beside his brother Piero, who had died in 1496. Their graves lie in San Pedro en Vincula, Florence.

Andrea del Verrocchio as a Painter

The sculptor Andrea di Cione, known as Andrea del Verrocchio, was born in Florence in 1435 and died in Venice in 1488. He is the creator of the very famous *Equestrian Statue of Bartolomeo Colleone* (1488 and cast in 1496) and was also a notable master of painting, who counted Leonardo da Vinci among his pupils, in whom he instilled his artistic sense of form. This and his taste for the ornamental are the contributions that Verrocchio made to the art of color at the end of the *Quattrocento.* Nevertheless, his sense of form, as evidenced in his sculpture, was not an obstacle to the development of a notable use of color, best

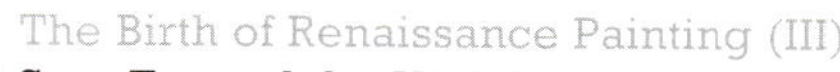

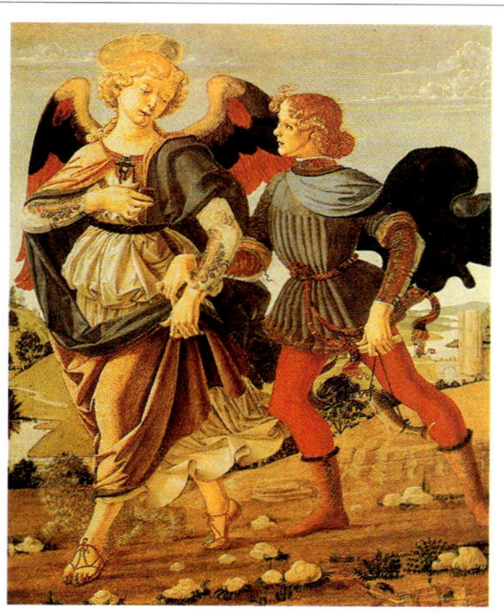

Verrocchio. The Archangel and Tobias *(c. 1670). Oil on panel, 26 × 33⅛". National Gallery, London. As well as its sense of shape and light, the work of Verrocchio is notable for its a ccentuated taste for ornamentation and the recreation of detail; this is an element he possibly borrowed from Ghiberti.*

seen in his paintings *Tobias and the Three Angels* and *The Archangel and Tobias,* both in the National Gallery, London. In these oil paintings the same human character can be seen that the artist developed as a sculptor in *David* (Florence). However without a doubt the best-known painting attributed to Verrocchio is *Baptism of Christ* (Uffizi Gallery), painted between 1470 and 1480. It is a beautiful example of his work, although paradoxically its attribution is the subject of controversy. The Uffizi Gallery attributes it jointly to Verrocchio and Leonardo da Vinci, who apparently painted the angels located to the left of Christ and the landscape in the background. According to Vasari, as a result of this collaboration Verrocchio decided to never again pick up his paintbrushes, since "Leonardo, who is so new to this art, has performed better."

Another work that must be mentioned for its pictorial interest is *Santa Monica among the Nuns of her Order,* an oil painting for the Church of Santo Spirito in Florence, which has an original coloring: blacks, greens, and grays are counterpointed with tones of ocher and sienna. The artistry of Verrocchio can be seen in the folds of the clothing and his ability to give his figures character, with the facial study of each one showing a deliberate psychology.

Lorenzo di Credi

Born in Florence in 1465, he was the chosen pupil of Verrocchio. Like Verrocchio, he was a goldsmith and sculptor before becoming a painter, although as a painter he can be accused of a lack of imagination. He was an eclectic artist who gave painting at the end of the Florentine *Quattrocento* and the beginning of the *Cinquecento* a style that combined his master's vitality of form with the Flemish delicateness and naturalism of Leonardo, his fellow apprentice.

His known pictorial work of the fifteenth century deals exclusively with religious themes. A follower of Savonarola, his religious puritanism led him in 1497 to burn all his profane works, which almost certainly included the best of his painting, as his *Self-portrait with Venus* (Uffizi Gallery), which escaped being burned, would seem to suggest. From 1503 there is his *Virgin and Child with Saint Julian and Saint Nicholas of Myra* (the Louvre) painted for the San Cetello in Florence. From 1510 there is his *Adoration of the Shepherds* from the Church of Santa Clara, *Annunciation* (both in the Uffizi Gallery) and *Madonna with Four Saints* from Santa Maria de las Gracias. Of unknown date there is a *Madonna* known as *The Virgin with the Vase of Flowers* in the Borghese Gallery in Rome.

One of his final works is *Saint Michael* from Santa Maria dei Fiore in Florence, where he died in 1537.

Lorenzo di Credi. Annunciation *(1510). Oil on panel, 28 × 34⅝". Uffizi Gallery, Florence. He was an artist who owes a great deal of his success to the proximity of the workshop of Leonardo and the circle of Verrocchio. His painting is a compromise between the mathematical space of the former and Flemish detail: it was a formula that had success in the early decades of the fifteenth century.*

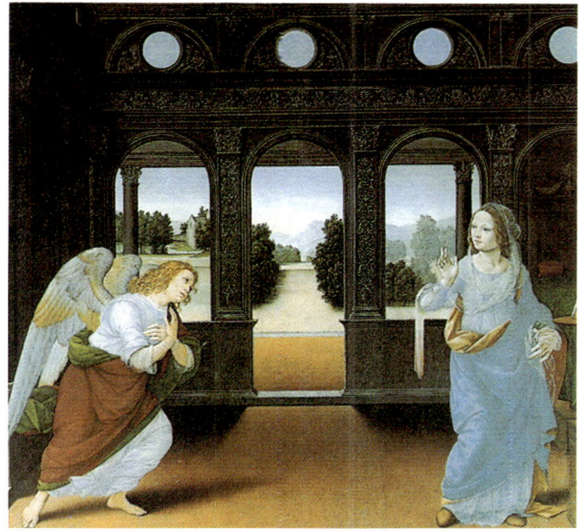

A STEP TOWARD THE HIGH RENAISSANCE (II)

SANDRO BOTTICELLI

The humanist thought that reigned in the intellectual atmosphere of the court of the Medicis found its most genuine artistic expression in the work of the painter Sandro Botticelli. Neoplatonic philosophy, which places more importance on the intellect than the senses, can be seen in Botticelli's iconographic repertoire. Botticelli had studied literature, and can be considered one of the humanists of his period, destined to live through the political and religious turmoil in Florence immediately prior to the fall of the Medici (1494) and the tragic end of Savonarola (1498). Savonarola was a Dominican friar who, with his prophecies and sermons denouncing perverted behavior, greatly troubled the consciences of many Florentines, including Botticelli. According to Joan Sureda, director of the National Museum of Art of Catalonia, Barcelona, "with Botticelli came to an end the first creative cycle of the art of the Renaissance."

The Painting of Botticelli

In terms of his treatment of form, the painting that can be considered characteristic of Botticelli is more poetic than artistic. It is an approach that is governed by the enormous subtlety of the linear rhythms that describe the bodies, clothes, and windswept hair, and that is more suited to sketching than painting.

In the evolution of Botticelli's painting, one can clearly see the influence of Filippo Lippi, who was almost certainly his first master and from whom he inherited the unequalled elegance of his linear treatment. Pollaiolo is evident in the consistency of his relief, and in his landscapes are influences by del Verrocchio.

> "Botticelli is the greatest of the Western artists who have searched for and found the grace of a linear art, which is firmly rooted in his precise and incisive outlines."
> A. Cirici Pellicer

The first works of Botticelli (between 1460 and 1470), almost all Virgins with Child, are a reflection of the art of Filippo Lippi, who lends him both the intimacy his figures emanate and also his great sense of elegance. From 1470 is *Fortitude* (Uffizi Gallery), a clear reminder of the works that Piero Pollaiolo had painted the year before. It is after this first stage, which can be considered to have ended with *The Discovery of the Body of Holofernes* (Uffizi Gallery) and of *Saint Sebastian* (State Museums, Berlin) that the first traces of Botticelli's own artistic world can be seen: a world peopled by amazingly agile and fluid bodies, whose heads gently tilt and whose smiles seem to show a poetic inspiration of exquisite lyricism.

Sandro Botticelli. Fortitude *(1470). Tempera on panel, 34¼ × 65¾". Uffizi Gallery, Florence. This is one of Botticelli's first works. While it owes a great deal to its influences, it nevertheless shows the distinctive characteristics of his artistic personality.*

It could be said that the true Botticelli is the painter who moved around the circle of intellectuals that surrounded Lorenzo de' Medici, and who were prime movers in the neoplatonic Renaissance. This is the Botticelli who participated directly in the veneration that humanist Florence felt for the classical world, complete with its myths and philosophies. Nevertheless, it is a Botticelli who, before becoming a part of the "circle" of the Medici, had already perfected his unmistakable linear patterns through religious painting that showed vitality, elegance, transparent colors, and boundless tenderness.

However, there is another type of Botticelli painting that, without losing its innate sense of rhythm and elegance, loses the spark of genius that had illuminated the artist's work from the eighties on. This is a painting that was influenced by the religious crisis inspired in Botticelli by the sermonizing of Savonarola, and in which there was no room for pagan myths. The figures lose their grace and sensuous beauty to return to a world of tense bodies, tragic faces, and thick colors.

The Work of Botticelli

As with other great artists who have left behind a great body of

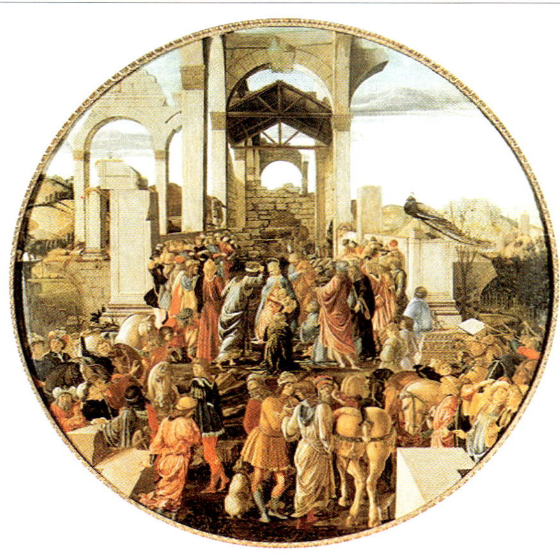

Sandro Botticelli. Adoration of the Magi *(1472–1473). Tempera on panel, 51½" in diameter. National Gallery, London. The flowing movement of the figures and the recreation of the atmosphere, in which biblical tradition and the ancient classical world are present, reflect the neoplatonic theories put forward by Botticelli's contemporary, Marsilio Ficino.*

work, history and the critics have taken it upon themselves to select those of Botticelli's works that constitute, so to speak, an anthology of his art. It is an anthology that, responding to personal criteria, is open to discussion.

In chronological order (with the exception of *Primavera* and *The Birth of Venus,* which will be considered at the end, due to their importance), there follows a brief commentary on those of Botticelli's works that, according to most accepted criteria, are considered the most representative.

The National Gallery in London houses the *Adoration of the Magi* of 1472–1473, in which Botticelli's style is completely encapsulated. It is an extremely notable circular panel (called a tondo) of exquisite beauty, painted in tempera. Approximately two years later, in about 1473, the artist painted another *Adoration of the Magi* (Uffizi Gallery) for the Lami chapel in Santa Maria Novella. This is a composition of notable documentary interest, as the figures are portraits of personalities of the period: the painter himself (wearing a yellow cloak), located on the right side of the painting, Cosimo de' Medici the Elder, Lorenzo the Magnificent the Younger, his brother Giuliano, Piero il Gottoso (the gouty), son of Cosimo, and others. Botticelli was an outstanding portraitist, as is shown by his *Portrait of Lorenzo the Magnificent* (National Gallery) or *Young Man with a Medal* (Uffizi Gallery), a supposed self-portrait, and *Portrait of a Young Man* who could be Simonetta Vespuci (National Gallery).

In 1482, after painting *Primavera,* Botticelli painted two of his most beautiful Madonnas (both in the Uffizi Gallery), which are overflowing with tenderness and in which the unmistakable drawing of the artist reaches superb levels of quality, precision, and emotion. These are *The Madonna of the Pomegranate* (almost certainly a commission for the Palazzo della Signoria) and *The Madonna of the Magnificat,* a painting that is highly notable for its smoothness, warmth, and very careful, sweeping composition. Its figures describe patterns that gather around the Virgin and stretch to the circumference of the sumptuous carved golden frame that borders the painting.

We have said that the religious crisis that Botticelli experienced caused the birth of another type of painting. This

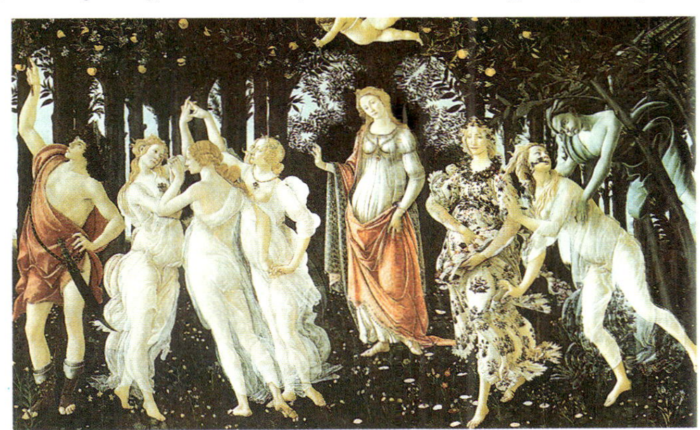

Sandro Botticelli. Primavera *(1480–1481). Tempera on panel, 123⅝ × 79⅞". Uffizi Gallery, Florence.*

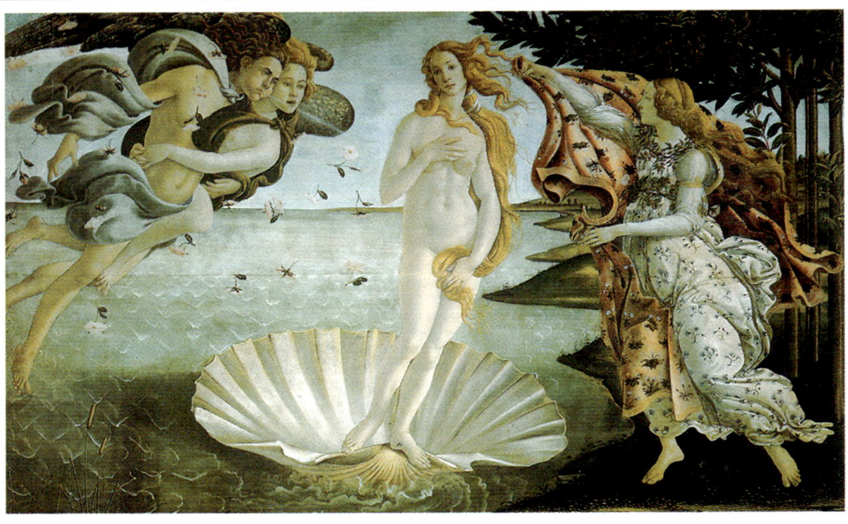

Sandro Botticelli. The Birth of Venus *(1485). Tempera on canvas, $109\frac{1}{2} \times 67\frac{5}{8}$". Uffizi Gallery, Florence. The pinnacle of Botticelli's painting, together with* Primavera, The Birth of Venus *reaches a high point in his expressive language. After this work there could only follow either academicism or crisis in Florentine art. This is the crowning point in the moralist and idealist spirit of the* Quattrocento, *and from this moment art returns to a reality of worried faces and contorted figures.*

was realistic and dramatic and began to appear around 1490. The artist left classical themes, with the exception of *Calumny* (Uffizi Gallery) of 1494 or 1495, which illustrates, in an idealized manner, the work of the Greek Appelles (fourth century B.C.) who was described by Lucan (second century A.D.). Within a very conventional architectural setting, naked Truth is being questioned by Calumny (who is hidden within thick, ragged clothes), who in turn is being guided by Envy, Suspicion, and Ignorance. In the painting the symbol for Truth is a female nude who is formally correct and classically beautiful but who is far from the ethereal beauty and sensual intelligence with which Botticelli had been able to infuse his mythological characters.

From the last years of his life, mention must be made of works such as the intensely dramatic *Pietà* (c.1500) in the Alte Pinakothek in Munich and the *Mystic Nativity,* also from 1500 (National Gallery, London), which faithfully reproduce Botticelli's state of mind, now completely enthralled by the apocalyptic discourse of Savonarola, who had been tried and executed in 1498.

Primavera

Between 1480 and 1481, Botticelli painted the masterpiece of his artistic maturity, whose title, due to the interpretation that Vasari gave it, is one of many interpretations that have appeared over the centuries. Painted for the Villa de Castello, commissioned by Lorenzo de Pierfrancesco de' Medici, a cousin of Lorenzo the Magnificent, this painting, $123\frac{5}{8} \times 79\frac{7}{8}$", is painted in tempera with unsurpassed technical mastery. It is considered to be the greatest triumph of painting that places idealism (ideal beauty) above rationalism (realistic beauty). The artistic values of *Primavera,* particularly following its latest restoration, are so clear to the observer that there can be no argument whatsoever. The transparency of color and light (in a painting almost devoid of shadow), and the dancing rhythms suggested by the hands, figures, and diaphanous clothes that swirl around and en-

Sandro Botticelli. Madonna of the Magnificat *(1482). Tempera on panel, $46\frac{1}{2}$" in diameter. Uffizi Gallery, Florence.*

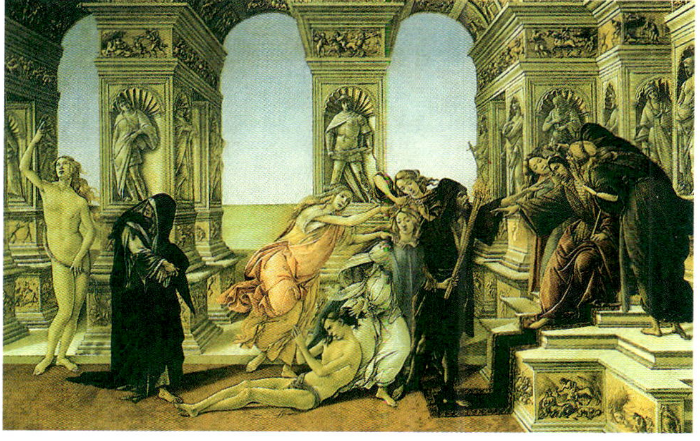

Sandro Botticelli. Calumny *(1494–1495). Oil on panels, 36 × 24⅖". Uffizi Gallery, Florence. In the reproduction of the ancient painting of Apeles, the elements of the crisis of Neoplatonic Florentine idealism are already outlined. The ideal beauty is undressed, the rash truth by sin, old age, and reality.*

circle the magnificent youth, create an artistic symphony that is almost audible, and fills the whole of the painting with absolute harmony.

As far as its significance is concerned, there are many differing views. Some have tried to make the allegory allude to the theme described by Ovid of the metamorphosis of the nymph Cloris into Flora (the moment of spring that the gods send to the world at the appointed time). However, it seems certain that the theme was taken from *Stanzas Begun for the Tournament of the Magnificent Giuliano de' Medici* by the poet and Latinist Angolo Poliziano (1454–1494). The allegory refers to the goddess Venus (in the center, in a garden scattered with flowers and fruits) surrounded by Mercury, the three Graces dancing (to her left), and to her right Cloris pursued by Zephyr, who makes her conceive with his breath and turns her into Flora, spreading flowers everywhere. Its final aim is the exaltation of the humanism that was triumphant in Florence at the time of the Medici.

The Birth of Venus

In 1485, five years after painting *Primavera,* Botticelli painted *The Birth of Venus* also for the villa of Castello. Venus, born from the water, floats on a shell blown by the winds. On land, the figure of Spring (Flora) awaits her, to cover her with her blanket of flowers. Although five years separate the two paintings, the second one displays the same melancholy, light, and purity of description as the first. The body of the goddess is one of the most beautiful and noble nudes in the history of art. She expresses a double aspect of love. On one hand, there is the chaste pleasure of the contemplation of her beauty. On the other hand, there is the sensual aspect of love. Together they create an erotic and intellectual whole that brings together human and divine.

THE ARTIST'S LIFE

1445. Alessandro de Mariano Filippeti, son of a Florentine craftsman, is born. He takes the name Botticelli from the goldsmithing master with whom his father placed him, although his training as a painter seems to be due to Filippo Lippi.

1470–1473. In 1470 he already has his own workshop, and works with Pollaiolo. At the age of 28 he belongs to the Council of the Company of San Lucas of Florentine artists, together with Andrea della Robbia, Verrocchio, and the brothers Antonio and Piero Pollaiolo.

1479. He leaves Florence and moves to Rome, where he collaborates on the mural paintings of the Sistine Chapel in the Vatican, together with Ghirlandaio and other painters.

1481. Back in Florence, humanist ideals powerfully affect his art. He paints *Primavera* and in 1485, *The Birth of Venus.*

1491. The success of Botticelli and his workshop is unanimously recognized by Florentine society. From the nineties on, his painting becomes more realistic and dramatic. Commissions dry up and his decline as a painter begins.

1494. It is known that Botticelli bought a house on the outskirts of Florence in this year, which would seem to contradict Vasari's assertion that the artist had an impoverished old age.

1510. He dies in Florence in May. The inexplicable unpopularity of Botticelli begins. Among other criticisms, Leonardo bemoans his poor knowledge of perspective. Vasari only deigns to recognize the grace of some of his figures.

A STEP TOWARD THE HIGH RENAISSANCE (III)

PIERO DELLA FRANCESCA

With its humanism and its artistic splendors, Florence shares the triumph of the Renaissance with other Italian cities. Siena gave the world painters such as Giovanni di Paolo (1403–1482), Il Sassetta (1392–1451), Il Vecchietta (1412–1480), Natteo de Giovanni (1430–1495), and others. They left subsequent painting with the memory of the exceptional lyricism of the Gothic school of Siena. Umbria, which received the direct influx of painters from neighboring Tuscany, also played an important part in Renaissance painting, thanks especially to Piero della Francesca.

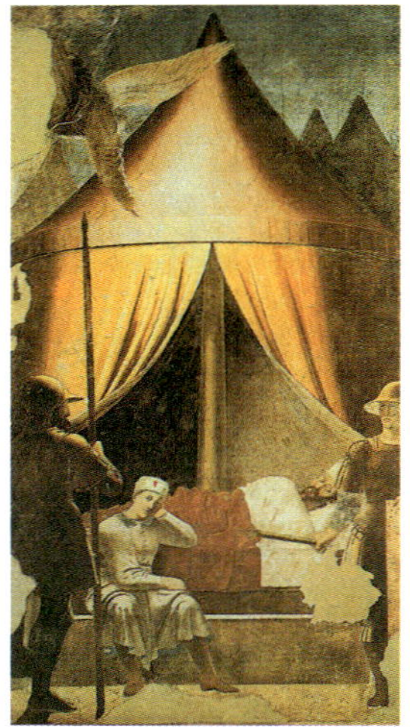

Piero della Francesca. Scene from the Legend of the Cross *(1452–1459). Fresco painting, 53½ × 294⅛". Church of San Francisco, Arezzo. For Piero della Francesca, more important than the faithful reproduction of ancient medieval myths was the creation of secular epics with religious and political connotations for his contemporaries. The artist focuses on the pure artistic arrangement of space; geometry plays an essential role in the distribution and ordering of his groups and characters. In this way the figures are reduced to mathematical structures: an oval for the head, a cylinder for the neck, and regular volumes for the bodies.*

The Painting of Piero della Francesca

The style of Pierro della Francesca was almost certainly forged in Florence, when at the age of 23 he discovered the work of Masaccio and studied with Paolo Uccello, in whose painting he found artistic ideas that complemented his talent for mathematics. Like Uccello, Piero della Francesca was an intellectual of form, who dedicated himself to its refinement. His figures are like synthetic bodies, reduced to elemental volumes that are defined by polished, convex surfaces. His bodies are emotionally aseptic and are conceived more as architectural forms than living masses. However, these architectural forms assume beautiful tones, entirely bathed by a diffuse, nourishing light. The mathematician in Piero della Francesca is evident in the minute calculation of his compositional ideas. He sees composition as the result of a relationship of measurements in which each figure and each void is an absolutely vital element for maintaining an order that otherwise would cease to have artistic meaning.

The Work of Piero della Francesca

The clearest evidence of the influence of Masaccio in the youthful painting of Piero della Francesca is possibly the *Misericordia altarpiece (The Virgin of Mercy),* tempera and oil on panel from 1445, Municipal Museum of Borgo San Sepolcro (Italy). Its carefully composed

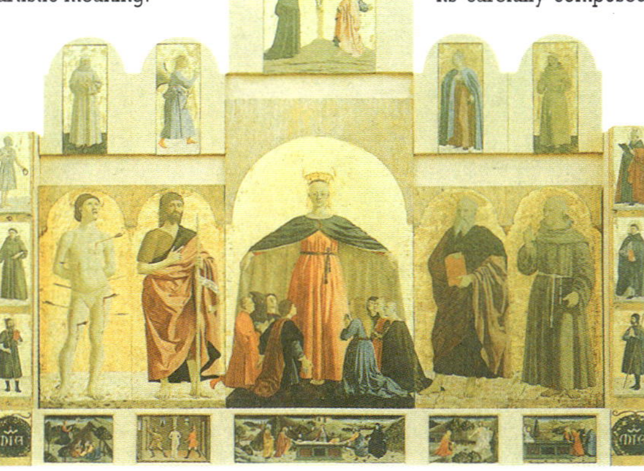

Piero della Francesca. Misericordia altarpiece (The Virgin of Mercy) *(1445). Tempera and oil on panel. Municipal Museum, Borgo de San Sepolcro (Italy). One of the few existing works from the beginning of this painter's career. The influence of Masaccio can be deduced here, although it is a work done under strict medieval guidelines, as evidenced by the positioning of the figures.*

Piero della Francesca. The Flagellation of Christ *(c. 1459). Oil on panel, $31^{7}/_{8} \times 23^{1}/_{4}$". Galleria Nazionale delle Marche, Urbino. Iconographically it is unusual that Piero della Francesca should give more importance to the three contemporary characters than to the actual flagellation. In this way it could be interpreted that the biblical scene appears as a dream to these characters, or that it is some kind of vision. There is no lack of interpretations that try to put the painting into the context of the history of the period.*

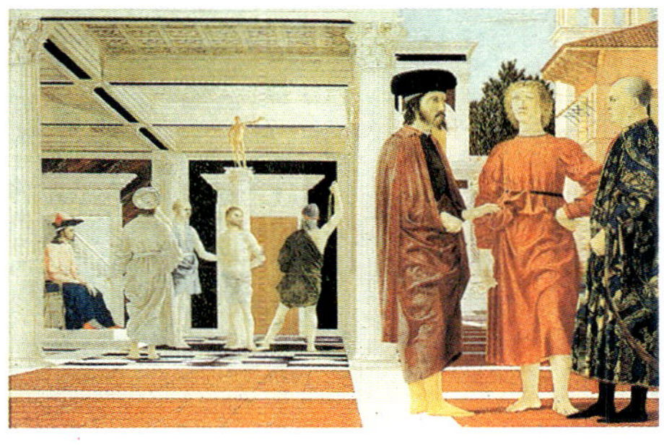

figures offer the solemn appearance and typical statuary of Masaccio. Between 1448 and 1450 della Francesca painted the *Baptism of Christ* for the Abbey of San Juan Bautista de San Sepolcro (National Gallery, London). It is an oil-painted panel that demonstrates the characteristics of the artistic language of the artist's mature painting: order, geometric balance that governs all the elements in the painting, and uniformity of light, which creates an atmosphere of extraordinary translucence. The same formal completeness and luminous presence appears in *The Flagellation of Christ* (c. 1459) in the Galleria Nazionale delle Marche, Urbino. It is an oil-painted panel that represents two realities at different times in two architecturally different spaces, one interior and the other exterior. Within a covered space there is the actual flagellation and, right in the foreground, drawing attention away from the evangelical scene, three people are talking. Many people have speculated about the meaning the artist wanted to give them, but no supposition has been backed by faithful evidence.

The most notable works by Piero della Francesca are his frescoes of the *Legend of the Cross,* which decorate the choir of the Church of San Francesco, Arezzo. He began them in 1452 and dedicated seven years to them, with the help of some of his pupils, so that they were finished in 1459, at the same time as *The Flagellation of Christ.* The medieval legend of the miraculous discovery of the cross of Christ is shown in different scenes with a very clear, unreal light that dilutes the shapes in an atmosphere that places a barrier between the observer and the depth of the painting. The artistic space of Piero della Francesca is impenetrable and advances toward the observer.

Notable also are his portraits of *Battista Sforza and Federico de Montefeltro,* panels located in the Uffizi Gallery, as well as *The Virgin with Child and Two Angels* in the Galleria Nazionale delle Marche, Urbino. In his later works, his obsession with metrical relationships in composition gives way to a greater naturalism that combines drawing light, and color in a unique overall space.

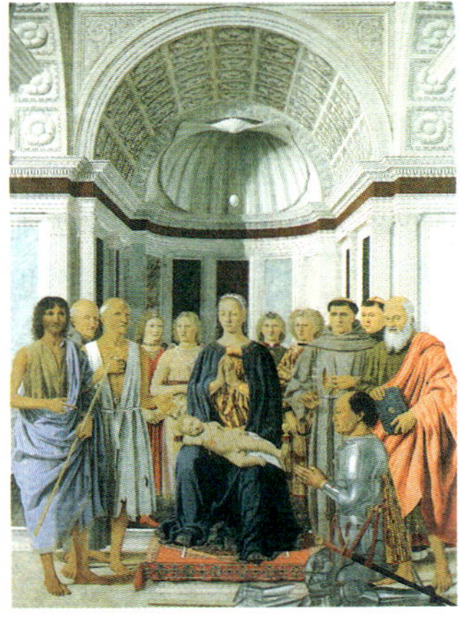

Piero della Francesca. Virgin with Child adored by Federico de Montefeltro *(1472–1474). Oil on panel, $66^{7}/_{8} \times 97^{5}/_{8}$". Pinacoteca de Brera, Milan. A major example of geometric ordering. The painting takes its organization from the egg hanging above the Virgin. From this point the space is arranged in circles that move from the egg emerging from the shell (a symbol of the perfection and origin of the world) to the Virgin's head. This structure is repeated in concentric circles from the background of the room to the distribution of the figures.*

THE ARTIST' LIFE

c. 1416. Born in Borgo San Sepolcro.

c. 1429. He moves to Florence, where he collaborates with Domenico Veneziano on the frescoes of San Egidio. He meets Masaccio and he studies with Paolo Uccello.

c. 1442. He moves back to Borgo San Sepolcro.

1451–1452. He paints in Rimini and in Arezzo, the frescoes for the Church of San Francesco.

1459. He paints in the Vatican. The work is now lost.

c. 1465. He is found in the court of Urbino, painting for Federico de Montefeltro.

1482–1492. Almost blind, he writes his theoretical tracts *De Perspectiva Pingendii* (1482) and *Libellus de Quinque Corporibus* in the same year that he dies (1492).

FORERUNNERS OF THE PAINTING OF THE *CINQUECENTO*

For Italian painting, the last two decades of the fifteenth century represent the definitive entry of classical naturalism into the aesthetic conceptions of all its painters. From Masaccio to Botticelli and from Botticelli to Piero della Francesca, *quattrocentist* painting acquired the characteristics that would define the great painters of the *Cinquecento*. By the 1480s and 1490s these qualities were already present in the drama of Luca Signorelli, the formal classicism of Perugino, and the perspective and anatomy of Mantegna.

The Pathos of Luca Signorelli

A student of Piero della Francesca, Signorelli's painting shows the assimilation of his master's ideas about geometrical simplicity and the abstract sense of space. Nevertheless, even in the works of his youth, the stillness of his master's figures gives way to tenser and more expressive ones. With time, the painting of Signorelli takes pleasure in the pathos of gestures, and his characters, whether nude or dressed, reflect the aesthetic tastes of humanist intellectualism of the end of the *Quattrocento*. This can be seen in the classical naturalism of his *Holy Family*, Uffizi Gallery, a tondo (circular panel) some have seen as a forerunner of Michelangelo's famous *Tondo Doni*, and in the frescoes of the *Santa Casa de Loreto* (c. 1480) in the Santuario della Santa Casa, Loreto, in which the painter emphasizes movement and the eloquence of the gestures.

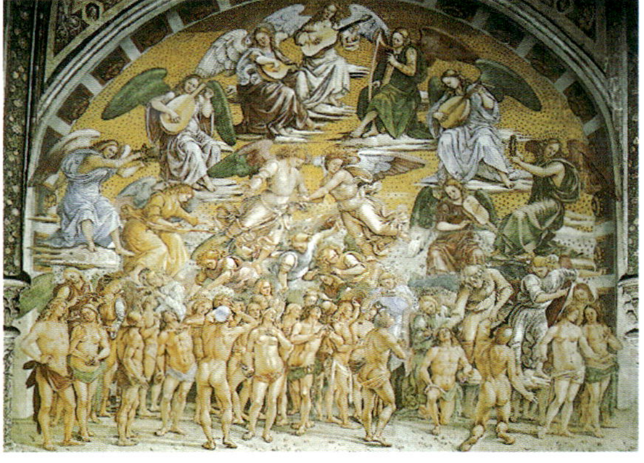

Signorelli. The Last Judgment *(1499–1502). Fresco painting. Chapel of San Brizio. Orvieto Cathedral, Italy. In this scene the painter from Cortona concentrates on the pathos of the bodies. Based on Dante's inferno, it does not intend to represent the magnificence of the heavens but rather the feelings of men, taking pleasure in the contorted bodies, the unrealistic foreshortenings, and the expressions of pain.*

Between 1497 and 1498, Signorelli finished his monumental frescoes of the *Scenes from the Life of Saint Benedict* in the cloister of the abbey of Monte Oliveto Maggiore. In these grandiose frescoes Signorelli developed his scenic ideas with complex compositions in which he applied all the techniques of geometric perspective and color, and his own vision of the ordering of forms, the positioning of space, and the treatment of light with which his master had experimented.

However, the work by Signorelli that contributes most to what would be the classicism and mannerism of the *Cinquecento* is without question his decoration of the chapel of San Brizio in Orvieto Cathedral, Italy. From

Signorelli. The Holy Family *(c. 1490–1495). Oil on panel, 48⅞" in diameter. Uffizi Gallery, Florence. Signorelli was a great drawer and painter of nudes. Vasari, a contemporary historian of the Renaissance, relates a dramatic anecdote about the life of the artist that confirms this fact. After the murder of one of his sons, Signorelli "had the body uncovered and painted it with incredible strength of determination and without shedding a tear, with the aim of being able to see it whenever he wished."*

1499 to 1502 the painter dedicated himself to completing the mural decoration that Fra Angelico had left unfinished fifty years previously. On the ceiling he painted the *Choir of the Patriarchs,* the *Doctors of the Church,* and *Virgins and Martyrs,* taking pains to adapt his style to the characteristics of the Dominican's work. On the other hand, in the decoration of the walls, Signorelli gave free rein to his capabilities as a great draftsman, with five frescoes that summarize Christian doctrine concerning the final judgment, all painted with his intrinsic pathos: *Preaching of the Anti-Christ, Resurrection of the Dead, Last Judgment, Damned Consigned to Hell,* and *Paradise.* The scene of the damned, inspired by Dante, concentrates all the artistic knowledge of the painter. He treats the contorted figures with an incredibly artistic line, accentuated foreshortening, and a linearity that is reinforced by parallel strokes as if it were an enormous engraving. The painful, supplicating expressions depict the pathetic situation of a humanity that writhes and begs without hope. History will have to wait for Michelangelo to see another such artistic expression of the terror of man confronted by his own destiny.

Luca Signorelli, born in Cortona around 1441, the son of Egidio de Ventura Signorelli and a sister of Vasari's grandfather, was also a painter with public responsibilities. He was a magistrate in his home city, and acted as an ambassador in Florence and Rome, in the period in which the Vatican was the focus for the dissemination and reception of Renaissance art. He is known to have worked for Pope Julius II in the decoration of the Vatican apartments. However, this work disappeared when it was substituted by frescoes by Raphael.

Signorelli died in Cortona in 1523, three years after Raphael, and when Michelangelo had already painted the ceiling of the Sistine Chapel.

The Classical Taste of Perugino

In Umbrian painting of the *Quattrocento,* after Piero della Francesca and his pupil Luca Signorelli comes another excellent painter, Pietro Vannuci (called Perugino because he was born in Citta della Pieve in the region of Perugia). He was a painter of eclectic tastes who learned from the hand of Piero della Francesca and was also influenced by his workshop colleague Luca Signorelli, and from Verrocchio, with whom he worked in Florence. The work of Botticelli, Ghirlandaio, and Leonardo da Vinci himself had a marked influence on the young Perugino, although his early works predominantly show the constructivist ideas of his master. However, this constructivism soon disappears to make way for the personal style of Perugino: painting that is clear, simple (he never entered into the ideological debates of his time), and conveys an ideal of classical beauty, tending to languid expressions. According to Vasari, Perugino "was not a very religious man" although even so he became one of the most appreciated painters of religious themes of his period. In his Virgins and saints he reflects his taste for forms that are gentle, even a little "soft," with which he builds figures who inhabit a world that is aesthetic, harmonious, pleasant, and charmingly poetic. There is an aesthetic gap between the constructivist rigidity of his early works, such as *Tableaux in the Life of Saint Bernard* (1473) in the National Gallery of Umbria, and his first religious and profane works, from the eighties on.

The fresco of the Sistine Chapel in the Vatican, *Christ Giving of the Keys to Saint Peter* (1481–1482, and one of his most important works) is evidence of a mature art that is capable of combining in a single work all the qualities of the Renaissance. It is impossible to look at this fresco without seeing the source of inspiration of Raphael's famous painting *Marriage of the Virgin* (1504). In Perugino's painting there is an anticipation of Raphael's classicism (Raphael was one of his pupils), with similarities that can be seen in many of his canvas works. Of these, mention must be made of the oil on canvas *The Vision of Saint Bernard* (1488–1489) in the Alte Pinakothek in Munich, and the final versions of his paintings of Saint Sebastian, in which the naked body of the young martyr, with all the appearances of classical configuration, appears as a kind of Apollo of the Christian Renaissance. His *Saint Sebastian* (alone) in the Louvre (1493), one of the most beautiful nudes in the painting of the *Quattrocento,* is

Perugino. Christ Giving of the Keys to Saint Peter *(1481–1482). Fresco painting, 216½ × 131⅞". Sistine Chapel, The Vatican, Rome. In this work, which accompanies the famous frescoes of Michelangelo in the Sistine Chapel, Perugino shows he has completely absorbed the principal achievements of the* Quattrocento: *visual space, theoretical space, the real limits of perspective, the synthesis between architecture and landscape, and the positioning of figures.*

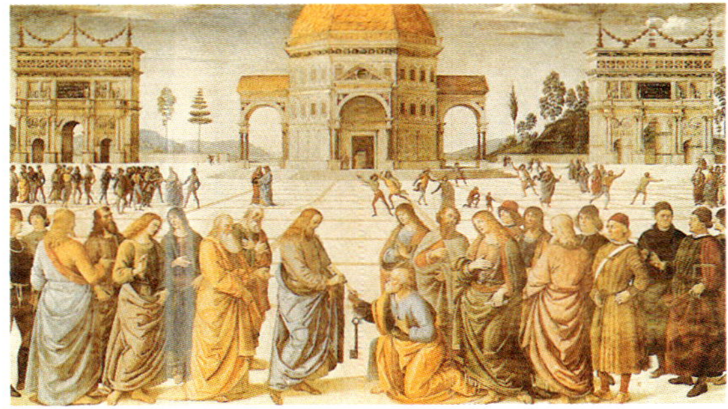

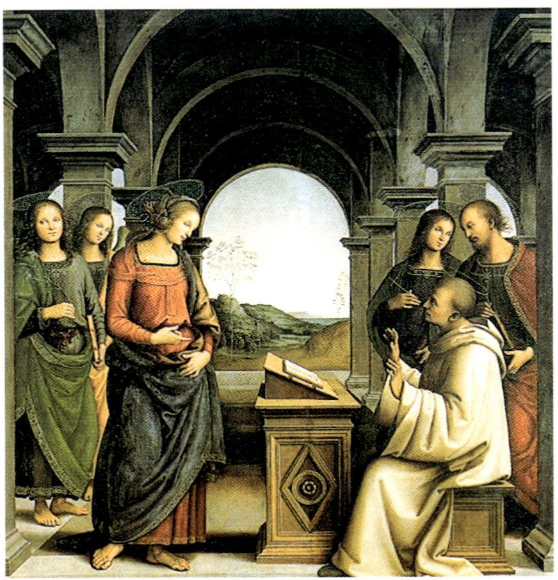

Perugino. The Vision of Saint Bernard *(1488–1489). Oil on panel, 66⅞ × 68⅛". Alte Pinakothek, Munich. Perugino is a painter who tends to summarize the transcendental and religious experiences that feature in his paintings with a minimum of figures. In this way he achieves a harmonious whole in which the story and the emotions being depicted are harmoniously condensed.*

repeated in the panel of *The Virgin and Child with Saint John the Baptist and Saint Sebastian* (Uffizi Gallery) also of 1493.

Between the years 1490 and 1500 Perugino decorated the Sala dell'Udienza of the Guild of Bankers in Florence with frescoes in which his painting seems to renew itself, possibly influenced by the youth of his pupil Raphael Sanzio.

The success of his work, and the large number of commissions he received, led him to repeat his models excessively and to use his pupils to serve interests that were more commercial than artistic. Vasari affirmed that Perugino "would have been capable of anything for money" and, referring to his collaborators, said that "none of them ever matched the diligence of Pietro, or his graceful application of color." Referring to Raphael, he made an exception: "by dedicating himself fully to the noble art of painting, he far exceeded his master."

Pietro Vannuci, Perugino, came from a very humble family, and before his Florentine period was trained in Perugia beside Benedetto Bonfigli (who died in 1496). He is one of the most recognized painters of his time. In 1523, three years after burying his illustrious pupil Raphael, he died in Fontignano.

The Original Classicism of Mantegna

The first Italian Renaissance forged a cultural atmosphere in the republic of Venice inspired by humanism, which created among the intellectuals a true veneration for Ancient Greece and Rome. The University of Padua was one of the main centers of culture, where the great scholars of the ancient world taught and studied.

Some of them frequented the workshop of the painter and antiques collector Francesco Squarcione (1397–1468), who was also at that time the master and godfather of a young painter named Andrea Mantegna. Both of them shared a love for ancient objects. The young Mantegna was soon passionate about antiques and was a keen admirer of the sculpture of Donatello. These influences defined the style that Mantegna kept throughout his life. In his paintings he rescues the architectural motifs and ornaments of antiquity and uses them to create the decoration of his works: columns, entablatures, and reliefs are added to the structures of temples, triumphal arches, and colonnades. In his paintings the stonework seems to extend itself to the landscape

Mantegna. The Agony in the Garden *(c. 1455). Tempera on panel, 31½ × 24¾". National Gallery, London.*

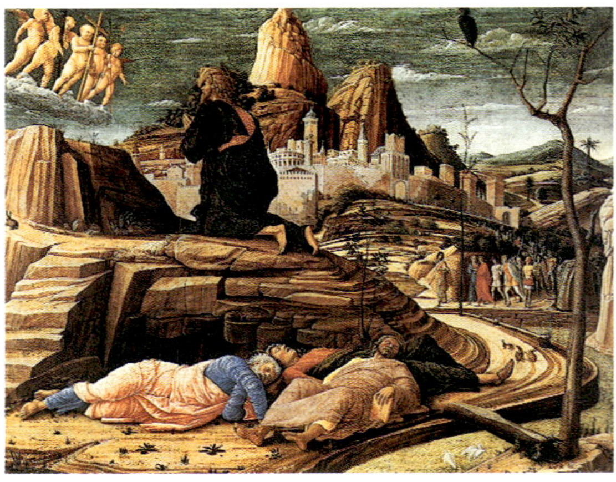

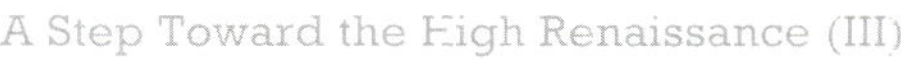

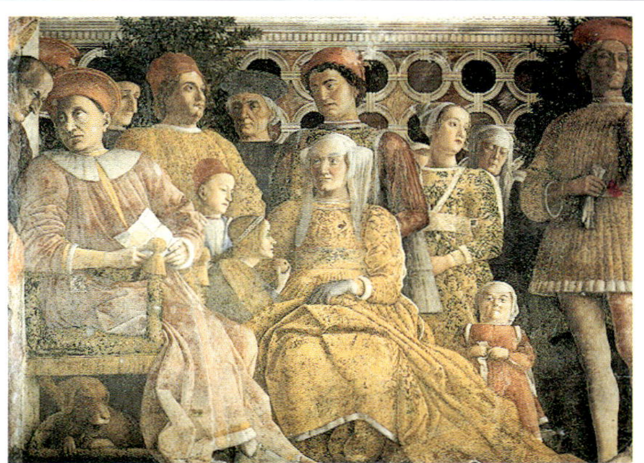

Mantegna. Ludovico Gonzaga with his Family and Court *(1473–1474). Fresco painting. Camera degli Esposi, Ducal palace, Mantua. In the Camera degli Esposi (or Room of the Bride and Groom), a cycle to which this scene belongs, Mantegna searched for a total fusion between art and reality. In fact, these scenes appear to the observer behind false, painted frames, on which the artist has represented curtains. In this way Mantegna paints an optical illusion in which he invites the observer to enter and take part in the life of the Gonzaga family.*

and to all the living beings in it.

In 1448 Mantegna began to work for himself on the frescoes of *The Life of Saint James and Saint Christopher* (Ovetari chapel of the Eremitani Church, Padua). In these early Venetian works, the figures, their clothing, the marble, and the plant motifs are drawn with exquisite detail and painted with superb colors, all within a materially uniform pictorial space.

This type of stony landscape, containing all the components of the painting, is reflected emphatically in the painting in the National Gallery (London) *The Agony in the Garden,* c.1455, and in the impressive *Crucifixion* in the Louvre. This is a scene that takes place in a landscape that borders on the idealized, and that seems to be cut from the same stone that covers the peak of Calvary, and that also seems to be part of the bodies of the crucified men. From the altarpiece for the great altar of San Zenon, the panels of *Saint Peter and Saint Paul* and of *Saint John and Saint Laurence* are notable. They both show figures within an architectural space, with an obviously romantic flavor, drawn from a low point of view that places the horizon at ground level, to increase the sensation of grandeur of the whole. This was a trick that Mantegna used on many of his works, whether small or large. Among these latter are some of the frescoes from the Camera degli Esposi (Room of the Bride and Groom) in the palace of the Duke of Mantua (1473–1474), referring to the life of the Gonzaga, and the nine canvases of *The Triumph of Caesar* (1486–1492) painted in tempera, which Federico I Gonzaga commissioned and which are currently in Hampton Court Palace, London. Notable among his small-scale works is the famous canvas *The Dead Christ* in the Pinacoteca of Brera, Milan (1470–1480) one of the most impressive foreshortenings in the history of art.

Andrea Mantegna was born in Isola de Carturo, between Padua and Venice, in 1431 and according to Vasari, he was the son of a certain Biagio, a poor man who died when Mantegna was still a child. He was then taken up by the painter Francesco Squarzione, who, on realizing the boy's talent, not only taught him but also adopted him as a son.

Up to the age of seventeen, Mantegna worked for his step-father, whom he eventually left after many problems.

After his early works in the Eremitani Church in Padua and the altar of San Zenon of Verona (in the period 1448–1456), he received so many commissions that he was forced to postpone his introduction into the court of Ludovico Gonzaga, marquis of Mantua. He had been summoned in 1456, and did not enter until 1460–1466, after spending a long period in Florence.

The court of Mantua benefited from the most fruitful and important stage in the art of Mantegna, until, from 1488 to 1490, Pope Innocent VIII employed him in Rome to decorate the chapel of Velvedere in the Vatican, which now does not exist.

Returning to Padua, he died in 1506.

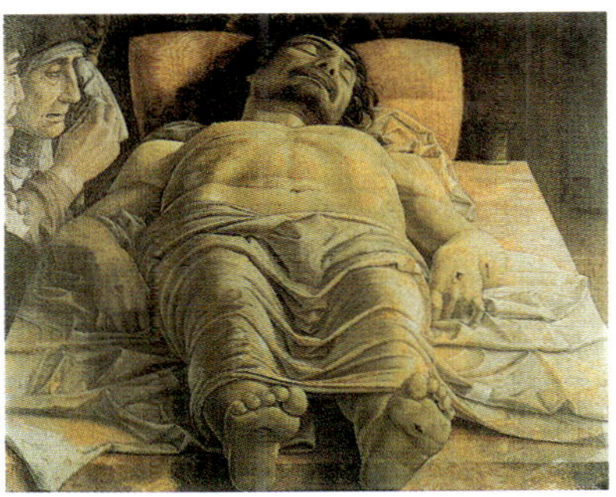

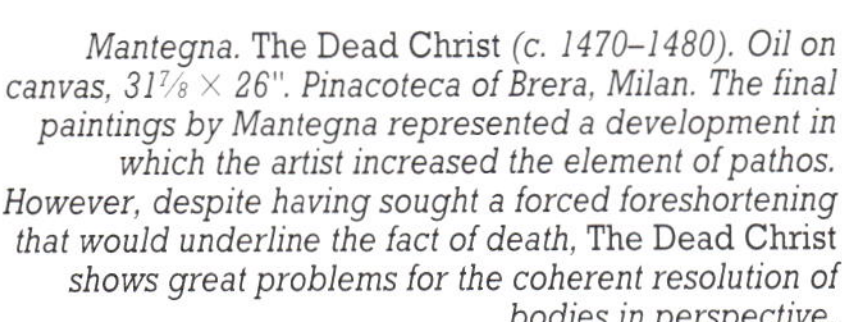

Mantegna. The Dead Christ *(c. 1470–1480). Oil on canvas, 31⅞ × 26". Pinacoteca of Brera, Milan. The final paintings by Mantegna represented a development in which the artist increased the element of pathos. However, despite having sought a forced foreshortening that would underline the fact of death,* The Dead Christ *shows great problems for the coherent resolution of bodies in perspective.*

FOUNDERS OF FIFTEENTH-CENTURY VENETIAN PAINTING

During the first half of the fifteenth century, Venetian painting continued in the tradition of late Gothic, until the Vivarini brothers, Antonio (1420–1484) and Bartolomeo (1432–1491), began the change toward the robust naturalism of Mantegna, their contemporary and neighbor from Padua. In Venice, the point of confluence between East and West, a type of painting took shape in which the influence of Mantegna was combined with the luminosity of the landscape and the chromatic tradition of Byzantine painting.

The Painting of the Bellini Family

The evolution of Venetian painting, from flamboyant Gothic to the modernity of the Renaissance aesthetic finds its greatest protagonists in the Bellini dynasty, father and sons.

Jacopo Bellini

As a painter he was trained under the influence of Gentile da Fabriano, to whose tendencies he tried to add the presence of Byzantine taste in the Venetian tradition, and the new ideas coming from the naturalists of Tuscany. Jacopo Bellini (1400–1470 approximately) is, in effect, the first person to try to incorporate Renaissance perspective into the tendencies of late Gothic.

Of his painting, little survives, although his *Madonnas with Child* (the Louvre and Accademia, Venice) are evidence of the level of primitivism that his painting still displays, despite their undeniable naturalist intentions.

As a painter of murals, he created frescoes in Verona Cathedral (1441) and in Venice. There, together with his sons, he painted at the Scuola de San Giovanni Evangelista (1452–1453) and in the Scuola Grande.

Gentile Bellini

Possibly born in 1429, Gentile, the youngest son of Jacopo, became known as a portrait painter in 1465, when he signed his first great work—a portrait in tempera of the first patriarch *Lorenzo Giustiniani* (Accademia, Venice). In 1474 he was named the official painter of the city and was commissioned to travel to Constantinople to paint his *Sultan Mohammed II* (1480). Gentile left Constantinople after being invested as a knight of the Golden Spur.

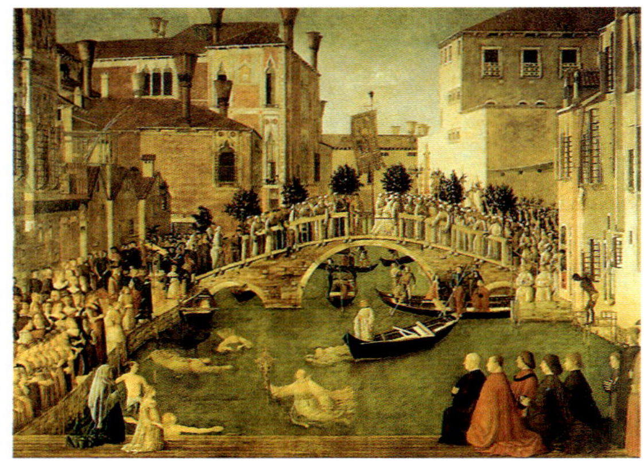

Gentile Bellini. Miracle of the Cross *(1500). Oil on canvas, 16⅞ × 12⅝". Accademia, Venice. Gentile Bellini was a painter of commissions who, as in this case, dedicated himself to creating detailed descriptive scenes of the city of Venice, beginning a genre that would continue all the way to Canaletto.*

In Venice, apart from his collection of portraits of the Doges, he painted the likenesses of many other people. His *Portrait of a Mathematician* in the National Gallery (pre 1474) stands out for its verisimilitude and psychological depth. Over and above his dedication to the portrait, Gentile was the unequalled painter of the events of his city in the fifteenth century. In the form of graphic chronicles, Gentile Bellini portrayed Venice as a proud, beautiful, and complacent city and he perpetuated its great events and characters and the urban scenes where they took place. With Gentile Bellini, Venice began the "vedutista" genre (from the Italian for view) so beloved of its citizens. *Procession in Saint Mark's Square* (1496), *the Miracle of the Cross* (1500), and *the Miraculous Cure of Pietro Ludovici* (1501) are events that occurred in a real urban landscape, reproduced with an ineffable descriptive detail that is rigid in terms of line, but beautifully harmonious in color.

Six years after painting the *Miraculous Cure of Pietro de Ludovici,* Gentile Bellini died in Venice.

Giovanni Bellini

Giovanni Bellini was the greatest painter of the Venetian *Quattrocento.* His long life allowed him to continue painting from Gothic archaism (which despite everything still breathes in the work of his brother Gentile) to the modernity and complete assimilation of his humanist ideals.

Born, it is thought, in 1426, he was possibly an illegitimate son of Jacopo. This supposition arose from the fact that he did not figure in his mother's will, and that he was always mentioned after his brother.

In his youth, of which little is known, he adopted the geometrical ordering and perspective of Mantegna, who had married his sister Niccolosa. This artistic decision surfaced around 1460, after working with his father and his brother Gentile in Padua and Verona. Examples that show the influence of his brother-in-law are *The Transfiguration* (1460) in the National Museum of Capodimonte, Naples, and *The Agony in the Garden* (also c. 1460).

From the 1460s, the hardness of his painting gives way to new ideas about volume, still in the tradition of Mantegna, but with a softer creation of forms, although nevertheless delineated by precise lines. Examples of this are the paintings in oil, *Pietà* in the Pinacoteca of Brera and *The Presentation in the Temple* in the Querini-Stampalia Gallery in Venice. Between 1475 and 1480 Giovanni Bellini worked on the renovation of the mural decoration of the chamber of the Grand Council of Venice, which made him the equivalent to the official painter of the city, in which capacity he remained faithful to grandiloquence. However, his official work did not prevent him from becoming a fashionable painter, capable of painting Madonnas as tall, svelte women with humanly beautiful faces, which proclaim the prime of the Renaissance. *The Virgin with Child* in the Carrar Museum in Bérgamo (1460) and the so-called *Madonna degli Alboretti* in the Accademia in Venice are a clear expression of the degree of softness with which he could paint when not working as an official painter.

The evolution of his painting can be appreciated clearly in one of his greatest works: *The Transfiguration,* a work that is almost the polar opposite of the one he had painted in 1460.

In the last years of his life, Bellini showed his unreserved humanism. His *Female Nude* or *Woman before a Mirror* represents a step toward the Venus of the *Cinquecento,* and for its anticipation of the *sfumatto* of da Vinci.

He died in Venice in 1516, never having lost public and official recognition of his position as the city's foremost painter of the period.

Giovanni Bellini. The Agony in the Garden *(c. 1460). Oil on panel, 50 × 31⅞". National Gallery, London. This work follows the model of the same theme by Mantegna, Giovanni Bellini's master, which is also to be found in the National Gallery. Placed one opposite the other, the landscapes of the Venetian painter are softer and open to the horizon, and suffused with the light of the city, Veneto.*

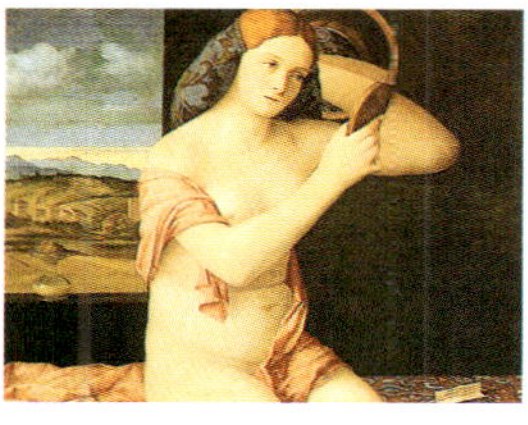

Giovanni Bellini. Female Nude *or* Woman before a Mirror *(c. 1510). Oil on panel, 31⅛ × 24⅜". Kunsthistorisches Museum, Venice.*

Giovanni Bellini. The Transfiguration *(1480–1485). Oil on panel, 59½ × 45¼". National Museum of Capodimonte, Naples. An example of the mature art of Giovanni Bellini, this painting represents a real landscape containing architectural works such as* Sant'Apolinar. *In the middle are divine figures bathed in an unreal light that underlines the metaphysical nature of the scene. They contrast with the three figures in the foreground on whom a different light falls, referring to faded human existence.*

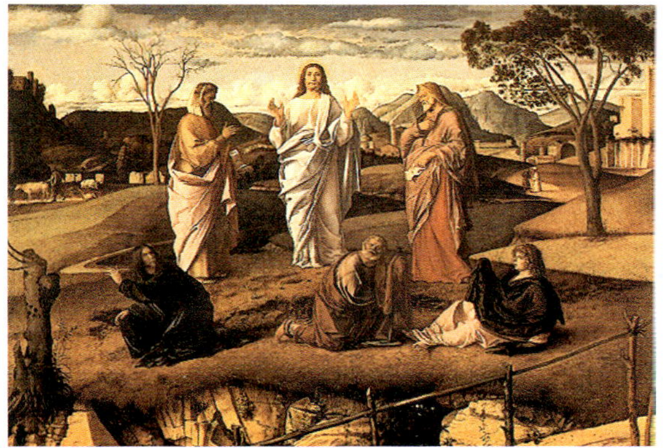

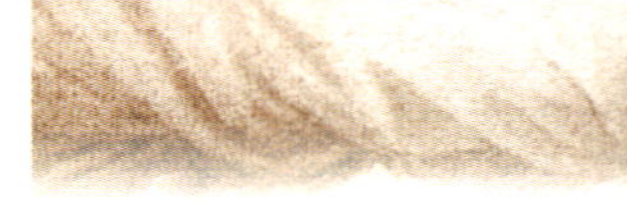

CONTEMPORARIES OF GIOVANNI BELLINI

ANTONELLO DA MESSINA

Giovanni Bellini had a great deal of influence on Venetian artistic creation. His work was applauded and followed by those who frequented his workshop (Bartolomeo Montagna, 1450–1523, and Cima da Conegliano, 1459–1517), and by other painters who, without having worked with the master, discovered the traces that he and his brother Gentile left imprinted in the Venetian aesthetic of the first Renaissance. Many of the Bellini brothers' contemporaries achieved fame, such as Vittore Carpaccio (1465–1525), a follower of the pictorial virtuosity applied to the "vedutista" genre begun by Gentile.

The Painting of Antonello da Messina

The painting of this Sicilian, trained in the artistic environment of the Two Sicilies, shows a convergence of the elements of late Valencian, Catalan, and Flemish Gothic that was fashionable in the court of Alfonso of Aragon, together with the new customs of the *Quattrocento,* which the artist discovered in Rome, Florence, Arezzo, and finally Venice. There the ideas of Pietro della Francesca and the palette of Giovanni Bellini ennobled his work, to the point that Bellini himself felt a great admiration for Messina, to the detriment of his liking of Mantegna.

The importance of Antonello in the artistic evolution of the Renaissance (apart from his excellent religious work) rests on the fact that he introduced to Italy Flemish oil techniques and naturalist portraiture, which delved into the personality of the model. In general, all the portraits of Antonello share the same features: they are three-quarter portraits, with the head turned to the left of the observer but with the eyes looking right. The portrait is always cut off below the shoulders. This standardization seems to satisfy the need to inhibit any details that did not concern the capturing of the model's personality.

Antonello da Messina. Altarpiece of Saint Cassiano *(1476). Oil on panel, 13¾ × 21⅝", 24¾ × 45¼" and 14 × 22⅜". Kunsthistorisches Museum, Vienna. A recomposed altarpiece of which only three parts survive: the central part representing the Virgin with child, and on the lateral pieces the saints Nicholas, Magdalena, Ursula, and Domingo.*

The Work of Antonello da Messina

Among the early surviving works, without either date or signature, can be mentioned the *Virgin with Child* (National Gallery, London) and *Saint Zosimus* (from the Forti Collection in Italy). These show clear references to the painting of his master Colantonio (born around 1420 and very well known in Naples between 1450 and 1453), in which there is a prevalence of the elements of late Flemish, Provencal, and Catalano-Aragonese Gothic. His first dated and signed work (1465) is a representation in iconic form of the *Salvador Mundi,* in the National Gallery (London), which shows the first signs of his interest in the new customs of the Renaissance. His polyptych of *Saint Gregory* of 1474 (National Museum of Messina) and *The Annunciation* of 1475 (National Museum of Syracuse) show the influence of Piero della Francesca in the conception of the figures. But it is in his short Venetian period that the painting of Antonello da Messina shows his modernizing concerns, although he does not abandon the Flemish detail that charac-

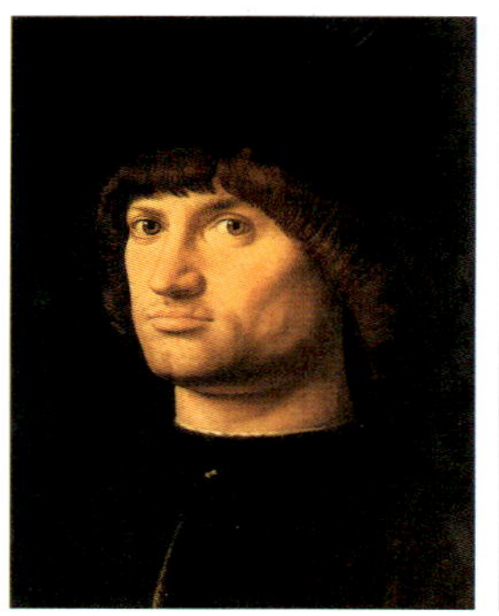

Antonello da Messina. Condottiero *(1475). Oil on panel, 13¾ × 15". The Louvre, Paris. The work of Antonello da Messina is a clear example of how the arrival of the High Renaissance was due to the combination of a series of influences. On one hand, he shows the advance of spatial representation in Florentine painting and on the other, the oil painting and naturalist techniques of the Flemish painters. The work of this Venetian artist combines both aspects in order to achieve lifelike portraits with great psychological depth.*

terizes his work.

The *Altarpiece of Saint Cassiano* of 1476 (Kunsthistorisches Museum, Vienna), is a true marvel of pictorial sensibility in form and color, and the most ambitious of the works he created in Venice. The figures are bathed in a light that affects absolutely every detail of the painting, and really appear to "live," although in a space that could be called metaphysical. The paintings of *Saint Sebastian* (1475–1476) in the Gemäldegalerie, Dresden, from an altarpiece that is now lost, and *The Virgin Annunciate* (1475) in the Reginal Gallery of Sicily in Palermo, summarize his Renaissance spirit.

From this period his best known works are the *Portrait of Trivulzio* (1476) in the Civic Museum, Turin, and the portrait of a young man that, because of its hard, scornful expression is known as *Condottiero* (1475), the Louvre. It is a marvelous psychological study of which the following has been said: "It is impossible to express better the daring of the sharp nose, whose nostrils seem to pulsate; the appetite for pleasure and the scorn of the lower lip...the lucid cruelty that appears in the depths of the shining eyes..."

One of the most fully Renaissance paintings of Antonello da Messina, despite its Gothic forms, is the oil painting *Saint Jerome in His Study.* Because of the exquisite Flemish detail with which the artist has filled the whole of this small painting, some writers have doubted that it comes from the last period of his artistic activity, and have tended to locate it between 1460 and 1474, the decade when he was most influenced by Flemish customs.

The observer enters the pictorial space by means of a large door that occupies the entire space of the painting, so that there is a separation between the real world and the symbolic world that follows Gothic tradition. The painting's structures multiply in perfect frontal perspective as far as the windows, which allow a glimpse of a landscape that stretches as far as infinity. A cube-shaped space, centered in the nave, symbolizes the intellectual world of the saint.

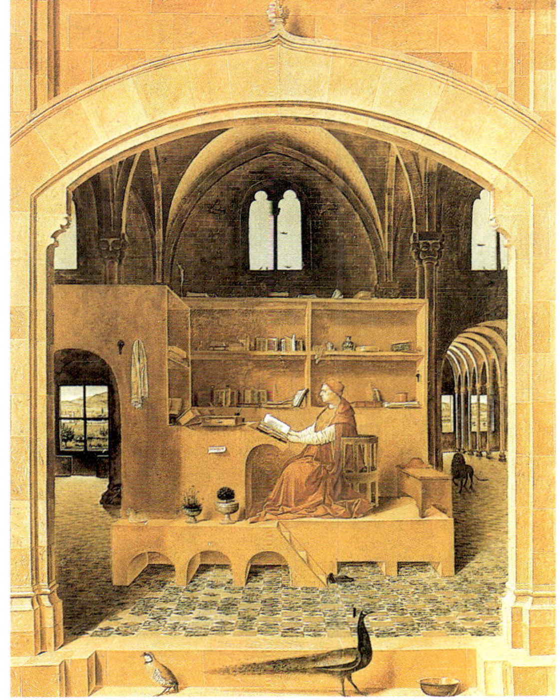

Antonello da Messina. Saint Jerome in His Study *(c. 1460–1474). Oil on panel, 14⅛ × 17¾". National Gallery, London. The painting is open like a window to show off its minute detail that stretches from the foreground, where two birds are represented in the real space of the observer, right to the background, where it is possible to make out each element of the landscape. In the central scene, Saint Jerome sits surrounded by all the elements of his library, including books, instruments, and plants.*

THE ARTIST'S LIFE

c. 1430. Born in Sicily, the son of a sculptor named Giovanni and his wife Garita, he is called Antonello degli Antonii.

1440–1450. The approximate period of his training at the hands of Colantonio.

1450–1453. During this period he almost certainly works with his master in Naples, Messina, Palermo, and Reggio in Calabria. (Vasari's assertion of a supposed journey to Flanders to study the secrets of oil painting is doubtful.)

1465–1472. In this period he travels to the main artistic centers of the *Quattrocento:* Rome, Florence, Arezzo, and Milan.

1475–1476. Years of frenetic activity in Venice, when he paints his most significant works, and the ones that most distinguish the Venetian painting of the *Quattrocento.*

c. 1479 He dies in Messina.

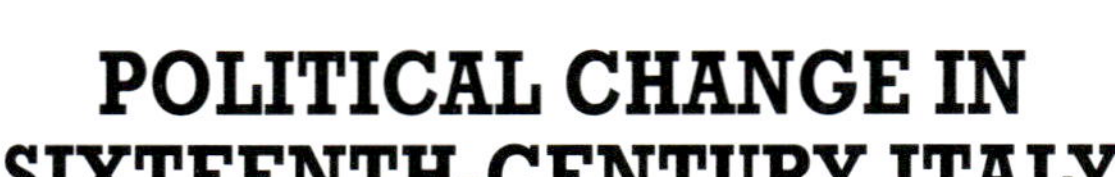

POLITICAL CHANGE IN SIXTEENTH-CENTURY ITALY

The political map of Italy in the *Quattrocento* was a varied mosaic of city-states, each one a center for the production and dissemination of art. Either in order to maintain their political prestige, or purely through a desire for show, the great families bestowed literary and artistic patronage within the geographical boundaries of each republic. As we have seen in the preceding pages, this gave rise to different stylistic developments; however, at the beginning of the sixteenth century the political panorama of the Italian peninsula changed notably. The territorial interests of Spain, France, and the church reduced the number of states, which then became a part of their dominions. This in turn led to a great loss of cultural focus points, thus producing a greater concentration of effort and a greater unity of artistic criteria. Padua and Urbino lost their *Quattrocentist* importance. These and other cities stopped being great producers of art, although they still produced artists such as the architect Bramante and Raphael Sanzio or "de Urbino," who were artists of major importance in the key centers of the sixteenth century. The result of this "concentration" was the arrival of an unrepeatable creative achievement, to which European culture (which had its foundations in Greece and Rome) owes the impulse that propelled it toward modernity.

The Great Artistic Centers of the *Cinquecento*

Modena, Mantua, Ferrara, and Parma

Whereas some cities, such as Rimini, Pienza, and Turin (as well as the above-mentioned Padua and Urbino), lost their innovating and pioneering style, others held on to it. Some of the states situated between Venice and Liguria, which had received the benefits of the patronage of the Gonzaga and Este families, continued to be important centers of artistic production. This is the case with Modena, Mantua, Ferrara, and above all Parma, which provided the impulse for a veritable school of painting.

The Republic of Venice

As a consequence of its confrontation with the Ottoman Empire and the changes in foreign trade that took place following the discovery of America, Venice

Raphael. Portrait of Pope Leon X with Two Cardinals *(c. 1518). Oil on panel, $46\frac{7}{8} \times 60\frac{5}{8}$". Palazzo Pitti, Florence.*

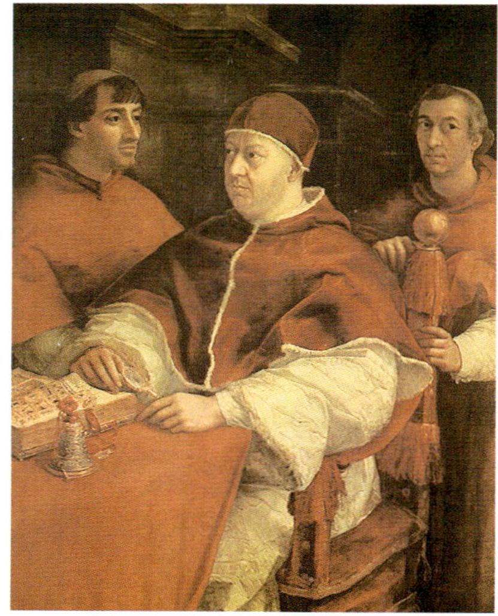

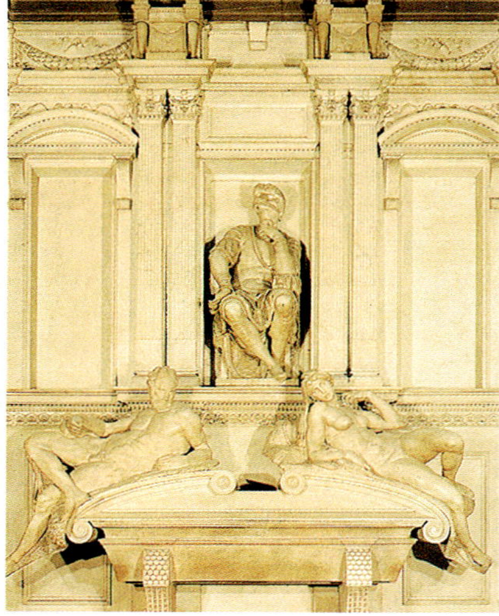

Michelangelo. Tomb of Lorenzo de' Medici (1524–1531). *Marble sculpture. New sacristy of San Lorenzo, Florence. In his works of art, Michelangelo embodies the concept of the "Universal Man" of the Renaissance, creating work in painting as well as sculpture and also carrying out some architectural projects.*

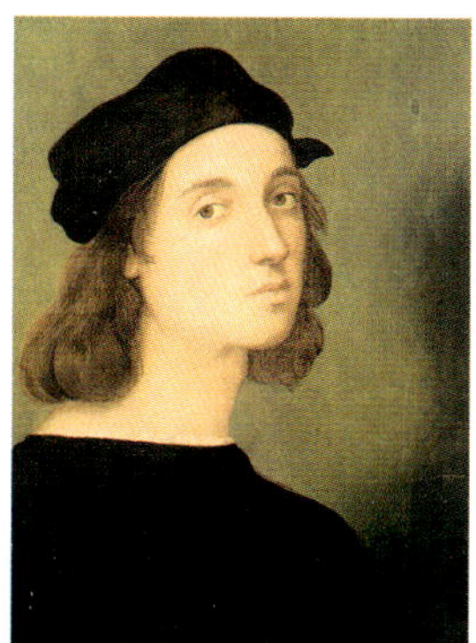

Raphael. Self-portrait *(c. 1506). Oil on panel, 13 × 17⅜". Uffizi Gallery, Florence.*

lost its naval dominance in the Mediterranean and found itself distanced from the new commercial routes. However, despite these setbacks, the Serenisima Republic did not give up its vocation for political and cultural power. It reaffirmed itself in the lands of northwest Italy and on the Adriatic coast: from Istria and Dalmatia, to Crete and the Peloponnese, territories in which it distributed (and received) artistic resources of prime importance in the history of art.

Florence

When the power of the Medici family ended (Lorenzo the Magnificent and his successors), Florence became a republic, until, with the backing of the Empire and of France, the Medici recovered power in 1511. Under Cosimo the Magnificent, Florence annexed Siena, and held the capital of the great dukedom of Tuscany.

Although the new Signoria lacked the creative vitality and innovation that it had shown in the *Quattrocento,* it maintained its avant-guard position and was instrumental in the appearance of Classicism and Mannerism in the sixteenth century.

The Supremacy of Rome

As a consequence of the transfer of the seat of the papacy to the city of Avignon (1305–1378) and the later schism of the so-called Antipopes, which continued until 1408, when Julius II became Pope in 1505, Rome had still not developed into a great city. It was with the papacy that Rome became a force capable of confronting the great absolute monarchies and of establishing powerful papal states that would allow the popes to intervene in the political rule of the rest of Italy. Thanks to their "earthly power," Julius II and the popes of the Medici family turned Rome into a military and political power, but also into the indisputable capital of art and culture of the sixteenth-century Renaissance.

Nevertheless, Rome never created its own school of painting, despite the fact that history often refers to the Roman school. The church of Rome, above all, was a great consumer of art. The popes and other dignitaries had an exceptional capacity for securing the services of the greatest artists, who arrived in Rome from the rest of Italy and Europe to work in the Vatican and the other palaces of the great families and cardinals of the church.

Under Julius II, named Giuliano della Rovere (1433–1513), the city witnessed the construction of the Basilica of Saint Peter's, the Vatican palace, and the embellishment carried out on the great rooms of the residences of the *Quattrocentist* popes. Pope Julius II had the intelligence, or luck, to commission the three great artists who made this transformation possible: Bramante, Raphael, and Michelangelo.

The architect Donato d'Agnolo di Pascuale, known as Bramante (1444–1514) was the unarguable heir of Brunelleschi, the artistic genius who gave new energy to the old classical legacy and who initiated the great classical architecture of the *Cinquecento.* The great importance of Bramante for sixteenth-century art was, naturally, in his particular buildings and monuments with which the new classicism began: *Santa Maria presso San Satiro* of 1482–1486, *Santa Maria delle Grazie* of 1490, both in Milan, the project for the *Basilica of Saint Peter of the Vatican* (1505–1506), which he did not see finished, the *Patio of San Damaso* (1505) in the Vatican, the *Tempietto of San Pietro in Montorio* (1503) in Rome, and many others.

Since both painting and sculpture, in their most monumental expression, were subordinate to architecture, one can conclude that the sculptural and pictorial classicism of the first quarter of the sixteenth century developed in parallel with the architecture of Bramante. Due to the three artists mentioned above, Rome was able to convert itself into the great monument of the *Cinquecento,* the acropolis of Renaissance art.

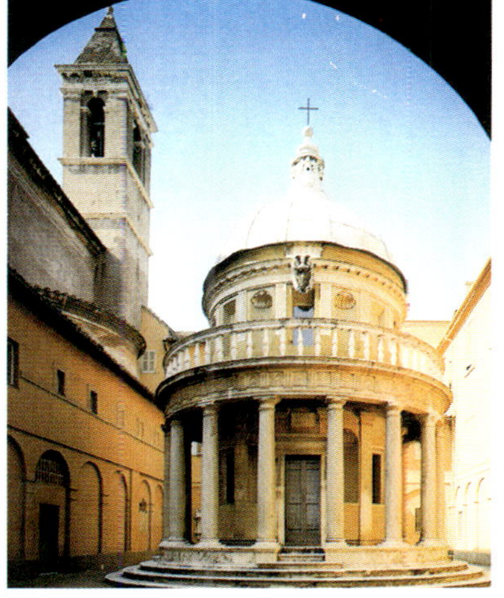

Bramante. Tempietto of San Pietro in Montorio *(1503). Rome. The small shrine of Bramante is now located in the Spanish Academy of Fine Arts in Rome, and is a complete demonstration of* Cinquecento *classicism. In a very small space Bramante employs all the main techniques of classical architecture. The work is an exercise in style, executed with great simplicity and perfect balance and harmony, all carried out on a human scale.*

GENIUSES OF RENAISSANCE PAINTING

LEONARDO DA VINCI

The change from the fifteenth to the sixteenth centuries saw the culmination of Renaissance art, in the work of a few artists who were capable of expressing themselves in what are considered the "major" arts (architecture, sculpture, and painting). History had given them the unique opportunity to put man and the human figure at the center of thought and artistic creation. The great *maniera* (style in Italian) of conceiving of and creating an artistic work developed, treating the human figure with grandeur so that it became monumental and archetypal, and thus leaving behind the creative achievements of the *Quattrocento.* Four extraordinary talents appeared: Bramante, Leonardo, Michelangelo, and Raphael. Bramante was an architect and also had a great talent as a painter. This is demonstrated in his very few surviving works, such as the figures of *Philosophers and Soldiers* for the Panigarola palace, now in the Pinacoteca Brera in Milan.

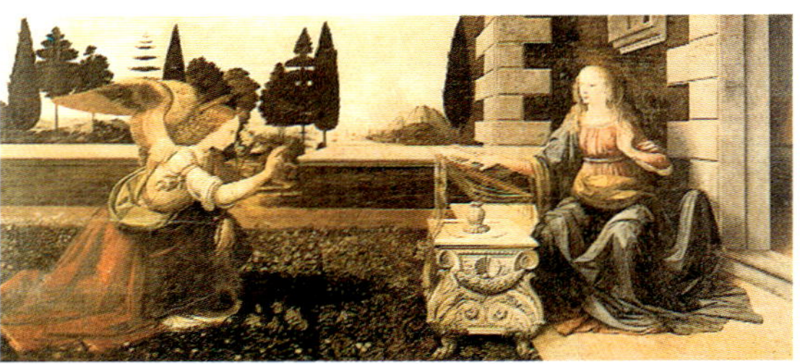

Leonardo da Vinci. The Annunciation *(1472–1475). Oil on panel, $85\frac{2}{5} \times 38\frac{1}{2}$". Uffizi Gallery, Florence. One of the first works by Leonardo, although it is already possible to see the interests that he will gradually develop. In the first place, the search for atmosphere, both by means of the representation of the perspective of space and in the light that shapes the figures. Secondly, the configuration of unreal space, in which the geometric and the mathematical join with the detail.*

Leonardo's Painting

When defining the work of Leonardo, the first thing that can be said is that he was the archetypal *Renaissance Man,* interested in all branches of human knowledge. From military engineering to philosophy, arts, and science, he was equally concerned with discovering new techniques for painting as with designing a machine that would fly. Leonardo was possibly an engineer more than a pure artist. He was a theorist who was able to demonstrate his theories with results. Leonardo came to a style of painting not through accumulated experience but rather by means of scientific reasoning. According to A. Cirici Pellicer,

> "Leonardo began the artistic flow that was to last until Impressionism in the nineteenth century: the search for atmosphere, the primacy of values over volumes; movement made into a presence, not shaking solid objects, but making them pulsate continuously with the spaces."

Leonardo was a tireless designer of buildings that were never constructed and the creator of sculptures that time has not preserved. However, he is unarguably one of the pillars of universal painting, with a wide repertoire of themes and techniques, although few of his paintings survive. With his constant experiments, Leonardo himself was mostly responsible for the ruin for most of his paintings.

As a theorist, author of *Tratto della pittura,* he produced the first reasoned definition of pictorial form and structure, from which evolved the concepts that led to the classicism of the *Cinquecento.* The primacy of drawing, as a base for any artistic creation, is the real essence of Leonardo's art. He was one of the greatest draftsmen who has ever lived, a great master of all the techniques related to drawing and tonal values. His virtuosity is unparalleled in his use of *sfumato,* the soft blending

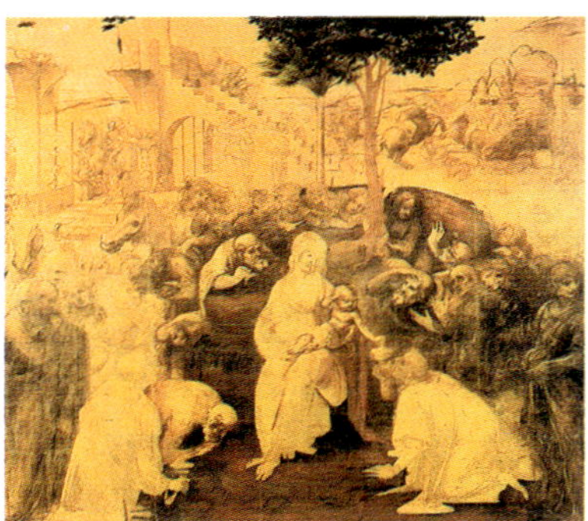

Leonardo da Vinci. Adoration of the Three Kings *(1481–1482). Oil on panel, $96\frac{7}{8} \times 95\frac{5}{8}$". Uffizi Gallery, Florence.*

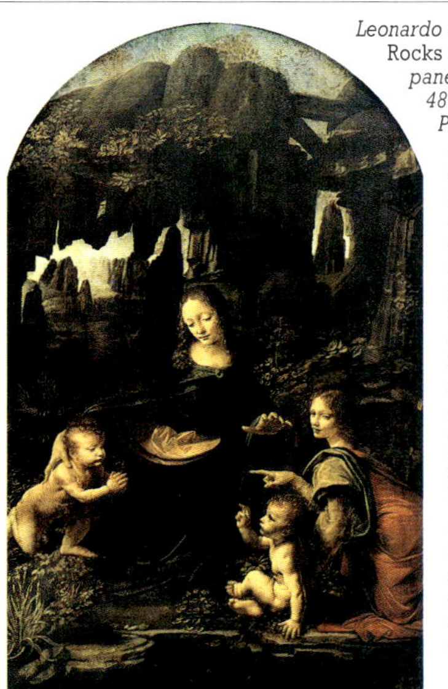

Leonardo da Vinci. Virgin of the Rocks *(1483–1486). Oil on panel transferred to panel, 48½ × 78⅜". The Louvre, Paris. In this masterpiece by Leonardo the influence of neoplatonism is clear. In addition to the mystical atmosphere that surrounds the holy scene, the presence of the Virgin in the strange surroundings of a rock-filled cave alludes to the famous platonic cave. According to myth, all that humans can perceive are the shadows of the divine. Thus, the surroundings of the Virgin correspond, in a certain sense, to the celestial truths of heaven itself, from where the shadows are projected onto the world.*

of one tone into another.

Leonardo came to pictorial representation by means of empirical knowledge, which led him, for example, to the dissection of corpses in order to study human anatomy, of which he ended up becoming a great expert. This is clear not only in the robust musculature of his male nudes, but also in the true genius with which he paints the softness of his female figures, and in every other detail, from the divine expression of the lips of his Virgins and paintings of Saint Anne to the marvel of the *Mona Lisa.*

The Work of Leonardo

Leonardo's artistic creation developed in Florence, Milan, and Paris, with occasional visits to Rome and Venice. In the last stage of his life (which corresponds chronologically to the *Cinquecento*) he was a tireless traveler.

On the other hand, we have to imagine that the inexhaustible imagination of Leonardo and his genius as a draftsman and painter is shown both in the surviving work and in the information we have of his failed experiments as a painter, and the other reasons that led him to destroy his work. A good example of this is the terrible condition in which *The Last Supper,* one of his most representative works, survived. Leonardo had the idea of applying egg tempera to a prepared surface in order to paint the fresco.

Of the works that survive, the following are the most representative:

From his first Florentine stage, which took place between 1472 and 1482, we must mention above all his first known drawing: *Valley with Mountains and Castles* of 1473 (Uffizi Gallery). This was done with quill and watercolor, with notable effects of atmospheric perspective, an aspect in which it exceeds the landscapes of the *Quattrocento.*

From his collaboration with Verrocchio, between 1470 and 1480, one must not forget his contribution to the *Baptism of Jesus* (Uffizi Gallery): the figure of the blond angel to the left of Jesus, and the background landscape.

Between 1742 and 1743 came *The Annunciation* (Uffizi Gallery) painted for the Convent of San Bartolome de Monteolivetto, near Florence. It is an oil panel that still shows Verrocchio's characteristic hardness, but with a group of trees defined sharply against the light in contrast to the diffusion of the distant landscape and against which the figure of the angel stands out. It is a formula that he repeated in some of his most representative works.

The Madonna with the Carnation, between 1472–1475, anticipates the compositional formula of placing the figures in a triangular, almost equilateral, scheme in the foreground. The background scene is lit from behind, for example, via a window through which the luminosity of the sky can filter and collide, so to speak, with the frontal light that illuminates the figures. It is a technique that he repeats in his portrait of *Ginevra de'Benci* (between 1474 and 1476) in the National Gallery, Washington. Her head and bust contrast with the dark leaves of a juniper, which the artist relates to the woman's name. It is important to

Leonardo da Vinci. The Last Supper *(1495–1497). Egg tempera on a preparation for* buon fresco, *346½ × 181⅛". The refectory of the Convent of Santa Maria delle Grazie, Milan. In* The Last Supper, *Leonardo's innovative spirit led him to experiment with a new technique of fresco painting.*

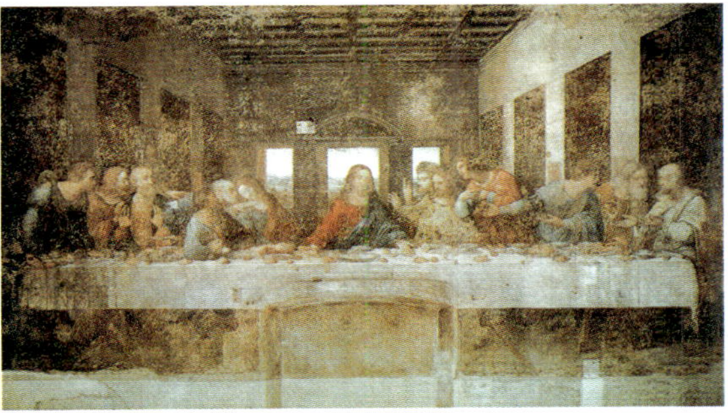

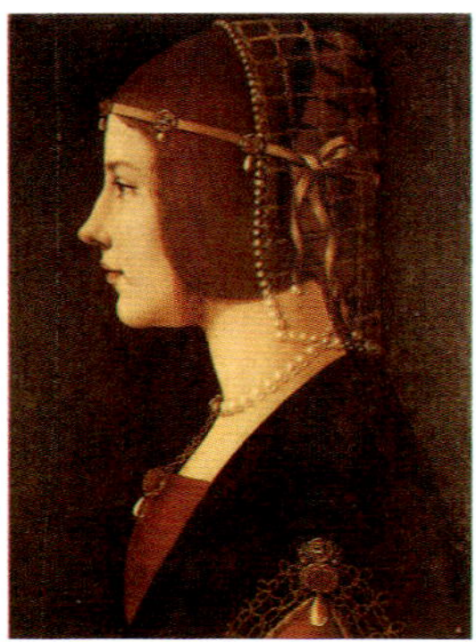

Leonardo da Vinci. Lady with a Pearl Hairpiece *(c. 1485–1490). Oil on panel, 13⅜ × 20⅛". Pinacoteca Ambrosiana, Milan. Leonardo sought accuracy in his portraits, which he achieved through the use of drawings previously taken from life.*

point out that in the works mentioned he begins to show *sfumato,* the particular treatment of chiaroscuro that characterizes his figures.

The first stage in Florence is brought to a close with two unfinished works of greater complexity. Despite being interruptions of his monochromatic phase, they feature the defining characteristics of Leonardo's artistic prime. The paintings are *The Adoration of the Three Kings* (Uffizi Gallery) and *Saint Jerome,* a commission for the monks of San Donato de Scopeto, near Florence, which he left unfinished when he departed for Rome. The first is without a doubt one of the most elaborate of Leonardo's compositions, based on the gestures of the characters who swarm around the Virgin and Child in a multicolored throng. The small arm that reaches out to the beautiful chalice that the adorer at the right of the painting is offering completes the diagonal that drops from the top corner. On this diagonal converge the curving patterns suggested by the heads of the different groups of people. The light-filled atmosphere is completed by an architectural background, with a staircase, trees, and horses, which fades into the distance.

Saint Jerome of 1482 (Pinacoteca Vaticana) is one of Leonardo's first examples of anatomic "description," a result of his scientific interest in the workings of the human body. It was an interest that previously had shown itself in the drawing of 1479, *The Body of Bernardo Baroncelli* (the murderer of Giuliano de' Medici) *Hanging from the Gallows* (Bonnet Museum, Bayonne).

The Milanese Period

During the sixteen years that Leonardo spent in the service of Sforza, he worked as an architect, sculptor, painter, and engineer of artillery and hydraulics, while his pictorial genius created, among others, two key works in universal painting:

The Virgin of the Rocks is an oil painting on panel, later transferred to canvas, painted between 1483 and 1486 (the Louvre). It represents a marvelous artistic composition and study of light. The composition of the figures corresponds to a closed format in the shape of an equilateral triangle, whose interior they fill. The observer's gaze covers the whole of the composition by following the broken line suggested by the magnificently drawn arms and hands, with the sensational foreshortening of the left hand of the Virgin. This was a technique previously practiced by Bellini, and that is recalled in the works of later painters. The light effect begun in *Saint Jerome* is repeated, more markedly, in this beautiful group, and the figures are bathed in the mysterious light that filters in through an imaginary crevice.

The Last Supper (1495–1497) is another of Leonardo's masterpieces, for its composition, its illumination (it repeats the formula of the two opposing light sources, one from behind, one from the front), and for the artistry and expressiveness of the figures, whose heads are all taken from natural studies. The perspective space in which *The Last Supper* takes place has its vanishing point almost in the center of the very noble head of Jesus. In this way, standing out against the sky that the central opening of the dining room reveals, the face of the Lord attracts the interest of all the people watching (the apostles as well as the observer), without this centrality making the painting monotonous. Leonardo's genius for composition divides the apostles into groups of three, each with its own dramatic action. Faces and hands are directed toward the vanishing point (the face of Jesus) while they express their confusion at their master's prediction: *Amen dico vobis me traditurus est.* The majesty and artistic grandeur of the figures of *The Last Supper* indicate the new great *maniera* or style of painting.

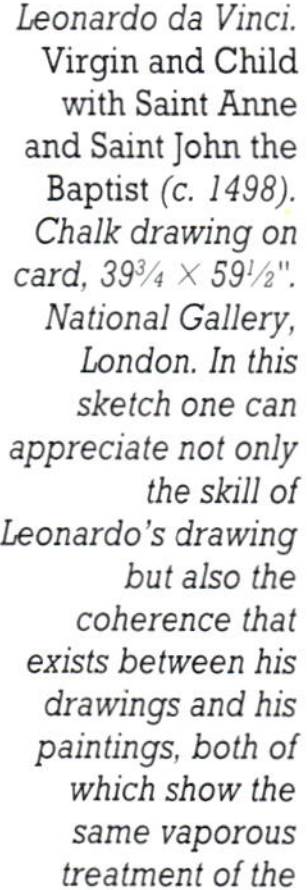

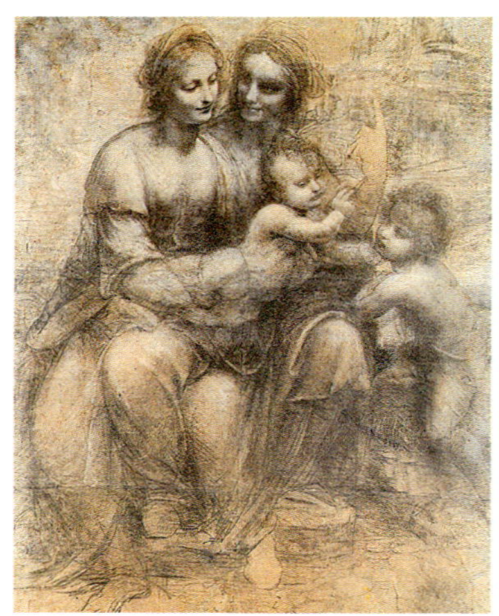

Leonardo da Vinci. Virgin and Child with Saint Anne and Saint John the Baptist *(c. 1498). Chalk drawing on card, 39¾ × 59½". National Gallery, London. In this sketch one can appreciate not only the skill of Leonardo's drawing but also the coherence that exists between his drawings and his paintings, both of which show the same vaporous treatment of the figures.*

Leonardo was a great portrait painter, and managed to achieve remarkable counterpoint with the inner selves of his sitters. In the decade 1480–1490, he produced some extraordinary works: *Lady with an Ermine* (thought to be Cecilia Gallerani) between 1485 and 1490, Czartoryski Gallery, Krakow. *Lady with a Pearl Hairpiece* (possibly Beatriz de' Este) of 1490, Pinacoteca Ambrosiana, Milan, which is a profile with an extraordinary power of suggestion, *The Musician* (possibly Franchino Gaffurio) of 1490, which is also in the Pinacoteca Ambrosiana, Milan. In all of these, Leonardo demonstrates his extraordinary capacity for detail of the highest quality and the atmospheric effectiveness of *sfumato,* which was to reach its pinnacle of attractiveness and expressiveness with the *Mona Lisa,* one of the most famous paintings of all time.

The Second Florentine Period

The fall of the Sforza family following the French attack on Milan forced Leonardo to return to Florence, passing through Venice and Mantua, and taking with him the drawing of *The Virgin and Child with Saint Anne and Saint John* (c. 1498), the marvelous charcoal drawing which is now one of the jewels of the National Gallery in London.

To this period belongs one of the great lost works, *The Battle of Anghiari,* a mural for the hall of the great council of the Palazzo Vechio, which was destroyed fifty years after being painted. What we know of it is a copy of the central group, made by Rubens, which is a scene of great power and dynamism in which Leonardo represents a clash of cavalrymen attempting to rescue their standard.

From the same period (1503–1505) comes the *Mona Lisa* (also known as *La Gioconda*), which is without question the most famous portrait in the world. It is essentially a face and two hands, about which innumerable claims and suppositions have been made. The truth is that despite hypotheses with greater or lesser evidence, everything is conjecture, not least of which is the identity of the model.

The application of *sfumato,* of which the *Mona Lisa* is the greatest example, can be seen in *Saint John the Baptist,* the Louvre (1513–1516), another masterly lesson in art. It is the naked torso of a young man with a languid, enigmatic expression emerging from darkness, as an anticipation of the shadowy world of Caravaggio.

From the last stage also comes *Virgin and Child with Saint Anne* (1508–1510), oil on panel, in the Louvre.

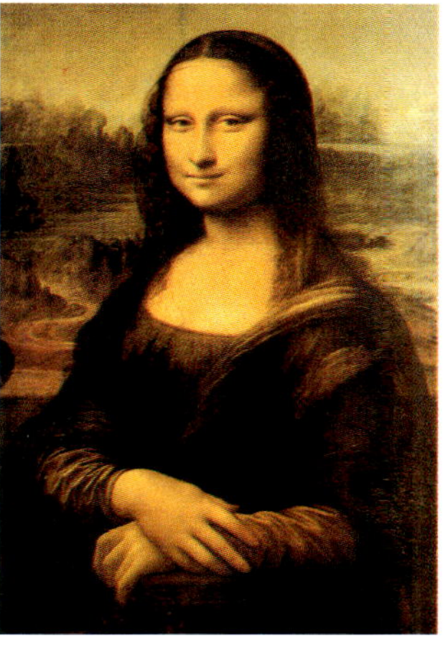

Leonardo da Vinci. Mona Lisa *(1503–1505). Oil on panel, 20⅞ × 30⅜". The Louvre, Paris. One of the masterpieces of the history of painting. In one brief image the smile of the Mona Lisa contains all of Leonardo's interests: the lack of definition of the smile caused by* sfumato, *which defines at the same time as it blurs, and the synthesis of sublime or ideal beauty, which is implicit rather than obvious and comes as a revelation.*

THE ARTIST'S LIFE

- 1452. Born in Anchiano, near Vinci, the illegitimate son of the lawyer Ser Piero da Vinci and a peasant woman called Caterina.
- c. 1470. His paternal grandfather, Ser Antonio, by whom he was educated, shows Verrocchio the sketches of the young boy. The sculptor has no doubt about taking him on as one of his apprentices.
- 1472. Leonardo da Vinci is already mentioned as an official painter in Florence.
- 1476. Still with Verrocchio he is accused of sodomy, an accusation of which he is completely absolved. Possibly in this year, and thanks to his supposed friendship with Botticelli, he receives the protection of the Medici.
- 1482–1487. He finishes his first Florentine period and begins his life in Milan, in the service of the Sforza family. For Duke Ludovico il Moro he works as an architect and engineer, as well as a painter and sculptor, creating an equestrian sculpture (of which only the preparatory drawings survive) of the founder of the dynasty Ludovico Sforza.
- 1498. He begins his second Florentine period, as a consequence of the arrival of French troops in Milan and the subsequent fall of Ludovico il Moro.
- 1506. He begins his wandering period. He travels to Milan, back to Florence and then again to Milan.
- 1514-1515. He lives in Rome, in the Vatican Belvedere.
- 1517. He travels to Paris, summoned by Francis I, a great admirer of his art. He takes with him the painting of the *Mona Lisa.*
- 1519. He dies on April 2 in the castle of Cloux in the Loire Valley.

THE MOST NOTABLE ARTISTS OF THE ITALIAN *CINQUECENTO*

THE PEAK OF RENAISSANCE CLASSICISM. THE DIVINE RAPHAEL

Raphael lived to the age of only thirty-seven. He had a short artistic life but one that was enough for his fellow citizens to refer to him as divine. Whether this was an exaggeration or not, the appellation is witness to the portentous and precocious skill that allowed a young man of twenty to reach, as a painter, the peaks of popularity and recognition among intellectuals and those in power. Raphael was an authentic prodigy in his mastery of the techniques of the art of painting, just as later Mozart was in the art of music. A unique sense of intuition allowed the young man to rapidly assimilate the achievements of Renaissance art that Leonardo and Michelangelo (among others) had given the world. On the other hand, the young prodigy was endowed with an attractive personality capable of opening all the doors of society, another facet of his personality that explains the rapid trajectory of one of the most prestigious artists in the history of art.

Raphael's Painting

In a letter that Raphael wrote to the literary count Castiglione (1478–1515), a person whom he painted in a superb portrait, there is a significant sentence: "I must confess to you that, to paint a beautiful woman, I have to see a lot of them."

It is an expression in which, behind its apparent insignificance, hides the eclectic nature of his aesthetic thinking. In reality, the merit that history has rightly accorded Raphael does not correspond to an innovative genius who developed new approaches to painting, but rather to an artist who mastered all the skills of his specialty, and who created a body of painting in which the whole of the art of the Renaissance comes together with unsurpassable brilliance. Historical perspective today allows us to see in the work of Raphael ideas and forms taken from Leonardo, Michelangelo, Bramante, and the less well-known Fra Bartolomeo della Porta, a Venetian painter who lived between 1472–1517.

The physicality of Raphael's figures is the result of his particular application of the methods of Signorelli, of the above-mentioned Bartolomeo della Porta, and above all of Leonardo (*sfumato* included). With these influences he produces a figurative, artistic language of great physicality, in generous spaces that do not overwhelm the human figure.

In the composition of his Virgins, he repeats the pyramidal layout already displayed by Leonardo and other previous painters. However, unlike with Leonardo, rather than letting his figures suggest a zigzag pattern, Raphael points their axes toward the vertex of the pyramid. Another compositional technique that Raphael used frequently is what is called the isocephallic plane: the level of the heads in the different

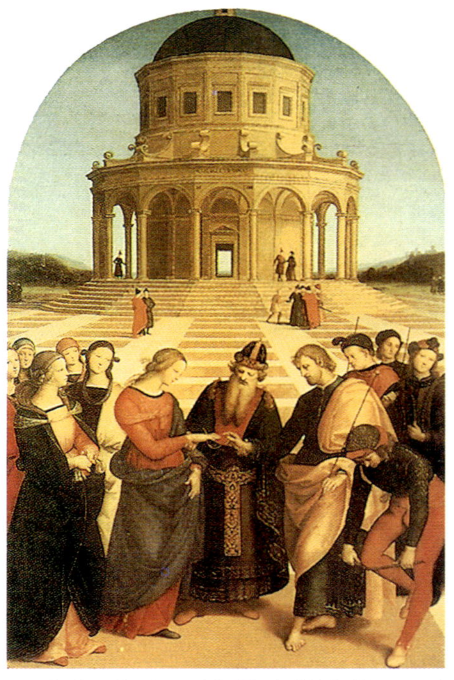

Raphael. Marriage of the Virgin *(1504). Oil on panel, 46 × 66⅞". Pinacoteca de Brera, Milan. The most important work of the painter's early period, during his stay in Umbria. Raphael has structured the surface of the painting in three parts, which are constructed by perspective and by the positioning of the figures. First of all, there is the scene of the Virgin getting married; then the perspective widens, guided by the flagstones on the floor, to a second group of people; to finish off there is the depth created by the space of the painting with the representation of a shrine that follows the models of Bramante.*

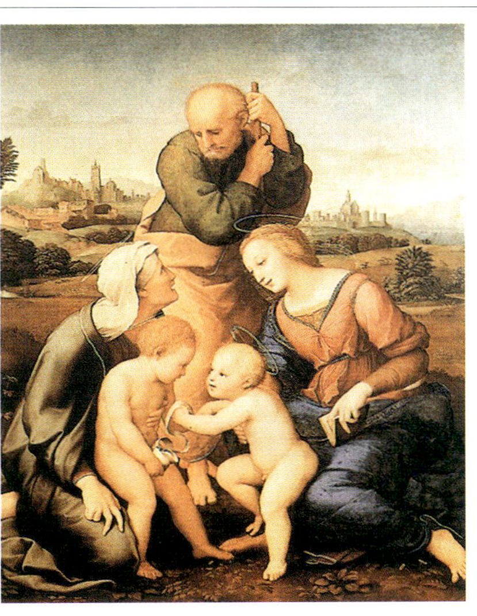

Raphael. The Holy Family with Saint Isabel and Saint John *(1507). Oil on panel. Alte Pinakothek, Munich. In this classical work, Raphael is at his purest, using a strict triangular framework and giving the bodies lightly twisting, harmonious movements, against a perfect landscape of aerial perspective opening out into space.*

groups of figures share the same plane of perspective.

As for color, Raphael's palette is richer than those of his predecessors, possibly because of the Venetian influence.

In summary, Raphael particularly stands out because of his balanced (one could say measured) application of painting's previous achievements, to become the greatest exponent of Renaissance classicism.

The Work of Raphael

The Work of a Young Man from Urbino

Orphaned at the age of eleven, the painter's apprentice grew up alongside Perugino, with whom he worked in Perusa. Having assimilated the methods of his master, he began to produce works in which he gradually left behind traces of the *Quattrocentists.*

There is the *Coronation of San Niccolò da Tolentino* (c. 1500), a work of which an angel survives in the Pinacoteca in Brescia, and two miracles of the saint, in the Museum of Capodimonte, Naples.

Also, *The Crucifixion* of 1502 (National Gallery, London) which still shows clear reminders of the angelic iconography of the *Quattrocento.* The *Coronation of the Virgin,* also of 1502 (Pinacoteca Vaticana, Rome), is a work infused with the spirituality of Perugino's painting.

Marriage of the Virgin of 1504 (Pinacoteca de Brera, Milan) is beyond doubt the masterpiece of Raphael's early period. The compositional formula of using the isocephallic plane in the three main groups of figures appears clearly, as do the ideas taken from Perugino's *Giving of the Keys to Saint Peter* and the architectural classicism of Bramante. This oil panel is a foretaste of later work by Raphael, with its luminosity, its perfect staggering of figures, its undulating, careless poses, and the grouping of its figures in isocephallic planes.

The Florentine Period

During the four years that Raphael stayed in Florence, he incorporated into his oil painting the influences of Leonardo concerning chiaroscuro and *sfumato* for outlines.

This was the period of his exquisite Virgins, of his most celebrated portraits, and the period in which the dynamic gestures appeared that he would exploit in his great murals in the Vatican.

Of his portrait work, mention must be made of:

His *Self-portrait* (Uffizi Gallery), which is unfortunately badly preserved.

Guidobaldo da Montefeltro (Uffizi Gallery)

The portrait of *Agnolo Doni* and his wife *Maddalena Doni* (1506) in the Palazzo Pitti, Florence. In its pose (including the hands) the portrait of Maddalena is a type of Mona Lisa though considerably more corpulent.

The Pregnant Woman in the Palazzo Pitti, Florence. In the anxious expression of the pregnant woman and the perfection of her sensitive hand spread out over her enlarged stomach, Raphael shows his ability to explore the psychology of his characters.

However without a doubt, the best-known work from Raphael's Florentine period is the wonderful series of images of the Virgin, painted between approximately 1505 and 1508. These Virgins correspond to earlier iconographic models but with Raphael reach an ideal of beauty based on formal and expressive serenity. The Virgin is seated, and behind her lies a landscape of soft colors that induce a relaxation of the spirit. She appears in thoughtful poses, as if protecting the innocence of the boys Jesus and Saint John, or alone with her son on her lap.

Raphael. Agnolo Doni *(1506), oil on panel, 17¾ × 24¾". Palazzo Pitti, Florence. In the series of portraits that he painted during his period in Florence, Raphael shows his pictorial ability in the treatment of realistic themes removed from religious topics.*

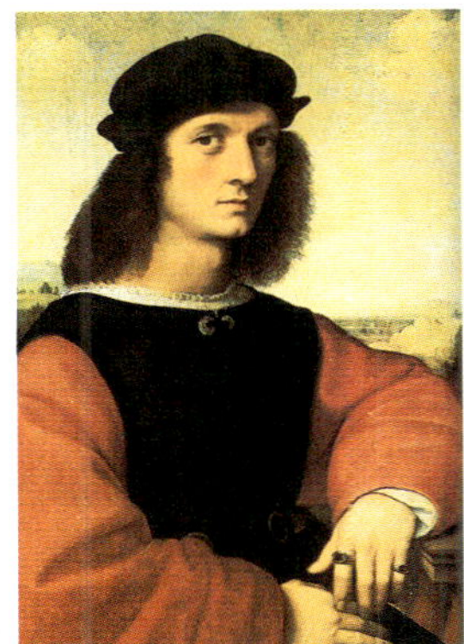

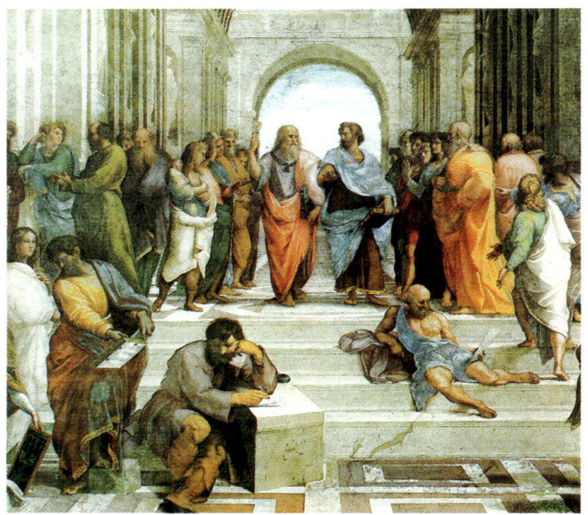

Raphael. The School of Athens *(1509–1510). Fresco painting, 303⅛" base. Stanze della Segnatura. The Vatican, Rome. Because of their location, the themes of the stanze, or rooms of Julius II's private apartment, had to be religious. Nevertheless, Raphael suggested a synthesis that included not only the teaching of the Bible but also of the ancient Greek and Roman thinkers. The fresco shows the classical philosophers reproduced with the faces of famous artists of the period, so Bramante represents Euclid, and Michelangelo Heraclitus. The ancient world is matched to the modern one, a true Renaissance sentiment.*

The Belvedere Madonna (Kunsthistorishches Museum, Vienna) and *The Madonna of the Goldfinch* of 1507 (Uffizi Gallery) or the Madonna known as *La Belle Jardinière* (the Louvre) are possibly the best-known paintings of the Virgin with Jesus and Saint John. From the same year is the *Holy Family with Saint Isabel and Saint John* (Alte Pinakothek, Munich), a work in which Raphael's pyramidal composition is very evident, and in which all the axes of the figures point toward the vertex of the pyramid.

The Madonna del Granduca (Palazzo Pitti) and the *Tempi Madonna* in the Alte Pinakothek in Munich are examples of Madonnas and Child in which Raphael's classicism reaches its purest expression.

Raphael's Roman Period

It was in Rome, specifically in what are known as the *stanze* (or rooms) in the Vatican, that Raphael created his most outstanding frescoes. This was the result of a commission from Pope Julius II, who decided to abandon the rooms of the Borgias and occupy others in the palace of Nicolas V. The great wall murals of these papal apartments are without doubt Raphael's most important work. They represent the culmination of his Renaissance classicism and the exaltation of classical humanism and the dogmas of the church.

The *stanze* or rooms are known by the most significant theme of each mural—The *Stanze of Heliodorus* and the *Stanze of the Fire*—except the first that he painted (1508–1511) called the *Stanze of the Signature,* because it features the dictates of heaven.

Of the grandiose frescoes that occupy the walls of these stanze (between 25 and 22 feet wide) the most famous are:

In the first *stanze, The Disputation of the Holy Sacrament,* a theme that is also known as *The Triumph of the Eucharist* or *Ecclesia* (assembly of Christians), is a composition that shows the relationship of the triumphant (celestial) church over the militant (earthly) one through the mystery of the Eucharist.

The School of Athens is a sensational depiction of architecture that recalls the magnificence of the great Roman baths. Plato and Aristotle, with other great figures from Greco-Roman thought, seem to be explaining their philosophy. The fact that this fresco was painted

Raphael. The story of Venus and Psyche *(c. 1517–1518). Fresco painting. Villa Farnesina, Rome. Raphael painted frescoes in the Villa Farnesina with the help of his pupils Penni, Romano, and Udine, who worked under the painter's instruction. In the cycle, Raphael forgets the centrality of the religious theme, opting instead for the treatment of sensual allegory and nudes.*

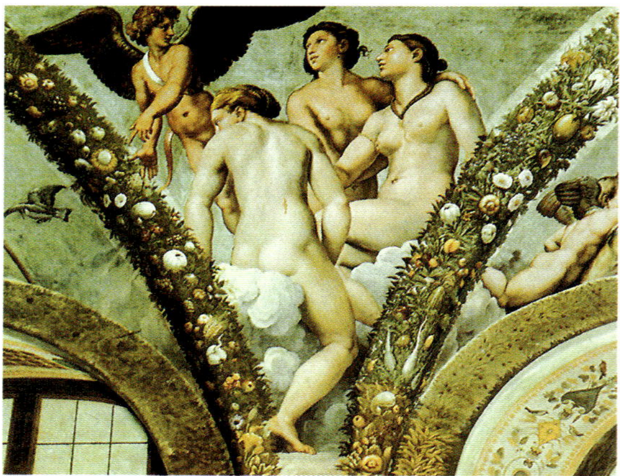

alongside *The Disputation of the Holy Sacrament* seems to correspond to the humanist idea of matching ancient wisdom (that was speculative and empirical) to revealed knowledge.

In the *Stanze of Heliodorus* (1511–1514) the outstanding theme is *The Expulsion from the Temple* and *The Mass of Bolsena,* showing the miracle of the Eucharist that gave rise to the feast of the Corpus Christi (1263). The episode of *Saint Leo the Great Stopping Attila at the Gates of Rome,* which could be interpreted as an allegory of papal power, and *The Liberation of Saint Peter* from the prison in Rome (a spectacular nocturnal scene) complete the murals of the *Stanze.*

The most beautiful part of the *Stanze dell'Incendio* (finished in 1514) and not all painted by Raphael, is the mural with the same name; this is the story of the fire of Borgo that was miraculously put out by Leo IV. The musculature in the style of Michelangelo and the dynamism of the female torsos are mannerist details that modify Raphael's classicism.

From Raphael's Roman period, one must also mention the frescoes that he created (with the collaboration of some of his pupils) for the villa Farnesina. The compositions for the pagan *Triumph of Galatea* (1511) and the *Story of Venus and Psyche* (1517–1518) contain beautiful nudes that, with their grace and opulence, seem to have emerged from the classical world.

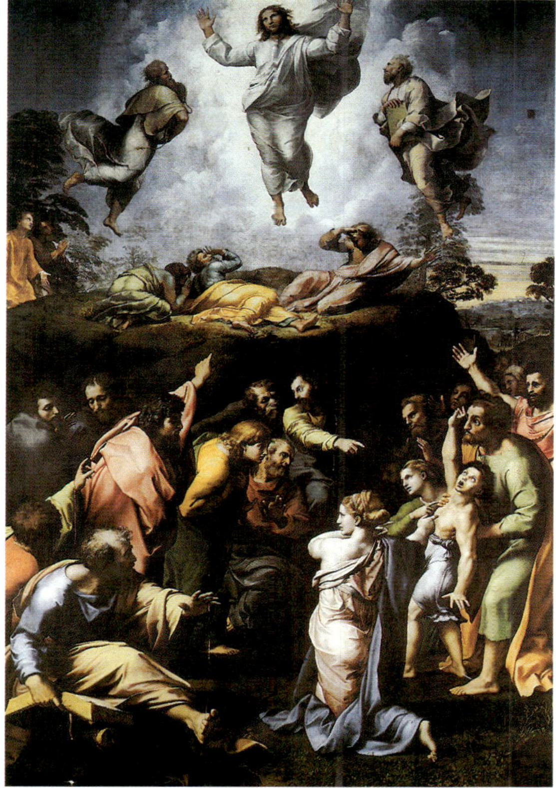

Raphael. The Transfiguration *(1513–1520). Oil on panel, 109½ × 159½". Pinacoteca Vaticana, Rome. A work commissioned for the Cathedral of Narbonne by Cardinal Julio de' Medici. Following the premature death of the artist, it was completed by his pupils Francesco Penni and Giulio Romano. It shows two miraculous episodes, one above the other. At the top, the transformation of Jesus on Mount Tabor, with the presence of Moses and Elias; at the bottom, Jesus curing a possessed child.*

A series of magnificent Virgins, portraits, and a great painting of *The Transfiguration,* which the premature death of the painter left unfinished and which his pupils placed at the head of his coffin, complete Raphael's work.

THE ARTIST'S LIFE

1483. Born in Urbino. His father, Giovanni Santi, a modest painter, dies when Raphael is eleven.

1499–1504. He lives in Perusa, with his mentors Pinturicchio, and more importantly Il Perugino, with whom he collaborates.

1500. He is recognized as a master.

1504. He ends his stay in Umbria, after painting the *Marriage of the Virgin.*

1505–1508. This is the fertile period in Florence. The well-known painter creates his most famous Virgins and portraits.

1508. He arrives in Rome, summoned by Pope Julius II. He begins the work of the decoration of the Stanze.

1511–1518. He paints the frescoes of the Villa Farnesina.

1517–1520. The last years of his life, in which he works on *The Transfiguration.*

1520. He dies in Rome.

GENIUSES OF RENAISSANCE PAINTING.

MICHELANGELO

To speak of Michelangelo purely as a painter is to have an incomplete vision of him. In the history of art he is essentially the sculptural genius of the Renaissance, and the architect of Saint Peter's in the Vatican. Paradoxically, though, of Michelangelo's most ambitious projects, only his pictorial works were executed entirely by him.

Michelangelo's Painting

In a note written to the humanist Benedetto Varchi, Michelangelo says: "I feel that painting is so much better the more it appears to be like relief, and relief is so much worse the more it appears to be like painting."

This is proof of the fact that he never denied his preference for sculpture. Moreover, he repeatedly demonstrated that painting was not his profession. He signed his letters and even his contracts for important paintings as "Michelangelo, sculptor." Even so, he was a genius at drawing, and his work as a painter occupies a foremost place in the history of painting, for the intensity of the internal feeling that informs it, for the beauty of its proportions, for the genius of the drawing of the figures, for the originality of its points of view, and for its delicate coloring.

The painter-sculptor Michelangelo, an indivisible association, made his debut as a painter with *The Holy Family* or *Tondo Doni* (c. 1503–1504) in Florence when he was already a well-known sculptor. He achieved the most beautiful expression of pictorial classicism in parallel with the sculptural classicism represented in the monumental *David,* finished in 1504.

Michelangelo's training as a youth, with Ghirlandaio, allowed him to achieve a pictorial art based on the volume of the figure, with the objective of depicting the beauty and grandeur of humanity. In his painting these are ideas that take priority over technique.

It has been said that grandeur was a malady in Italy in the first part of the sixteenth century, and there is no doubt that Michelangelo's painting, and indeed all his art, was affected by it. But the grandeur that Michelangelo imbues in his figures is so original and comes so sincerely from the depths of the artist's temperamental soul, that it achieves what we could call the most healthy expression of baroque art in history, prefiguring Venetian mannerism and the great Italian fresco painters of the seventeenth century.

The Pictorial Work of Michelangelo

If we measure the pictorial work of Michelangelo by the number of titles, we would come to the conclusion that it is rather limited. However, if we judge it by the number and size of figures, and their overwhelming dynamism and dramatic force, it would seem impossible that such a great achievement should be the work of just one man.

The Holy Family, a circular panel painted in tempera, which is also known by the names *Virgin Doni* or *Tondo Doni* (*tondo* from the Italian *retondo,* meaning round), is the true debut of Michelangelo in the art of color. It was painted between 1503 and 1504, very possibly for the wedding of Agnelo Doni to

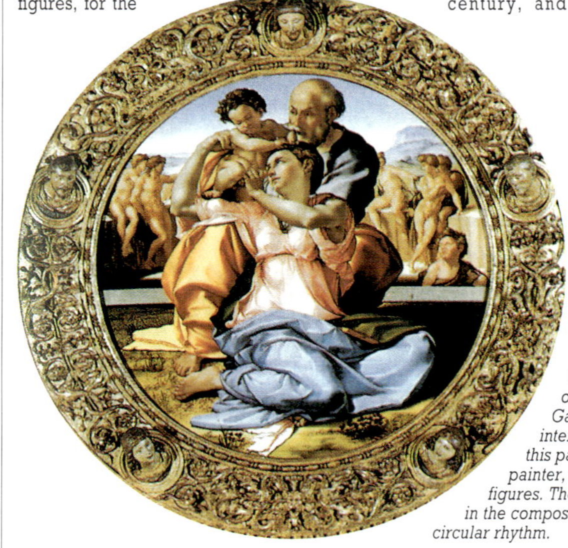

Michelangelo. The Holy Family, *or* Tondo Doni *(c. 1503–1504). Tempera on panel, 47¼" in diameter. Uffizi Gallery, Florence. Despite the little interest Michelangelo seemed to take in this painting, the work shows his genius as a painter, above all in the positioning of the figures. The round frame of the picture is echoed in the composition, full of curves that give it a circular rhythm.*

Maddalena Strozzi, and is today in the Uffizi Gallery. Michelangelo became known as a painter of pure classicism of a very high level. Evidently, in his painting in the Sistine Chapel, the artist, in the haste of his transcendental baroquism, produced more sublime creations, but it is in *The Holy Family* that Michelangelo essentially searched for beauty. The excellent composition draws the figures together into a block, and links them through patterns that center on the interest of the highly original face of the Virgin.

The twisting movement with which the artist paints the kneeling figure, and the harmonious positioning of her arms as she takes up her son, do not create a natural pose, but rather show Michelangelo's search for dynamic composition, with the result that this painting is seen as the origin of Mannerism.

The Paintings in the National Gallery in London. Given the lack of free-standing works that can be attributed to Michelangelo, mention should be made of two unfinished works on display in the National Gallery that show evidence of his hand. They are *Madonna and Child with Saint John and Angels* and *The Entombment* (of Christ). This is a panel of oil painted on tempera, 59⅛" × 63", that experts attribute to Michelangelo and to a master subsequent to him. The types of figures that are represented in the painting and the original dynamism created in the action of holding up the Lord as he is taken from the cross justify this attribution.

The Battle of Cascina. In 1504, soon after finishing *David*, Michelangelo received a commission for what could have been the first fresco of his early career. It was intended for the great hall of the Signoria of Florence, opposite Leonardo's *Battle of Anghiari*. It was a great occasion to show his unparalleled mastery of the representation of the male nude. He conceived of a troop of Pisan soldiers refreshing themselves on the banks of the river

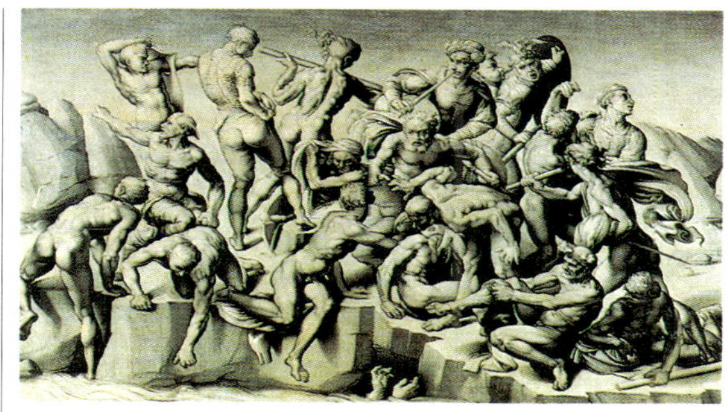

Michelangelo. The Battle of Cascina*, a copy by Aristoteles of Sangallo of an original drawing by Michelangelo (c. 1504–1505). Grisaille on panel, 52⅜ × 30¼". Leicester Collection, Holkam Hall, Norfolk. Great Britain.*

Michelangelo. General view of the ceiling of the Sistine Chapel *(1508–1512). Fresco painting. Sistine Chapel, The Vatican, Rome. In 1508 Michelangelo threw himself into the monumental task of painting the ceiling of the Sistine Chapel. First, he had new scaffolding constructed and quickly learned the technique of painting frescoes. Painting* al buon fresco *represented a series of problems that added to the physical difficulties of carrying out the work: it was necessary to work rapidly, with hardly any time to correct mistakes, calling for great precision and careful calculation of colors, which immediately became attached to the surface. Also, the posture required for painting meant that Michelangelo had to put up with the continual dripping of corrosive pigment in his eyes. The Sistine Chapel has recently been submitted to a polemical restoration that has uncovered previously unknown colors in Michelangelo's work, making it necessary to revise the theories that spoke of the artist's achromatism, which had been ascribed to his interest in sculpture.*

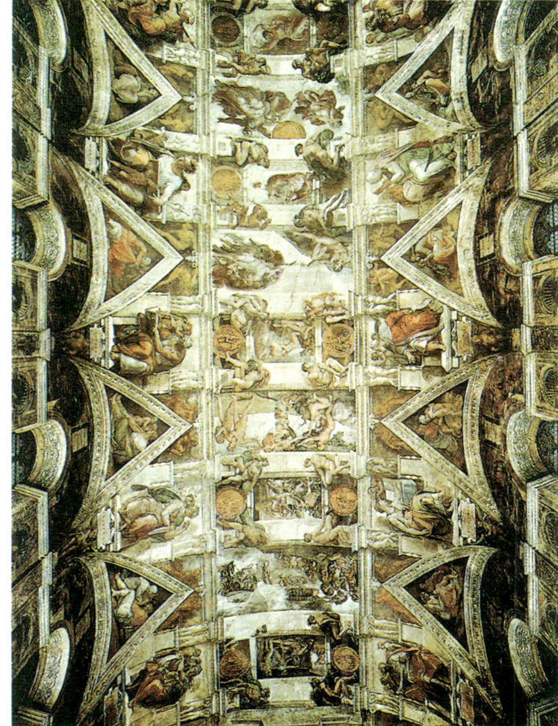

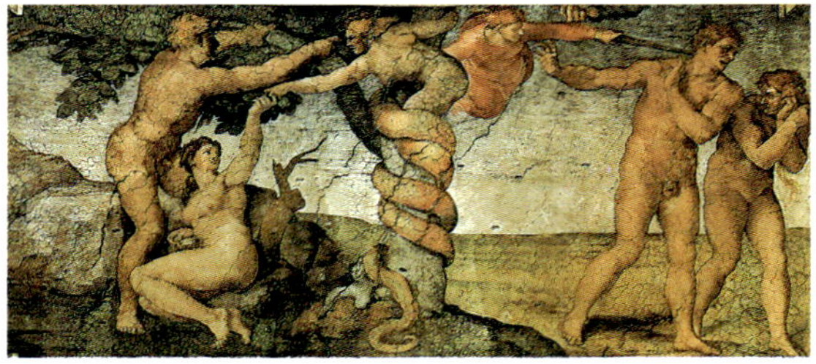

Michelangelo. Original Sin and the Banishment from Paradise *(1509–1510). Fresco painting. Sistine Chapel. The Vatican, Rome.*

Arno and being surprised by a sudden alarm. Of this painting we only know a preparatory sketch, thanks to a copy made by Aristoteles de Sangallo (Leicester Collection, Holkam Hall, Norfolk). The theme, trivial in itself, is converted into a very imaginative composition that visually relates all the components of a compact group of nude bodies, whose tense nervous movements throw their musculature into relief. However, the urgent summons of Pope Julius II left this project unfinished.

The Frescoes of the Ceiling of the Sistine Chapel of the Vatican (1508–1512). The minute study of this huge masterpiece of universal painting has caused rivers of ink to flow and can be found in the most erudite publications. Here follows a generalized commentary.

The ceiling of the Sistine Chapel is a space (when flattened) of 98'5" × 42'8", arranged by Michelangelo into nine transverse sections, which are subdivided into three registers by the longitudinal intersection of false cornices. From the top of the side walls, between eight windows, rise eight triangles, which, at the corners, have the form of huge shells. The organization of the pictorial surface, structured by painted architectural elements, means that the molding was completely integrated into the figurative work. Consequently, the Pope gave the artist absolute artistic liberty in the iconography of the paintings (something that was rare in this period), though not in its themes, which would have been left to a theologian.

The central registers of the vault, rectangles of different sizes, contain episodes from *Genesis;* the smaller rectangles are flanked by naked youths. In the side registers, the seven biblical prophets and the five sibyls of classical tradition, accompanied by youths, read or write, thus reiterating the humanist idea of a seamless link between the two usually contrasting worlds. The vaults, the triangles, and the shells of the ceiling contain other tales and characters from the Bible, forming the most surprising and grandiose imagery that has ever been conceived by an artist in the whole history of art.

Of the many admirable figures, that of *The Delphic Sibyl* stands out as one of the most vigorous, youthful clothed figures of the many that Michelangelo produced. In this figure his painting reaches the peak of his mastery of rhythm and form. The arms of this sibyl (especially the left arm) and the muscular back of the youth in the background count among the most beautiful examples of drawing that have ever been seen. In the scene of *Original Sin and the Banishment from Paradise* (on the left), the figure of Eve, reclining on rocks as she takes the forbidden fruit in her left hand, is a hugely impressive female nude and one of the figures with which Michelangelo achieves the definitive, solemn expression of corporal beauty. In the right half, the Eve who walks hunched over beside Adam, her face reflecting her intense anguish, seems to have lost her original beauty.

However, it is in *The Creation of Adam* that Michelangelo reaches his most perfect and impressive achievement as a painter. Never before and never since has painting shown such sublime figuration in the idea of God The Father, or of the nobility of the human being that begins to breathe as it receives the power that reaches it through the finger of the Almighty. It is the life of God entering into the body of man, a very noble body that is crowned by a beautiful head, with a frank expression not yet touched with malice. This is possibly the most beautiful male nude of the entire Renaissance, and possibly in the history of art.

Michelangelo. The Delphic Sibyl *(c. 1509),* The Persian Sibyl *(c. 1511),* the Cumaean Sybil *(c. 1510). Fresco painting. Sistine Chapel. The Vatican, Rome.*

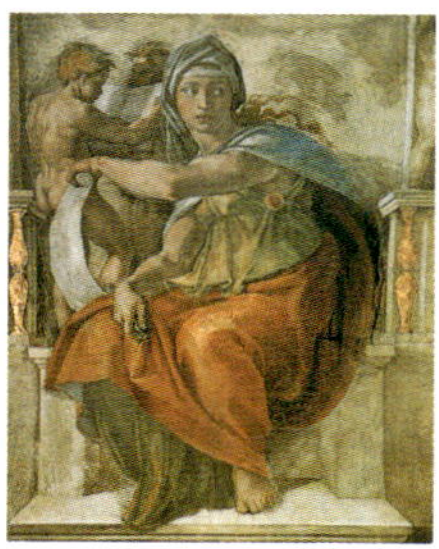

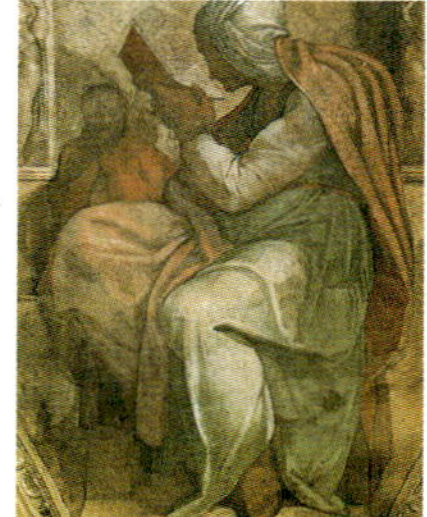

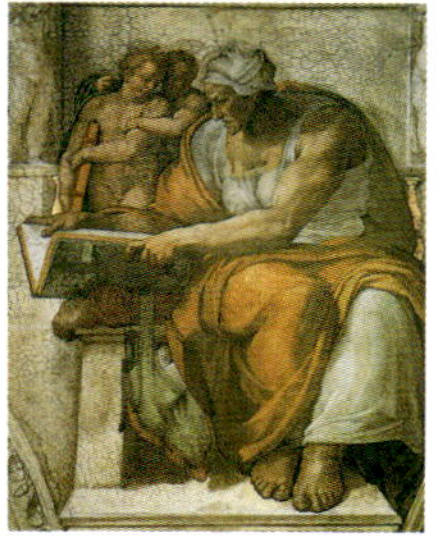

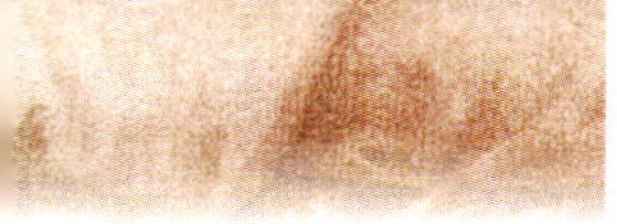

THE ARTIST'S LIFE

1475. Born in Caprese, a village in Florence, near the Apenines, of which his father Ludovico de Lionardo Buonarroti is administrator. When his mandate is over, Ludovico returns with his family to Florence.

1481. He is a student at a primary school of Francesco de Urbino.

1488. The painter Francesco Granacci presents him to Lorenzo the Magnificent. In the School of Art, he studies classical art and attaches himself to the Neoplatonic Academy.

1501–1504. Following his first stay in Rome (1496–1500), during which he sculpts his famous *Pietà* for the Vatican, he works again in Florence. He paints the *Tondo Doni*, sculpts the monumental *David*, and draws the sketch for the *Battle of Cascina* (1504).

1508. He builds the scaffolding to paint the frescoes of the Sistine Chapel, a work to which he dedicates himself with true frenzy and fury.

1512. After four years of incalculable effort, solitude, and claustrophobia, the scaffolding is removed and the work is revealed. The admiration it causes is enormous and universal, both then and ever since.

1534–1541. The Medici Pope Clemente II commissions the fresco of *The Last Judgment* for the back wall of the Sistine Chapel (1534). The death of the Pope postpones the start of work until 1537. It is finished in 1541.

1542–1545. He carries out his final paintings in the Vatican, commissioned by Pope Paul III: The frescoes in the Pauline Chapel, *The Conversion of Saint Paul*, and *The Crucifixion of Saint Peter*.

1564. He dies in Rome on the 18th of February. Before he dies he asks his friends to remind him about the death of Christ. On the 10th of March his body reaches Florence. It is buried in the Church of Santa Croce, in a tomb designed by Vasari.

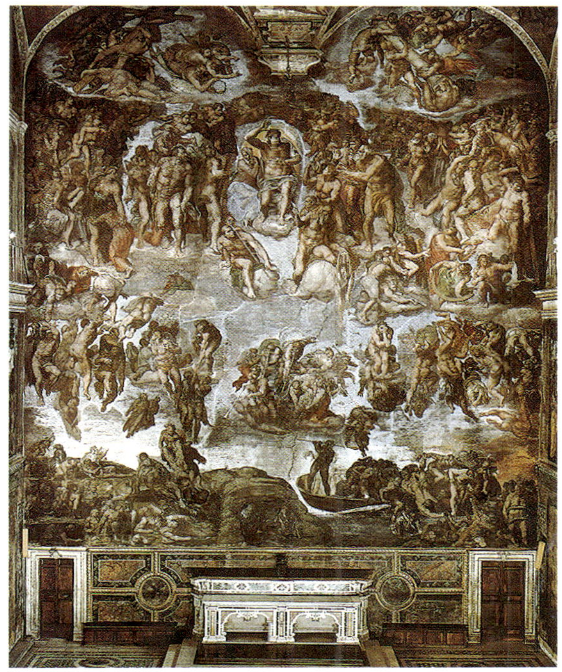

Michelangelo. The Last Judgment. *(1537–1541). Fresco. Sistine Chapel, The Vatican, Rome.* The Last Judgment *closes the cycles that Michelangelo designed for the Sistine Chapel. The now elderly artist fills this scene with all the drama of his tormented mind, particularly the scenes of Charon and the twisted bodies that lead their souls to Hell. Following the Council of Thirty, the entire cycle suffered moral censorship, and Daniele da Volterra was employed to cover the nudes with light cloths, earning him the nickname "Il Braghetone," The Breeches Maker.*

***The Last Judgment* (1537–1541).** Sistine Chapel, the Vatican, Rome. This is Michelangelo's last great fresco. Once again it breaks the molds left him by his predecessors and he paints a unified scene, presided over by Christ the judge. It is a fulfillment of the words written in Saint Matthew (24, 30-31)

"and they will see the Son of man above the clouds of heaven...who will come with great power and glory."

An enormous troop of powerful bodies, the triumphant and the humiliated, who seem to belong to a super-human humanity, are swirling up from open tombs to gather around Christ, or to throw themselves into the abyss with frenetic movements and expressions.

VENETIAN PAINTING OF THE *CINQUECENTO*

GIORGIONE

While the great *maniera* or style of painting was beginning in Rome with Raphael and Michelangelo, in Venice a school of painting was developing, which constituted the other great axis of Italian Renaissance painting. Due to the obsession of the Venetians for embellishing St. Mark's basilica and for finishing the Gothic work of the Doges Palace, the art of Venice had fallen behind until the appearance of Antonello da Messina. He brought to Venice the oil technique that in part gave rise to the specific coloration of *Cinquecento* Venetian painting. Where the great Florentine painters based their creativity on a mastery of drawing, Venetian painting found its own identity based on color rather than drawing.

The Painting of Giorgione

Giorgione was the arch exponent of Venetian classicism in the same way that Raphael, his contemporary, was of Florentine. Giorgione was a master of the art of oil painting, which he learned from Bellini. Perhaps this is the reason why his painting has a special brilliance of nuance (corals, emeralds, golds) in a diaphanous atmosphere highlighting the occasional use of carmine and pink. However, it is in his technical aspect that Giorgione makes his most singular contribution to painting. From 1507 (according to Vasari) he decided to start painting works with no previous studies or sketches. He is the first painter of the Renaissance to approach the canvas directly with paint and brush, something that represented a genuine revolution in this period. What Giorgione achieved was to sweep aside the traditional steps of painting (ideas, sketches and outlines) in a single creative action. Painting gained spontaneity, freshness, and color, although the influence of fashion led him to make subsequent alterations. It was an innovation that was significant in itself, and also because it was immediately adopted by Titian, the most important of the Venetian painters.

In thematic terms, in some of his works Giorgione is a disconcerting artist. Many of his most important paintings represent scenes that, despite their apparently narrative appearance, do not have a clear explanation. On the contrary, his arguments, or lack of them, have a surrealist air that have intrigued critics of all periods.

Giorgione. The Three Philosophers *(c. 1508). Oil on canvas, 56⅝ × 48¾". Kunsthistorisches Museum, Vienna. The great contribution of Giorgione consists of his way of painting, which was to have a direct influence on Titian. Without doing any preparatory sketches, he created his composition directly with paint on canvas, thus obviating the preliminary stages of preparation and execution of the idea, and gaining freshness and spontaneity.*

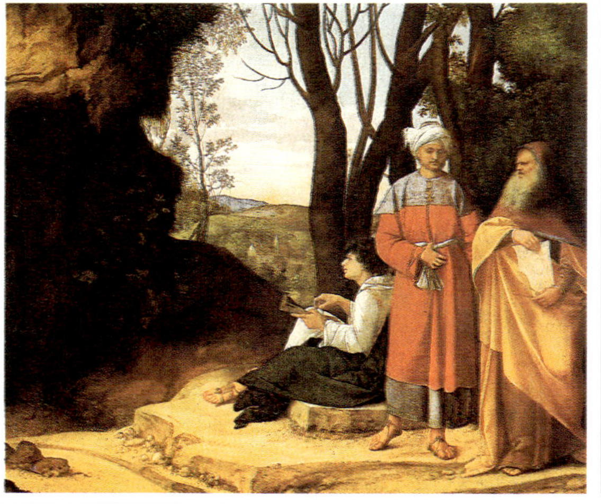

The Life and Work of Giorgione

Comparable to Raphael for the significance of his painting within Renaissance classicism, he is also comparable because of his short life, which was even shorter than that of his contemporary. His was an ephemeral life (of which there are few dates available) and not a very large output. This is complicated by the fact that there are doubts about the authenticity of some of the works attributed to him.

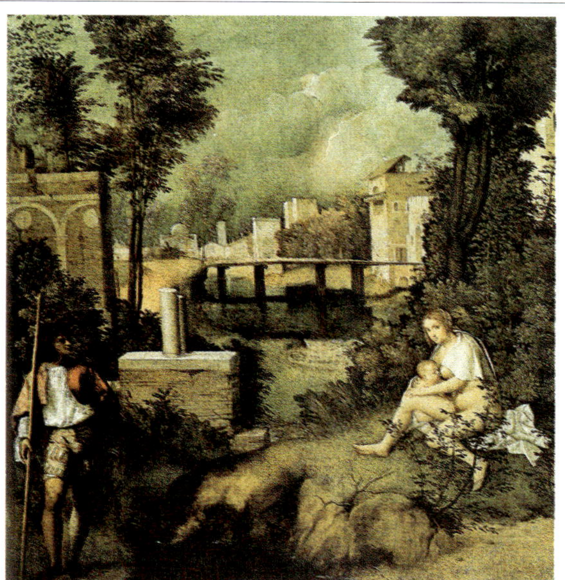

Giorgione. Landscape with a Gypsy and a Soldier *(c. 1508). Oil on canvas, 28¾ × 32⅝". Accademia, Venice. This enigmatic painting shows the connection with Giorgione's own pictorial theory. This landscape, directly painted with a brush, without any previous design, has a quality of immediacy. It also shows one single instant, a passing moment of nature in a flash of lightning. In a way, Giorgione relates art with nature, and also with the presence of mankind, which acts as witness to each event.*

Zorzon de Castelfranco, called Giorgione, was born in Castelfranco in Veneto in about 1478. It is almost certain that he was a pupil of Giovanni Bellini, whose influence is evident in the early works.

The Virgin with Child, Saint Liberalis, and Saint Francis (Castelfranco Cathedral, Veneto, Italy). An oil panel, of 1505, in which by playing with the effect of oblique light on faces and clothes he orders the painting into perfectly integrated areas. Both the figures and the golden light of the landscape in the background, which also bathes the enthroned Virgin, are similar to those of his master.

From the early stage, and showing the strong influence of Bellini, are the oil panels *Adoration of the Magi* (National Gallery, London) and the unfinished *Adoration of the Shepherds* (National Gallery, Washington).

Of the works that have been attributed to Giorgione without certainty, *The Storm* stands out, an oil on canvas c. 1508 (Accademia, Venice). Against a naturalistic and rational landscape, beneath a stormy sky, two figures that are unconnected take shelter, a young lancer and a nude mother, both completely unconcerned about the menace of lightning.

Another of these paintings is *The Three Philosophers* (Kunsthistorisches Museum, Vienna), an oil on canvas with three figures who have been identified as the three Magi, but who could equally be three philosophers (one is an Arab who could be Averroes). They stand in front of the dark entrance to a cave, referring to the cave of Plato. What is certain is that between the three figures there is the same lack of connection as between the figures in *The Tempest.* A young man, seated and studying geometry, seems to be unaware of the presence of the two people standing behind him. The landscape frames the scene, with a completely credible background for an inexplicable narrative.

Giorgione's greatest contributions to Renaissance iconography are his female nudes. His *Pastoral Concert* or *Fête Champêtre,* oil on canvas of 1510, completed by Titian (the Louvre) and his undulating Hellenic and sensual *Sleeping Venus* (Gemäldegalerie, Dresden), an oil on canvas also completed by Titian, show the true sensitivity of Giorgione, a passionate poet and rhapsodist, who died in 1510.

Giorgione. Sleeping Venus *(c. 1509–1510). Oil on canvas, 59 × 43¾". Gemäldegalerie, Dresden.*

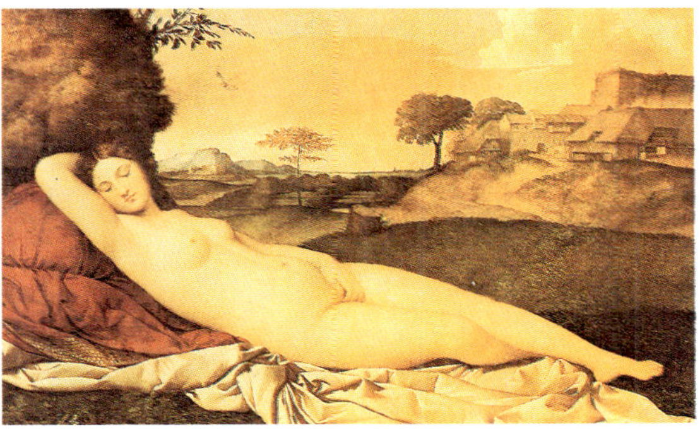

FROM VENETIAN CLASSICISM TO EARLY MANNERISM

THE GREAT FIGURE OF TITIAN

The classicism that Giorgione introduced to Venice, especially with his female nudes evoking the goddess Aphrodite, was inherited by his assistant Tiziano Vecelli, known as Titian. Between 1509 and 1510, Titian was steeped in his master's Hellenism as he completed his *Pastoral Concert* (or *Fête Champêtre*) and his *Sleeping Venus.* Titian was destined to be the greatest exponent of Venetian classicism of the sixteenth century, and the one who took it to the threshold of mannerism.

Titian's Painting

It has been said that in the history of painting there is a before Titian and an after Titian, which is true, above all, if one considers his way of working with color. Titian was the first painter who regularly used dull or uneven colors (dirty colors, as he called them) that were obtained by mixing complementary colors with white in unequal proportions. His method of working with oil, a technique he had learned from Giovanni Bellini and from Giorgione, was equally innovative. By substituting fine-tipped and soft-haired paintbrushes for pig-hair brushes, his oils gained texture and the painted material acquired a special dominance, which became an important factor in the nature and style of his paintings. From this, and from the fact that he finished his paintings with his fingers more often than his contemporaries did, was born the modern appreciation for the material qualities of painting. Titian did not illuminate forms he had drawn with existing colors, but instead created the forms and the colors at the same time, as the work progressed. It must not be forgotten that the great master enthusiastically adopted Giorgione's method of working, without previous sketches or outlines. Titian went one step further, and began to paint directly, drawing, sketching, and coloring as he went along. Commenting on his technique, he said, "Constructing too much disturbs my fantasies and does not let me paint." Thus he made it clear that for him it was one thing to draw (the flat interpretation of the shape of objects) and a completely different thing to arrive at the shape of things through their color.

In its themes, Titian's work is divided between mythology, Christian iconography, allegory, and his excellent portraiture.

Titian's Work

Titian's long life (he was said to be ninety-five in 1571, although he was almost certainly younger) left a great legacy of work. To summarize it would require selective criteria that would always be open to argument because of its inevitable subjectivity. However among Titian's most important works, the following would feature without question:

Titian's early work (up to about 1515) does not breathe with the same poetry as the work of Giorgione, who influenced him deeply. It must be remembered that the master died when the young Titian was working on the last of three of his works. *The Virgin and Child with Saint Roch and Saint Anthony of Padua* (1510), which is in the Prado in Madrid, the *Pastoral Concert* or *Fête Champêtre,* and the *Sleeping Venus.*

The Miracles of Saint Anthony (1511), three frescoes in the School of Saint Anthony in Padua are the first well-documented and conserved works by Titian. They reveal a Titian whose use of color (reds, oranges, and ochres on uneven blues and greens) and emotive gestures are a long way from Giorgione's placid immobility.

Sacred and Profane Love of about 1515 (Borghese Gallery, Rome) is a beautiful allegorical work in which Titian seems to

Titian. Sacred and Profane Love *(c. 1515). Oil on canvas. The iconographic interpretation of Titian's painting is always difficult, given that the Venetian artist enjoyed playing with complex references. In this case there is a certain parallel with the paintings of Raphael in the Stanze in the Vatican. As in those works, the classical tradition and the Christian tradition confront one another, here exemplified by Christian beauty wearing clothes and pagan beauty naked. The problem is that it is not known which morality the painter chooses.*

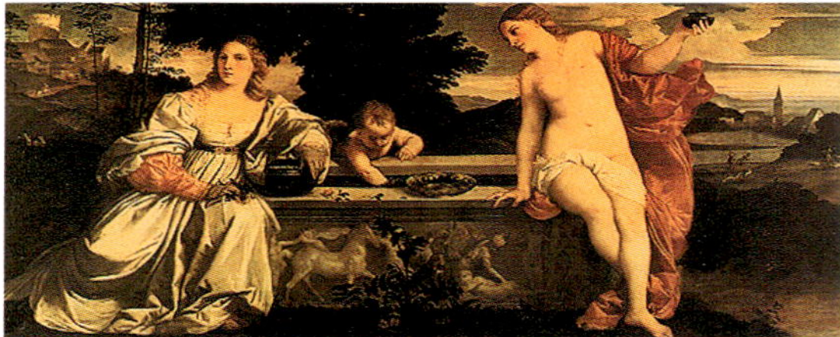

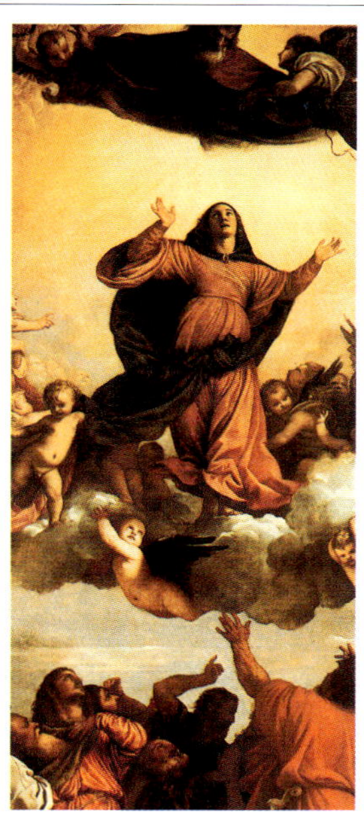

Titian. The Assumption of the Virgin *(1516–1518). Oil on canvas, 141¾ × 271⅝". Santa Maria Gloriosa dei Frari, Venice. One of Titian's most important works, and without question his greatest creation of the decade from 1510. It is an example of his compositional genius, although this was not free from controversy. The Franciscans for whom the work was destined were disconcerted by the tripartite structure between heaven, earth, and the transitional stage of the Virgin.*

have been infected by his master Giorgione's liking for inexplicable narratives. What is the meaning of the two beautiful women, one clothed, the other nude? They seem to show no intention of any type of contact as they sit on a Roman sarcophagus that has been turned into a fountain by a trick of Cupid. Is it an allegory of a supposed symbiosis between Christianity and paganism which, in a pastoral landscape, is divided between water and land?

Flora, oil on canvas, in the Uffizi Gallery, also of 1515, is the portrait of a magnificent woman (the image of a goddess) represented in Titian's classic coloring. With her torso half-covered, she recalls *The Fates of Phidias.*

Noli Me Tangere, oil on canvas, (National Gallery, London) is another of his works reminiscent of Giorgione, at least in its background landscape, which features the same composition that Giorgione, or maybe Titian himself, painted in the landscape of *Sleeping Venus.*

The Madonna and Child with Saint John and Saint Catherine in the Prado, Madrid is an oil on canvas that he must have painted in the years immediately after 1515. It is notable for the richness of its color, which shines in the silks and satins and with which Titian definitively abandons the much more hesitant coloring of his predecessors. It is possible that the head of the saint in this painting is a self-portrait.

Titian's long artistic maturity begins between 1516 and 1518, a period when he paints or starts to paint some of his best-known and spectacular works.

The Assumption of the Virgin (1516–1518) is a monumental oil on canvas (141¾ × 271⅝") for the main altar of Santa Maria Gloriosa dei Frari, Venice and is Titian's first great religious work. It is a composition that is designed to suggest the ascending flight of the Virgin on a pedestal of angels, through a sky that emanates golden light. Titian repeats the division between earth and heaven that Raphael had used in the *Disputation of the Holy Sacrament* and that will later be adopted by mannerist and Baroque painters. The clear gesticulation of the apostles, whose mortal condition keeps them firmly anchored to the earth, plays a large part in suggesting the momentum of flight, which stretches from the feet of the nearest observer to the welcoming arms of the Almighty.

The Pesaro Virgin, painted between 1519 and 1526 for the altar of the Pesaro family in the same church, Santa Maria Gloriosa dei Frari, is a superb painting in terms of color and composition, although it does not stand up to comparison with the great *Assumption* of the main altar, which to a certain extent diminishes it.

The *Averoldi Polyptych,* in the church of the Saints Nazario y Celso, Venice, painted between 1520 and 1522, is the third of Titian's great religious works of the period 1516–1526. Most notable are the male nudes of the resuscitated Christ and of Saint Sebastian being martyred,

Titian. The Bacchanal of the Andrians *(1518–1519). Oil on canvas, 69 × 60¼". The Prado, Madrid. In the representation of a classic bacchanal, Titian manages to unify the color and material aspect of the painting with a festive theme, in such a way that the work oozes from every part the vitality for which the Venetian master is famous.*

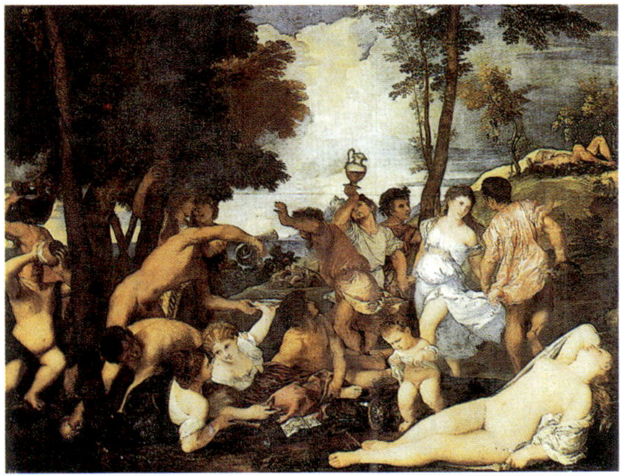

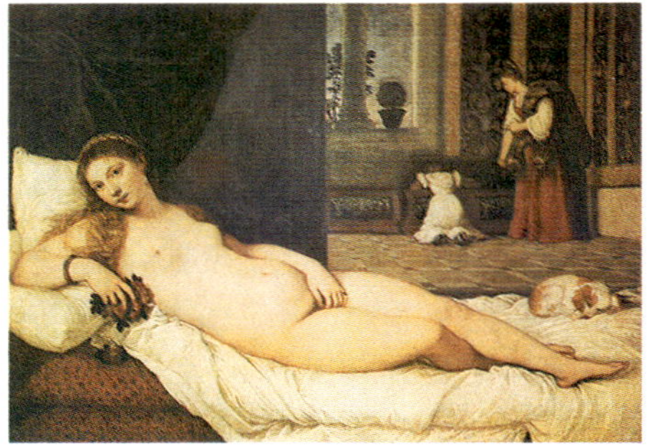

Titian. The Venus of Urbino *(1538). Oil on canvas, 65 × 46¾". Uffizi Gallery, Florence. Another example of the complex iconographic games that Titian offers, and that delighted his patrons. Taking the framework of Giorgione's* Sleeping Venus, *Titian painted a series of paintings in which he developed moral parables of the conflict between the classical pagan world and the contemporary world. Here the nude Venus in the foreground stands out against the young woman who is lying in the background of the image, victim of her own shame and the pagan immorality that has no place in the Catholic world.*

tied to a column, like the slaves of Michelangelo.

The Bacchanal of the Andrians and *The Worship of Venus,* of 1519, both in the Prado in Madrid, are two of the most important of Titian's pagan-themed works, painted for Alfonso de'Este. It is not until the 1530s and the 1550s that one gets to his more famous paintings of Venus and of the portentous Danäe. *The Bacchanal of the Andrians,* with the magnificent nude of Ariadna sleeping in the foreground and with the extraordinary movement and coloring of the figures taking part in the Bacchic celebration, is a tribute to wine, dancing, and song, which combine to produce the happiest party in the Renaissance. In *The Worship of Venus,* Titian reveals himself to be one of the best painters of children. A group of little cupids gather in a multicolored crowd at the foot of the Hellenistic statue of the goddess, in one of the most successful scenes of child nudes in history.

The Venus of Urbino (1538), oil on canvas, is a jewel of the Uffizi Gallery and one of the high points of the Renaissance. It is a masterly version of the pagan classic, featuring one of the most provocative and well-painted female nudes in the history of art. It is the outstanding successor, being more real and alive, to Giorgione's *Sleeping Venus,* which Titian himself had helped to paint. The pink hues of the goddess's hugely beautiful body emerge from the shadows of the luxurious house of the Della Rovere family, and are lit by the golden light reflected from the sheets and pillows on which she is reclining. The dark curtains against which the nude stands out, from her head to her hips, separate the pagan world of intimate reality from the chamber behind, underlined by two busy maids who appear at the back of the chamber.

Venus with Cupid and an Organist (1548), oil on canvas, the Prado, Madrid. In this composition, of which Titian made various versions (two of which are in the Prado and others in Cambridge, New York, and Berlin) again relates a real environment, in this case a Venetian landscape. The painting shows the classic symbolism and sensuality of the pagan world in the ivory-white flesh of the goddess, who receives the ethereal caress of music, while her attention is fixed on the tactile caress of love.

Danäe and the Shower of Gold (1553–1554), Kunsthistorisches Museum, Vienna, of which there exist other versions in Madrid and Naples. Another of the most successful nudes of the Renaissance, symbolizing the figure of Danäe, the mother of Perseus, being possessed by Zeus, who has metamorphosed into golden rain (in the form of coins) in an atmosphere charged with sensuality.

These nudes and others (such as *Venus* and *Adonis* in the Prado, for example) have remained in the history of art as some of the greatest achievements of Renaissance humanism.

The signs of mannerism that Titian incorporated into his painting began to appear in the decade 1550–1560, almost certainly as a result of his visit to Rome and his contacts with Michelangelo.

La Gloria or *The Last Judgment* (1551–1554), the Prado, Madrid, is an oil on canvas that the Emperor Charles V of Spain must have held in great esteem, since he took it with him on his

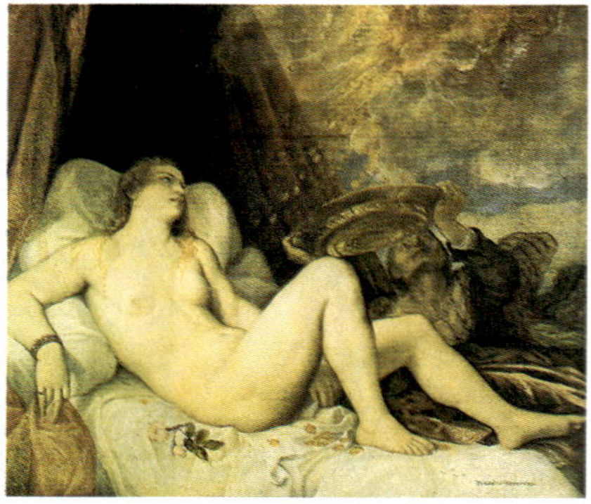

Titian. Danäe and the Shower of Gold *(1553–1554). Oil on canvas, 70⅛ × 50⅜". Kunsthistoriches Museum, Vienna. Titian was a great expert on classical mythology and reinterpreted many of its stories. In this case he focuses on a highly erotic, sexual theme in which Jupiter metamorphoses into golden rain to make love to Danäe.*

retirement to the Monastery of Yuste, following his abdication. The painting shows a saintly humanity, bathed in divine light. It includes representations of the Emperor, his wife Isabel of Portugal, and his children Phillip and Maria. It is a composition that, with its foreshortenings, gesticulations and twisted bodies anticipates the coming of mannerism.

The *Pietà* (Accademia, Venice), oil on canvas, begun in 1570 and that he left unfinished. Curiously both geniuses of the Renaissance finished their artistic life with the same theme: Michelangelo with the *Rondanini Pietà* (Castello Sforzesco, Milan) and Titian with the *Pietà*, Venice. It is a masterly, posthumous lesson in modern painting, left by a painter who was able to paint his final self-portraits by applying the paint purely by the touch of his fingers.

Titian's portrait painting is magnificent. He painted many half-body portraits, as well as full-body portraits, in addition to portraits that form part of a historical or allegorical scene.

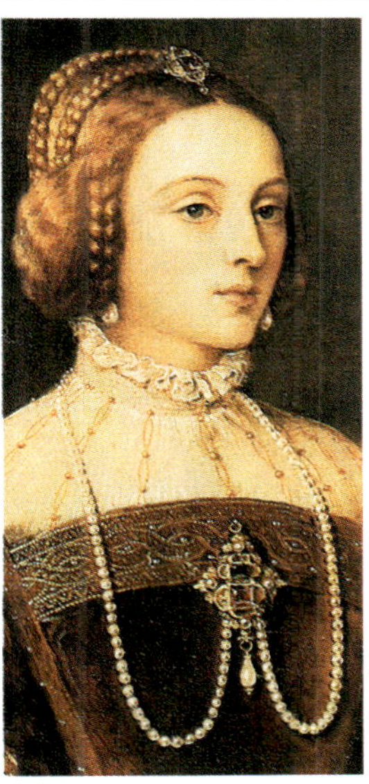

Titian. Portrait of the Empress Isabella of Portugal *(1548). Oil painting on canvas, 36⅔ × 46". Prado, Madrid. The art of Titian unfolds in the portrait of delicate qualities having already died when he depicted her. He gave her countenance a quality of health that obviously she no longer possessed.*

The notable psychological depth of his portraits does not distract the painter from the luxury of the clothes and jewels, which he is able to reproduce with admirable precision.

Isabel d'Este (1534–1536), Kunsthistorisches Museum, and *Portrait of the Empress Isabella of Portugal* (1548), the Prado, Madrid, are very beautiful portraits, unmatched in the detail of their blonde hair, full of jewels and embroidery.

Charles V on Horseback at the Battle of Mühlberg (1548), the Prado, Madrid, became the model for equestrian portraits for all monarchs of the period.

Pope Paul III with his Grandsons Cardinal Alessandro and Ottaviano Farnese (1546), National Museum of Capodimonte, is an original group portrait.

THE ARTIST'S LIFE

1477 or 1498. Titian's date of birth is uncertain. Born in Pieve di Cadore near the Dolomites between these years, the truth is that even he did not know the true date. In a note written in 1571 he was said to be ninety-five, although he couldn't have been more than in his eighties.

1505. He begins to work for Giorgione, having previously been with Bellini and his first master, the mosaic artist Sebastiano Zuccato.

1513. The city of Venice grants him an annual pension of 125 ducats, plus 25 more for each new portrait of the Duke.

1516. He is called to the court of Ferrara by Duke Alfonso de'Este.

c. 1520. He lives with Cecilia, who has already given him two sons, Pomponio and Orazio.

1525. Cecilia becomes gravely ill and, faced with the threat of imminent death, Titian marries her. But she survives and gives him two more children. The first one does not live long; the second, Lavinia, was her father's favorite, and the model for many of his works.

1532–1533. He paints the *Emperor Charles V with his Dog* (the Prado, Madrid) for the king's visit to Bologna. It is a full body portrait, which was to become the preferred model for kings and princes.

1546. He visits Rome and paints Pope Paul III. During his stay at the Vatican, he is distinguished with the title of citizen of Rome.

1548. The relationship between Titian and the imperial family is fertile and cordial. In Ausburg he paints the equestrian statue of Emperor Charles V.

1566. He receives a visit from Vasari, who wants to complete his *Lives of the Artists*.

1570. He begins to paint the Pietà, which he would leave unfinished.

1575. He writes to the Emperor for the last time, asking him for money he owes him.

1575. He dies on August 27, of the plague. He is buried in Santa Maria Gloriosa dei Frari.

THE MANNERIST AESTHETIC. PIONEERS OF FLORENTINE MANNERISM

Following the *maniera* ("style") of Raphael and Michelangelo, art sought to show a more dynamic approach to expression, leading to the style that has become known as mannerism. It should not be confused with the idea of affectation of the students and followers of Raphael and Michelangelo, who repeatedly copied the *maniera* of the masters; rather, mannerism was the result of a powerful artistic tendency that led to refined and highly humanist creations. This distancing from classicism, which Titian had attempted toward the end of his life, was practiced by painters in Florence, Rome, Parma, and Venice. Their work led to the high point of mannerism under Veronese and Tintoretto, and, at the beginning of the seventeenth century, joined with the first experiments of the Baroque. Andrea del Sarto, Pontormo, Rosso, Fiorentino, and Bronzino, among others, were pioneers of Florentine mannerism.

Andrea del Sarto

The Painting and Work of Andrea del Sarto

This Florentine painter, the first to show the hallmarks of the mannerists, was also responsible for the training of the two most significant artists of the new tendency in Florence: Pontormo and Rosso Fiorentino.

Andrea del Sarto was a painter with a classical background, who combines Raphael's *maniera,* Leonardo's *sfumato,* and Michelangelo's iconography. Narrative in his work develops with the monumentalism of the *Cinquecento,* sometimes inspired by the engravings of Dürer, and with a coloring that leans toward purples.

The most representative of Andrea del Sarto's work has a

Andrea del Sarto. The Sacrifice of Isaac Interrupted by the Angel *(c. 1529). Oil on panel, 27⅛ × 38½". The Prado, Madrid. This is one of several versions that Andrea del Sarto made of one of the most terrible scenes in the Bible: the sacrifice of Isaac by his father as proof of his faith, interrupted at the last moment by an angel. Despite the presence of mannerisms'* horror vacui, *the artist still uses the classical framework of formal, triangular symmetry.*

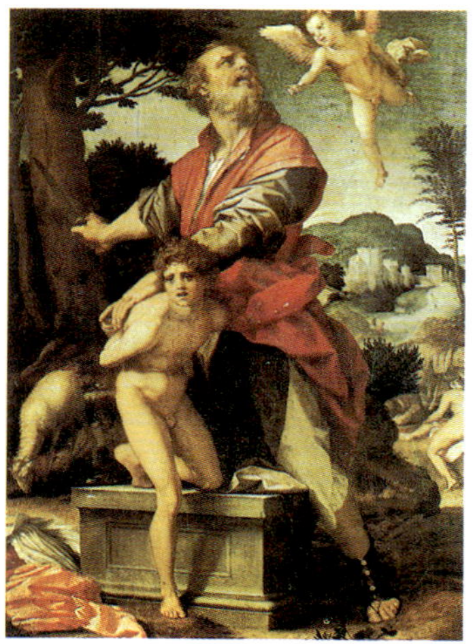

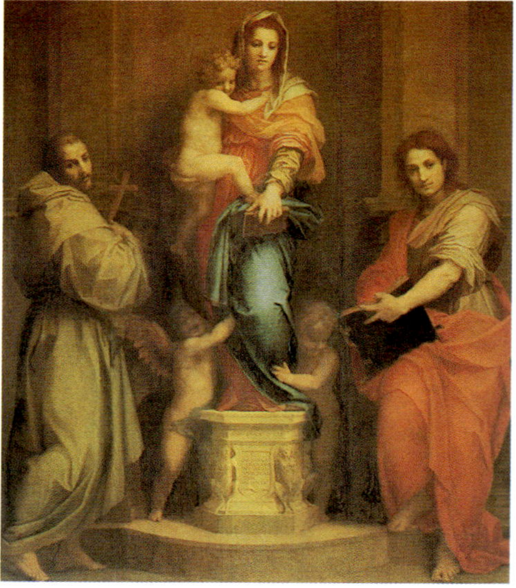

Andrea del Sarto. Virgin and Child, with Saint John and Saint Francis *(1517). Oil on panel, 70⅛ × 81⅞". Uffizi Gallery, Florence. This painting shows a monumental framework designed as an imitation bas-relief. A niche opens against a background suffused with a warm, shadowy atmosphere. The Virgin appears as a statue on a pedestal, lit by the light reflected from the bodies. The light not only gives shape and life but also color.*

tendency for what is called *horror vacui* (horror of space), which will grow with mannerism, and represents one of the excesses of Baroque. His composition is academic in style, often pyramidal and closed, with figures that tend toward mannerist *serpentinato.*

His most notable frescoes, paintings, and portraits are the following:

The frescoes in the cloisters of the Convent of the Annunziata (1509–1510) in Florence.

The Life of John the Baptist (1514–1526) in the small cloister of the Scalzi in Florence, a series that is surprising for its exclusive use of grisaille and the absence of color, composed of figures whose musculature is sharply defined, with hints of Dürer and Michelangelo.

The Virgin and Child, Saint John the Evangelist, and Saint Francis, 1517, in the Uffizi Gallery. This is an altar painting with a frontal, symmetrical composition, notable for its luminous color, the magnificent image of Maria on a pedestal with sculpted harp, and the exaggerated twisting poses of both the saints. The model of the Virgin was almost certainly the wife of the painter, and the figure of Saint Francis is thought to be a self-portrait.

Holy Family with an Angel (*Madonna della Scala*) in the Prado, Madrid, is a *sacra conversazione* of harmonious coloring, in which Andrea del Sarto uses roses, turquoises, dark greens, and violets in a pyramidal composition in the style of Leonardo and Raphael.

The Annunciation in the Uffizi Gallery and *The Sacrifice of Isaac* (c. 1529) in the Prado, are examples of Andrea del Sarto expressing himself with dynamic, snaking, mannerist forms.

A good portraitist, he was skilled in the use of *sfumato* as is shown in the portraits of his wife Lucretia del Baccio del Fede. In the one exhibited in the Prado, the painter seems to take pleasure in insinuating to the observer, in an ironic way, the sensual and somewhat unfaithful nature of his wife.

Pontormo

The Painting and Work of Pontormo

Thanks to this painter, a student of Andrea del Sarto, mannerism acquired a new personality and established itself as a style. Known as Pontormo, his real name was Jacopo Carrucci, a man whom Vasari defined as having an unstable personality, a complicated, tormented and dissatisfied character, and a tendency to question everything he had learned, starting with the work of his master and the ideas of Michelangelo.

In his painting, the heroic figures, although maintaining their grandeur, display a certain expressionism. The painter lengthened their bodies, applying unreal colors and exaggerating their dynamic postures and gestures to achieve a theatricality that, in spite of its formal beauty and the fine coloring of his compositions, ends up as excessively artificial.

Of his work, which was as variable as his character, the following, among others, are significant:

Virgin Enthroned with Angels (1518) in the Church of San Miguel Visdomini, Florence. Its disrupted patterns seem to fragment the body of the Virgin.

Pathos fills the expressionistic figures in his *Passion* (1522–

Pontormo. Lamentation *(1525–1528). Oil on panel, 75⅝ × 123⅛". Capponi Chapel, Santa Felicita, Florence. The painting has a characteristic rising pattern, created by lines alone and the growing scale of colors. Thus he fills the figures with emotion, not through their gestures and expressions, but rather by their deliberate inconsistency and by the way the image constantly dissolves away. Pontormo paints the very moment when the action is most intense.*

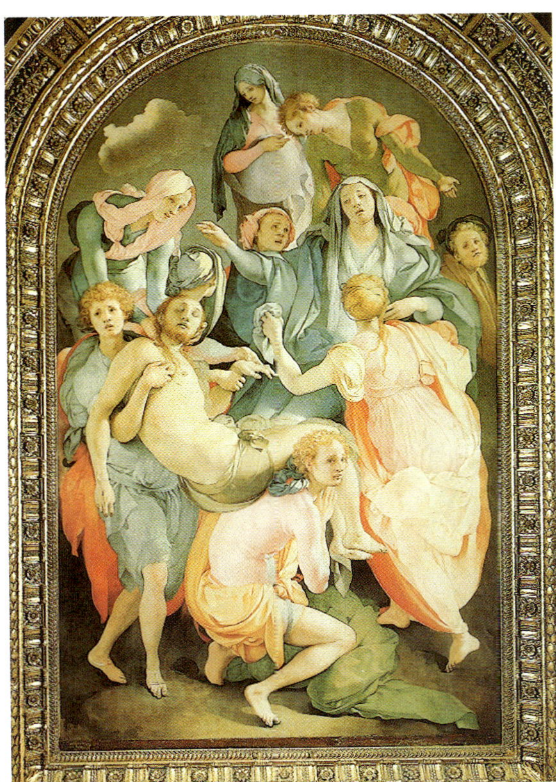

1525), badly deteriorated frescoes in the Cartuja de Val d'Ema that are elongated to the point of dislocation.

The same theatrical pathos can be seen in *Lamentation* (1526–1528), in the Caponi Chapel, Santa Felicita, Florence. Furthermore, the *horror vacui* that seems to have seized the painter, has led him to increase the group of Marys with the figures of other youths covered in light cloth, whose purpose seems simply to fill all the available space in the picture. Nevertheless, the beauty of the faces, the brilliance with which the clothes have been painted, and the often dissonant and unbelievable counterpoints of color give the painting an indisputable charm.

Pontormo himself offers an antithesis to this theatrical mannerism in another of his works, which he seems to have painted with a different personality. This is the painted window in the Medici Palace of Poggio, in Caiano, whose theme is *Vertumnus and Pomona* (1521), who are young or old depending on the season of the year. The painting features naked bodies, an old man with a dog, and clothed, reclining women, all painted with the atmosphere and diaphanous clarity of a country celebration.

Mannerism owes to Pontormo the counterpoint of colors in portraits. These are generally melancholic and introspective, as is the case with the *Portrait of Cosimo de' Medici il Vecchio* (1518) in the Uffizi Gallery, Florence, and the portrait of *Maria Salviati* also in the Uffizi.

Pontormo was born in 1494 in the city from which he took his name, and died in Florence in 1555.

Rosso Fiorentino

The Work and Painting of Rosso Fiorentino

Giovanni Battista di Jacopo Rosso (1495–1540) was known as Rosso Fiorentino because he was red-haired. Another pupil of Andrea del Sarto, he became, with Pontormo and Bronzino, the third of the pioneers of mannerism.

His mannerist tendencies can be seen in the violent dynamic of his compositions and figures, which have a volumetric geometry based on carefully determined planes and juxtapositions. In his *Deposition* of 1521 (Pinacoteca de Volterra, Tuscany) Rosso Fiorentino achieved a degree of formal abstraction that is truly remarkable. The complicated rhythms of his disrupted, swirling compositions, as well as the brilliance of color, which is close to the color of enamel, place him in a stylistic sphere that is very different from the one followed by his co-pupil Pontormo. However, the work that best characterizes his mannerism is *Moses Defending the Daughters of Jethro* (1523–1527), Uffizi Gallery, painted during his stay in Rome; the bodies are heavily twisted, with anatomies that are constructed on different, independently lit levels, something that is paradigmatic in Florentine mannerism.

In 1531 he was summoned by Francis I of France to work on Fontainebleau. Nine years later he poisoned himself, full of remorse for having unjustly accused his friend Pellegrino of theft.

Bronzino

The Painting and Work of Bronzino

Agniolo di Cosimo, known as Bronzino (1503–1563) is the representative of the first stage of Florentine mannerism who was destined to take the movement to the threshold of its full development in the second half of the sixteenth century.

A pupil of Pontormo, Bronzino tended toward a more balanced painting, removed from the improvisation and uncontrolled gesticulation of his master's work, although like him he felt the *horror vacui,* particularly in his religious work.

An eager follower of Michelangelo, he adopted his dynamism and the anatomic physicality of his nudes.

His contribution to mannerism can especially be seen in his portraits, which are highly disciplined and which pay careful attention to physiognomic reality, giving his subjects a distant

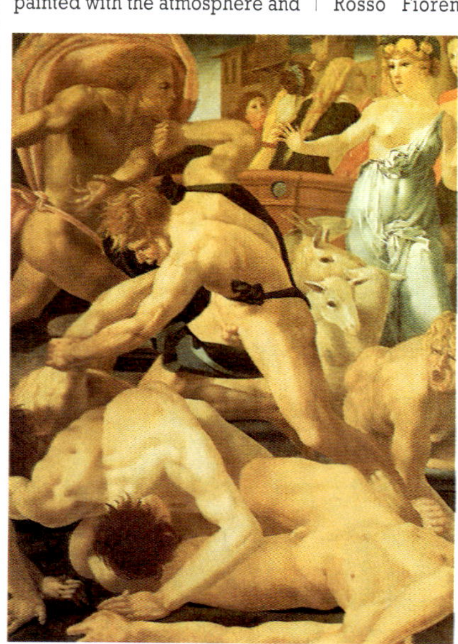

Rosso Fiorentino. Moses Defending the Daughters of Jethro *(1523–1527). Oil on canvas, 46 × 63". Uffizi Gallery, Florence. The dynamism, horror vacui, and strong coloring characteristic of Rosso Fiorentino turned him into the greatest exponent of mannerism. In this painting by the Florentine painter, the influence of Michelangelo is also perfectly clear, both in the treatment of color around the Holy Family and in the almost sculptural effect of the muscular bodies.*

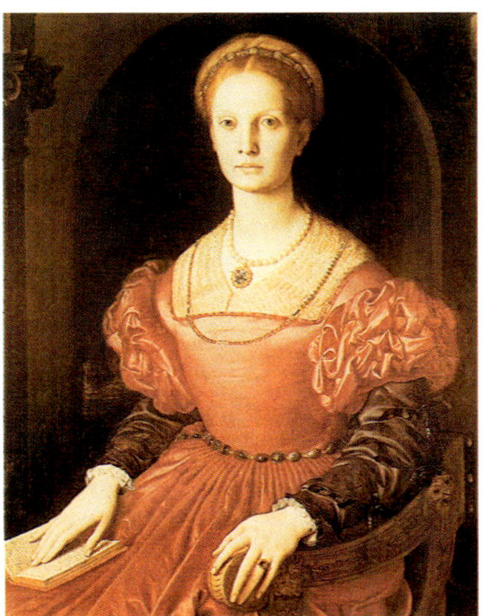

Bronzino. Lucretia Panciatichi *(c. 1540). Oil on panels, 33 × 41". National Gallery, London. The portraits of Bronzino are characterized by the search, more than the reliable representation, for the intellectual reconstruction of the model. In them, beneath the regular and geometric outline, is distinguished the clean and cold color, but with notes of brilliance and timbre. The characters of Bronzino are treated with great formal purity as if he were praising the subject as someone special deserving special treatment.*

Bronzino. An Allegory of Love and Time, Venus Embraced by Cupid or Discovery of Lewdness *(c. 1546). Oil on panels, 45¾ × 57½". National Gallery, London. Composition of undoubtedly erotic content, but full of references to the jealousies, deception, and betrayal in the figures and the focus that surround the central forms of Venus and Cupid.*

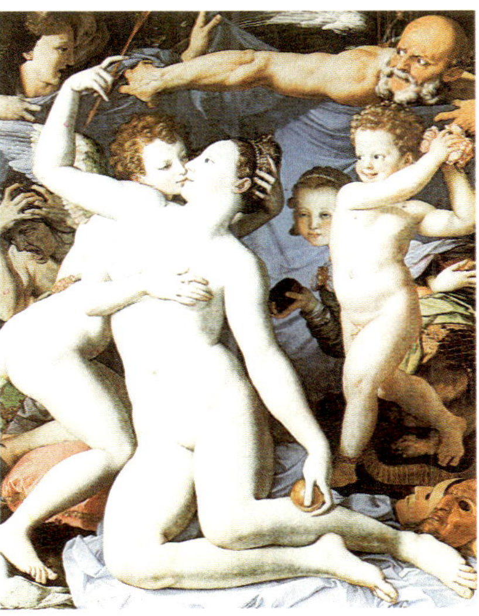

grandeur that greatly pleased the Medici and the ruling authorities. His portraits are rather sophisticated, minutely detailed images that are nevertheless emotionally silent and psychologically impenetrable.

Examples include the portrait of *Lucretia Panciatichi* (National Gallery, London), a woman who is notable for the elegance of her hands, the elegance of her luxuriously clad bust, and her very correct but rather inexpressive features. *Guidobaldo de Montefeltro* (1530–1532) and *Eleonora of Toledo,* wife of Cosmo I de' Medici (1545), both in the Uffizi Gallery, have the same air of scornful coldness in their emotions and the same minute detailing in the depiction of the material and ornamentation, seen in the armor of the former and the elaborate dress of the latter.

In his mythological paintings, Bronzino painted some of the most paradigmatic works of mannerism at the end of the first half of the sixteenth century. *An Allegory of Time and Love* (c. 1546) in the National Gallery, London, also known as *Venus, Cupid, Folly, and Time* is an oil on canvas painted for Cosmo I de' Medici, with unquestionable erotic overtones, despite the allegorical sense that is attributed to it (the presence of time and of luxury). The blue coloring and porcelain quality of the flesh of Venus and Cupid work powerfully with the sensuality of the figures.

The first stage of mannerism ended with Bronzino, giving way to full mannerism.

THE ARTIST'S LIFE

1486. Andrea del Sarto is born in Florence.

1493. At the age of seven he is apprenticed to a goldsmith, a profession he abandons in favor of painting. He trains as a painter in the workshop of Piero di Casimo and with Fra Bartolomeo. He marries the widow Lucretia del Baccio de Fede, who is blamed for his extravagant artist's life. He travels to the court of Francis I of France, who commissions him to buy works of art. On his return to Florence, he spends the money he received from the king.

1531. He dies in Florence, victim of the plague.

THE MANNERIST ARTISTS

TINTORETTO

Venice, which with Titian had achieved the greatest expression of its Renaissance classicism and the first glints of the new tendency, would see the peak of the new style. Full Venetian mannerism arrived in the shape of a painter who, for a short time, had been a pupil of Titian, who, according to some biographers, was jealous and envious of him. Nevertheless, the paths that the painting of each artist followed were sufficiently different to make it impossible for their work to clash. This talented, fleeting pupil was called Iacobo Robusti, known as Tintoretto.

The Painting of Tintoretto

Just as the work of Titian had had a particular clientele among kings, dukes, and senior government officials, Tintoretto painted for patricians, burghers, Venetian churches, and very occasionally for the official government of the Republic. Furthermore, Tintoretto's painting distances itself from Titian's classicism and assured grandeur, establishing instead an art that is full of energy, with a style in which form and color achieve fantastic results, combining the drawing of Michelangelo and the coloring of Titian.

It is said that in Tintoretto's workshop the following caption could be found: "Michelangelo for form, Titian for color." These few words sum up the pictorial scheme that created the greatest painting of Venetian mannerism, situated between the technical achievements of Titian, the pomp and theatricality of Veronese, and the efficient artistry of Michelangelo's best drawings.

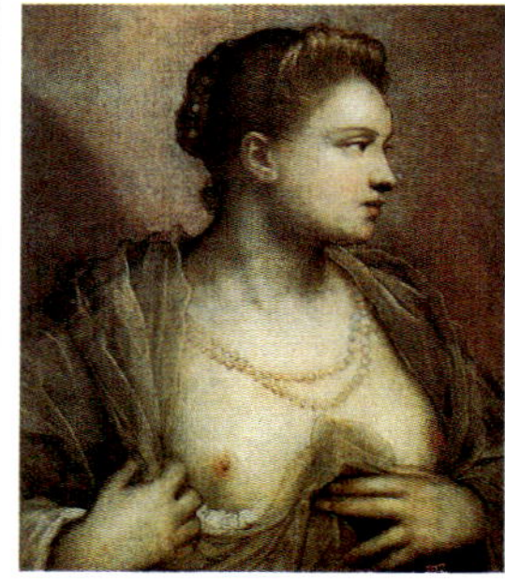

Tintoretto. Portrait of a Lady Revealing her Breast *(c. 1550). Oil on canvas, 21¾ × 24". The Prado, Madrid. This is one of the best female portraits in the Prado. It has variously been identified as Marietta Tintoretto, the daughter of the painter, but also as the famous Venetian courtesan Verónica Franco. The coloring in this work moves away from the artist's characteristic tones, reproducing a clear, pearl-like tonality that explodes in an infinite variety of grays.*

Tintoretto's painting is essentially religious. There are some five hundred works that the painter invests with his spirituality and an intense religious atmosphere. He uses the resources of mannerism: elongated figures, asymmetrical compositions that displace the subject or main group in favor of the overall composition, a heightened sense of depth in architecture and landscape, and twisted bodies, with poses and gestures that demand daring foreshortening. His temperamental brushwork leads to uneven finishes, with some forms scarcely finding definition and others perfectly finished.

Tintoretto. Christ Washing the Feet of the Disciples *(1547). Oil on canvas, 209⅞ × 82¾", the Prado, Madrid. A masterpiece, this painting shows the profound influence of mannerism in the displacement of the principal theme to one of the corners. What is most notable about this painting is the treatment of space, which undoubtedly influenced Velazquez. Tintoretto achieved a progressive deepening of space by means of a succession of shadows and lights, of the vanishing points that govern the painting, and of the spatial perspective.*

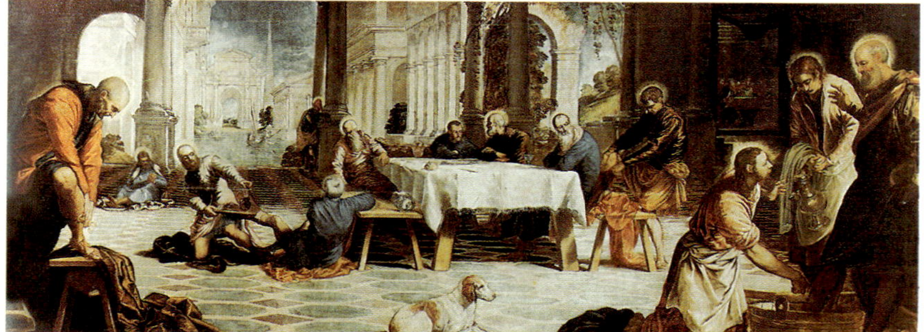

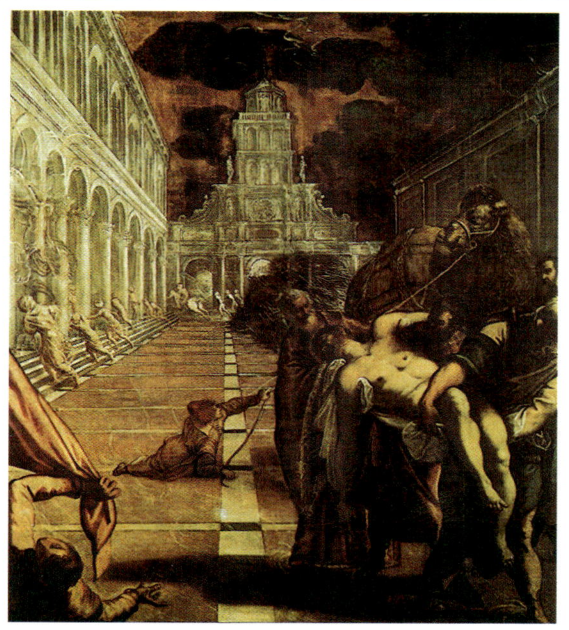

Tintoretto. The Stealing of the Body of Saint Mark *(1562–1566). Oil on canvas, 124 × 156¾". Accademia, Venice. In this work Tintoretto approaches the conception of drama as events that reveal a sense of humanity, which was a characteristic of Titian. The expression of* pathos *comes from the condensing of time and space of a series of dramatic events. These events are highlighted by an extended space that sends a sense of humanity into the world. The scenes are superimposed throughout a succession of Tintoretto's enormous aerial perspectives.*

The Work of Tintoretto

There are very few works by Tintoretto that can be dated with certainty, which makes it difficult to follow a line of evolution. Furthermore, his painting responds more to specific ideas than to repeated formulas. The only thing that is sure is that from the beginning, Tintoretto opted for a form of painting that was committed to the new techniques we call mannerist.

From his enormous output it is possible to mention here only a few of the works that are considered masterpieces of universal art in their own right.

Christ Washing the Feet of the Disciples of 1547, the Prado, Madrid. Together with *The Last Supper,* both painted for the Church of San Marcuola, this is one of the artist's first large-scale paintings (209⅞ × 82¾"). The enormous canvas, exaggeratedly wide, was ideal for Tintoretto to express his compositional ideas with a large scene. Its perspective extends toward the outside world through classical-style architecture. The light that pours in on the cenacle, designed by the artist with complete lack of concern for historical precedent, gives visual preference to one of the

According to Hernández Perera of the Universidad Complutense of Madrid: "The unique originality of Tintoretto's pictorial language, with his luminous naturalism, can be seen continued in El Greco, and is the antecedent of Caravaggio's tenebrism."

Also noteworthy in Tintoretto's work is the nocturnal setting of many of his paintings, doubtless due to his interest in the expression of color and in the effects of light, which in turn were the result of his particular liking for shutting himself away in his studio, and lighting it with lamps and torches.

Tintoretto. Judith and Holofernes *(1555). Oil on canvas, 46¾ × 22⅞". The Prado, Madrid. A work that is paired with* The Death of Holofernes, *also in the Prado. Both are from the artist's early period, and are notable for the clear coloring and the anatomy reminiscent of Michelangelo's attitudes and forms. The poses and movement of the figures and the play of light and shadow are already characteristic of Tintoretto.*

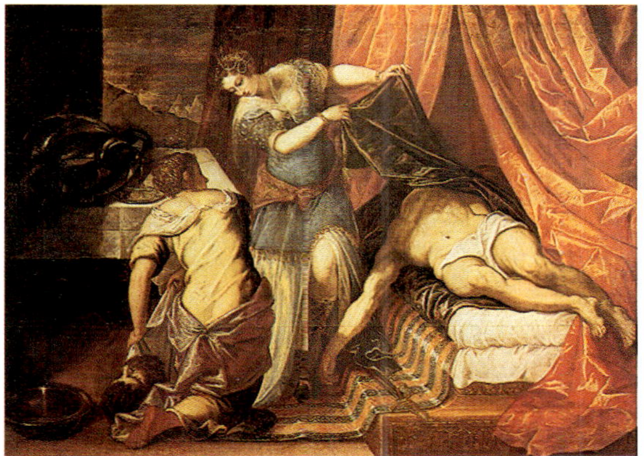

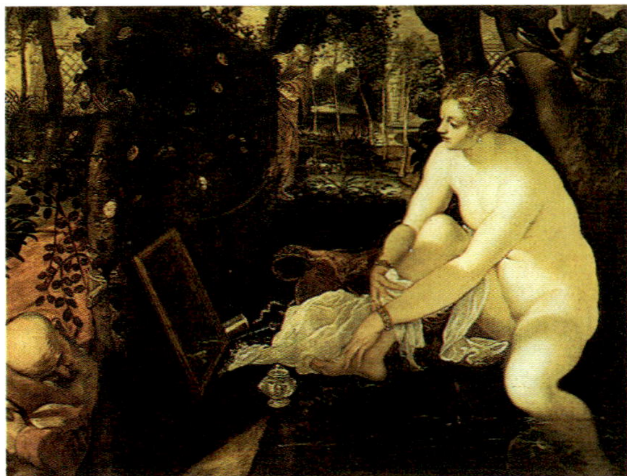

Tintoretto. Susana and the Elders *(1555). Oil on canvas, 95⅝ × 76". Kunsthistorisches Museum, Vienna. As with the* Portrait of a Lady Revealing her Breast, *Tintoretto's treatment of the female nude is always sensual. In the forms of the flesh with which he represents the nude Tintoretto is similar to Rubens, although the iconographic sophistication and the recreation of a world of perverse sensuality, very much to Venetian tastes, is closer to the paintings of Titian.*

apostles who, on the left of the painting, appears to be untying his sandal. In contrast, the group in which Jesus appears in the act of washing the disciples' feet is located on the far right of the picture, and is seen only after the eye has moved around the entire painting. This displacement to the extreme right of the picture of the group that should logically take the most important place is a formula that Tintoretto used on several occasions.

Freeing of the Slave by Saint Mark, 1548, Accademia, Venice. Painted for the Scuola di San Marco, this is one of Tintoretto's most mannerist, even Baroque, works and is very representative of the passion of his painting. The incredible foreshortening of the body of the saint is particularly notable as he hurls himself head first from heaven to save the slave. It is a wonder of drawing and chiaroscuro, used to capture the actual instant when the falling body is still held in midair.

The Stealing of the Body of Saint Mark, 1562–1566, Accademia, Venice. Also for the Scuola di San Marco, this is one of the most interesting of Tintoretto's works, showing the characteristic displacement of the main group to one side of the painting. The atmosphere in which the action develops is highly interesting. It is a desolate and phantasmagorical square, closed in by Renaissance architecture, and that could have been painted by the most committed metaphysical painter of the twentieth century.

Judith and Holofernes, c. 1555, the Prado, Madrid. This is an example of the series of biblical stories that Tintoretto painted during one of the periods of greatest expression and lyricism in his painting. It was acquired by Velazquez under the orders of King Philip IV of Spain. The scene is intentionally theatrical, with the *serpentinato* of the two female bodies, complemented by spectacular curtains, in anticipation of the aesthetic of the most fiery Baroque.

Susana and the Elders, 1555, Kunsthistorisches Museum, Vienna. When Tintoretto painted the female nude, something he did only rarely, he developed an iconography of generous flesh and rotundity that only Rubens could equal. In the subject of *Susana and the Elders,* of which there is another version of 1557 in the same museum, Tintoretto shows the ingenuity and imagination of his composition. In the 1555 version, the beauty of the

Tintoretto. Paradise *(1588). Work on paper. The Louvre, Paris. From the investigation into pictorial space, Tintoretto moved on to the investigation of light. In this work in progress, it is not perspective, but rather the light being radiated that gives the composition its depth and structure.*

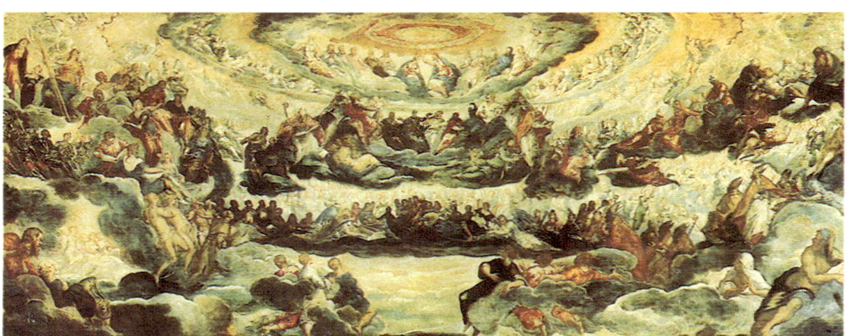

woman's body contributes to the beauty of a garden among whose plants the old men seem to be playing a game of hide and seek.

The paintings of the Scuola di San Rocco, Venice. These works show most effectively Tintoretto's grandiose conception of mural painting. *Christ before Pilate, The Road to Calvary,* and *Crucifixion* were painted between 1565 and 1566. Between 1575 and 1582 he completed the works that have been called the pinnacle of mural painting, with scenes from the Old and New Testaments.

Paradise (1588) is an enormous canvas, painted for the Doge's Palace in Venice. Here Tintoretto shows his grandiose concept of pictorial space, that appears layered among rocky clouds at different distances from the horizon, and that resembles a fantastical shot in a cinematic production filmed in cinemascope. There are versions of the same theme in the Louvre (a study) and in the Prado.

The Last Supper (1592–1594) in the church of San Giorgio Maggiore in Venice. Tintoretto's fertile inventiveness and pictorial talent did not weaken even in his last great paintings. The unreal light from a lamp hanging from a ceiling that is more intuitive than visible is reflected with powerful brilliance in the body of Jesus. It creates, in an extraordinary diagonal composition, contrasts, counter-lights, and color games that break the darkness and phantasmagoria of the grisailles that sketch out the almost imperceptible angelic beings that float near to the upper edge of the pictorial space.

In the field of portraiture also, Tintoretto left important works, among which stand out the portraits he made of important Venetians of his time, such as the portrait of the elderly *Alvise Cornaro,* the Doge of Venice (in the Pitti Palace, Florence), *Battista Morosini* (in the Accademia, Florence), and *Jacopo Soranzo* (in Milan) and the masterly *Portrait of a Lady Revealing her Breast* in the Prado (Madrid), all of which can be considered examples of his brilliant painting.

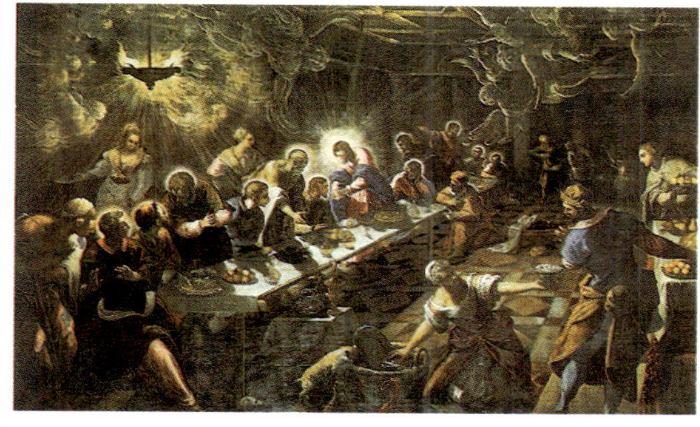

Tintoretto. The Last Supper *(1592–1594). Oil on canvas, 223⅔ × 143¾". Church of San Giorgio Maggiore, Venice. The last work by Tintoretto, in which he shows not only his investigation into a painting's levels of depth, but also demonstrates how light defines the forms. In addition, he creates a mystical atmosphere of figures drawn purely with smoke.*

THE ARTIST'S LIFE

1518. Born in Venice, son of Gian Battista Robusti. Small in stature and the son of a cloth dyer, he received the nickname Tintoretto.

In his relatively long life (76 years) there is nothing besides his painting that stands out. Just as his paintings are mostly undated, little information survives about his personal life, which he spent in Venice. He was rather uninterested in traveling. It is possible that he never went to Rome, and that he visited only Mantua, where he saw the work of Giulio Romano. He began his career decorating frescoes and selling his canvases outdoors.

From his brief apprenticeship with Titian he received his master's colorist influence.

c. 1547. He painted the *Miracle of Saint Ines* in the Church of Santa Maria dell'Orto, which set him on the road to fame.

1547–1548. He produced some of his most important work for the Scuola di San Marco.

1555. He married Faustina Episcopi, with whom he had eight children, three of them painters: Domenico, Marco, and Marietta, an excellent portraitist who was known as Tintoretta.

1560. It is known that more or less around this year he began to teach.

1565–1582. He painted, in two stages, the decoration in the Scuola di San Rocco.

1594. Death in Venice, of the plague, after delivering *The Last Supper* to the church of San Giorgio Maggiore. He is buried in Santa Maria dell'Orta, Venice.

NOTABLE ARTISTS OF MANNERISM

VERONESE

Italian mannerism in the last quarter of the sixteenth century preserved its prestige in Venice while little by little losing it in the rest of the Italian peninsula. Tintoretto is the first master of great mannerist painting, but was not the only one. Another painter, Paolo Caliari, known as Veronese, and ten years his junior, contributed to the prestige of the Venetian school with some of his most extraordinary works.

The Painting of Veronese

It is safe to say that the painting of Veronese is the most genuine expression of the unlimited appetite for luxury and opulence of high Venetian society in the sixteenth century.

When the tribunal of the Inquisition brought the painter to trial after he had painted the monumental painting *Feast at the House of Levi,* on the grounds that he had converted a passage from the Bible into a feast full of profane entertainment, Veronese defended himself with the following argument: "I had only painted what was convenient, since there is no irreverence in the fact that Jesus should be accompanied by the things that form part of everyday life in the city: affluent women, Oriental and African characters, dwarfs, dogs, exotic birds, etc."

Veronese was an outstanding painter of majestic architecture, creating work in his painting that was similar to that of the great architect Andrea Palladio (1508–1563). It provided a sublime background for his scenes that often featured huge numbers of people, dressed in ostentatious clothing, laden with anecdotal and atmospheric details, and without the least concern for

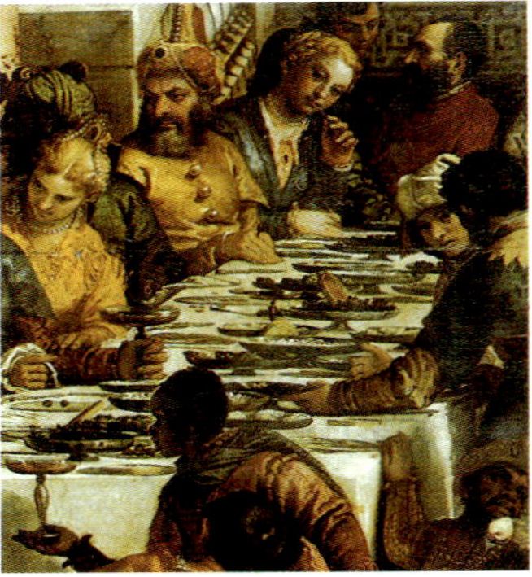

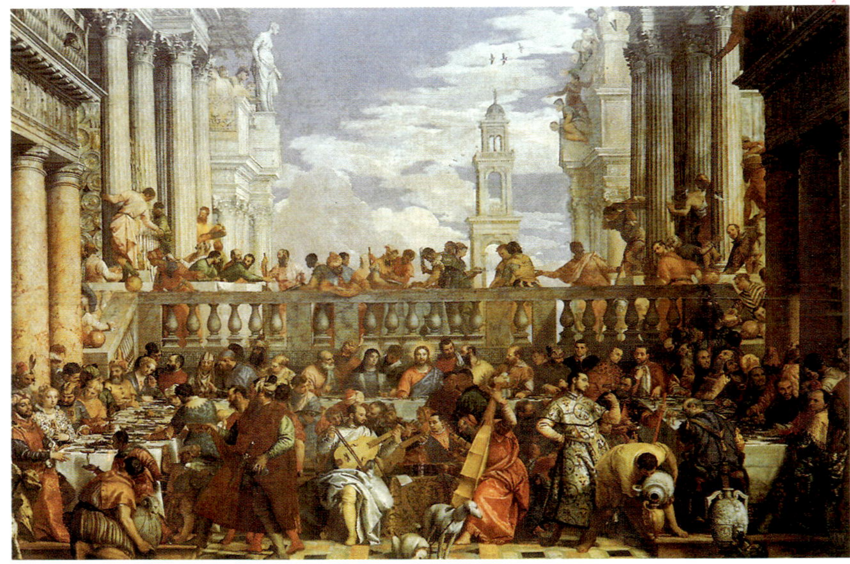

Veronese. The Marriage at Cana *(1562–1563). Oil on canvas, 32⅕' × 22'. The Louvre, Paris. One of the famous feasts that Veronese painted, in which he exhibits the Venetian taste for grand architecture, open perspectives, and lavish surroundings. In this painting the artist does not hold back on color or the superabundance of details, which situate him close to the most celebratory Baroque.*

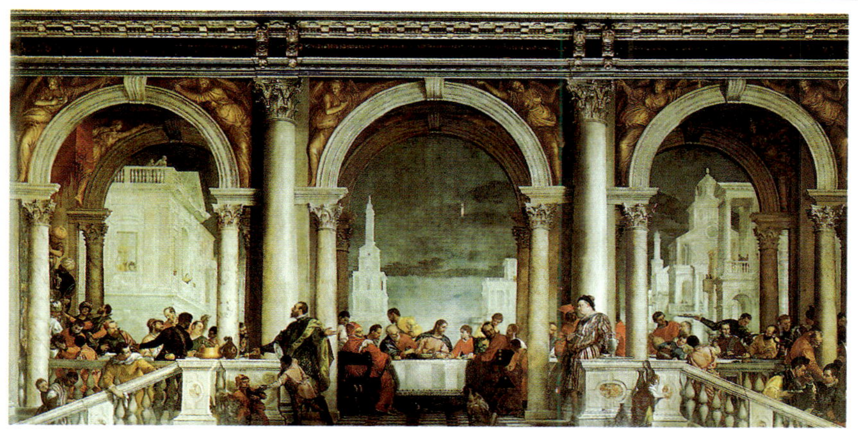

Veronese. Feast at the House of Levi *(1573). Oil on canvas, 42' × 18'. Accademia, Venice. The representation of Christ accompanied by dwarfs, Asians, Africans, children, affluent women, and dogs led to Veronese being accused of irreverence by the Inquisition.*

historical authenticity. For example, *Feast in the House of Levi* takes place in a magnificent Renaissance *loggia* or lodge, while in *The Marriage at Cana,* beside Christ and the apostles, who are dressed in tunics, are seated figures wearing turbans and Oriental jewels from wealthy Venetian society being served by African servants, along with dogs and in the center foreground a group of musicians playing Renaissance instruments.

Everything, from the horses to the bright clouds, is turned into an object of luxury, thanks to Veronese's paintbrush, which gives the images an extraordinary color.

Veronese's painting tends toward the monumental, from the enormous size of some of his work to the conceptual grandeur of everything within it. It is common for him to draw from a point of view below the line of the earth (or the bottom edge of the painting), thus foreshortening the figures and other elements in the composition, making them appear almost inaccessible, but this is a resource he does not always use. In his huge paintings, the horizon is near the line of the earth, but always within the frame of the painting.

The Work of Veronese

Veronese is the painter par excellence of the most spectacular feast scenes in history, without once relating them to passages from the Bible. Giving them a title related to the Scriptures is only a pretext to let his imagination fly in the depiction of huge scenes in which luxury and extravagance take place within grand Renaissance constructions.

The Marriage at Cana (1562–1563), the Louvre, Paris. This enormous canvas, of $32^{1}/_{5}$' × 22', is without doubt the archetype of Veronese's banquets. No fewer than 130 characters appear at the banquet that is being held in front of a balustrade that separates the scene from an imaginative architectural background. And as was traditional, among the guests can be found the most eminent faces of the period: Francis I of France is sitting next to Mary Tudor, Charles V is accompanied by the Marchioness of Pescara, who in turn is to the right of Suleiman the Magnificent. The Marquis of Avalos is sitting beside Leonor of Austria, Queen of France. It is a complete gallery of important people, whom the painter had no hesitation in seating at a table

Veronese. The Annunciation *(1548). Oil on canvas, 114½ × 56¼". Uffizi Gallery, Florence. The characteristics in the style and technique of this work demonstrate the early Venetian works of Veronese, and his knowledge of Palladian architecture in which the scene takes place. The arrangement of the characters is done from a perspective that goes from bottom to top, emphasizing the various expressions of the faces.*

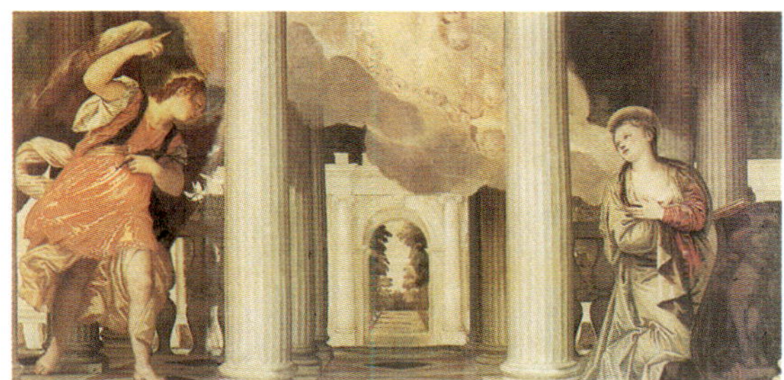

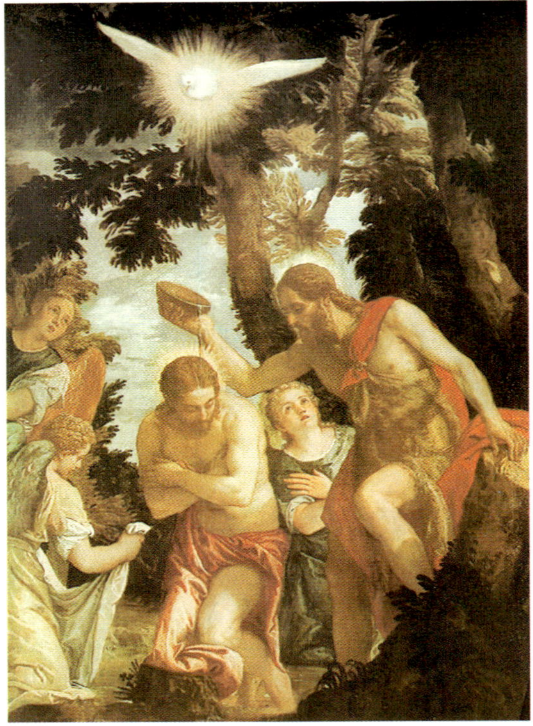

Veronese. The Baptism of Christ *(c. 1560). Oil on canvas, 52⅜ × 77¼". Palazzo Pitti, Florence. This is a strange painting for Veronese, in which the elegance of the figures and the virtuosity in the detail attempt to catch the eye, which is subtly drawn to the background of the image by delicate perspective.*

presided over by Jesus of Nazareth with his mother Mary, who are in fact the least visible characters in the enormous composition. In the center foreground is a group of Renaissance musicians, including Veronese, Titian, and Jacobo Bassano, a painter contemporary with Veronese (1517–1591).

This enormous work was commissioned in 1562 by the Benedictines of San Giorgio Maggiore for their new refectory, which was the work of Andrea Palladio. Finished in 1563, it stood over the monks' meals until 1797, when the French authorities transferred it to the Louvre.

In 1570 Veronese painted another feast scene, *Feast in the House of Simon* (the Louvre, Paris) for the religious order. In 1665 the work was given to Louis XIV.

Feast at the House of Levi (42' × 18') is, after *The Marriage of Cana,* Veronese's other great banquet scene, and even richer in detail and anecdote. Painted in 1573 for the Convent of Saint Paul and Saint John (today it is in the Accademia, Venice),it is the painting that led to the artist's appearance before the Tribunal of the Inquisition, as mentioned previously. The scene takes place between the arches of a monumental Palladian-style lodge. It assembles a great number of people between the side arches and the double staircase that leads to them: German soldiers, servants, clowns with parrots, dwarfs, apostles cleaning their teeth with a fork (*la forchette alla veneciana,* whose use had become widespread in Venice during that century), dogs, and children. Veronese himself, making a dismissive gesture, stands in front of a

Veronese. Allegory of Love. *Oil on canvas, National Gallery, London. The foreshortened figures are characteristic of Veronese, who creates movement from his particular low point of view (known as* sotto in sú*).*

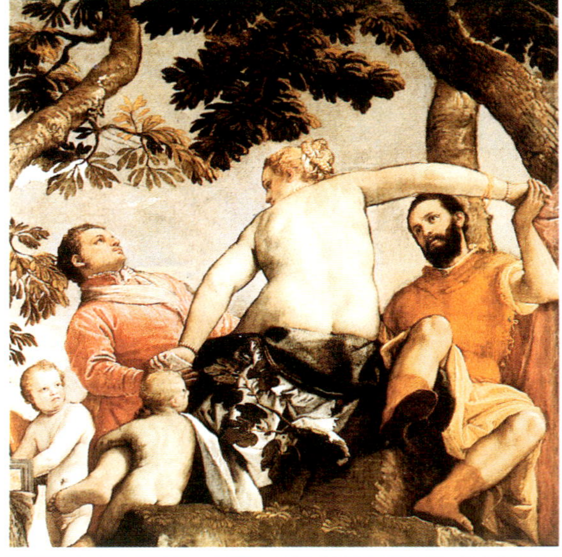

column, behind a small African servant.

In his canvas paintings, Veronese showed himself to be a consummate painter of detail, capable of concentrating on minutiae with the same magnificent splendor and the same exoticism he used in his enormous murals.

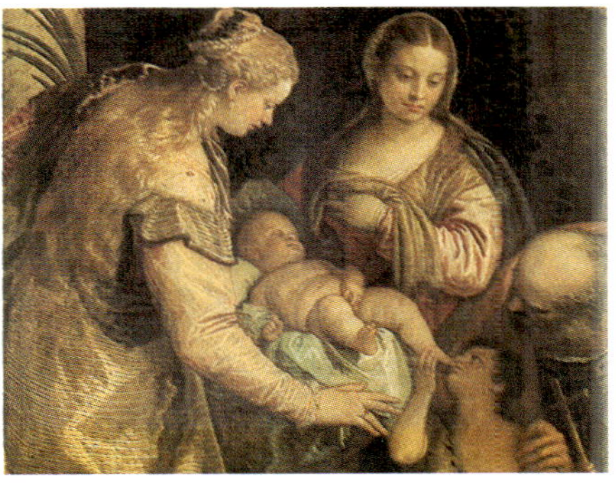

Veronese. Holy Family with Saint Barbara *(c. 1580). Oil on canvas, 48 × 33⁷⁄₈". Uffizi Gallery, Florence. It belongs to Veronese's late period. The painter's virtuosity in the depiction of the sense of air and space and the atmospheric vibration that suffuses the figures is admirable.*

Christ among the Doctors (or *The Presentation of Jesus*) is a large painting (169¼ × 92⅞") in the Prado in which the striking figure of the adolescent Jesus, who is presiding over a meeting of solemn, corpulent scribes and Pharisees, acquires the same solemnity as the Doric and Corinthian columns that surround him, increased by the foreshortening produced by a *sotto in sú* vanishing point.

Moses Saved from the Nile (1560–1570). Oil on canvas, 16⅞ × 19¾", the Prado, is a small painting in which Veronese transforms the Pharaoh's daughter into a Venetian duchess, dressed in the luxury of the times, within a landscape that includes a city that has nothing in common with ancient Egypt.

Venus and Adonis (1580). Oil on canvas, 75¼ × 87", the Prado. This is one of the few classical themes that Veronese painted. It shows his characteristic luminosity and brilliant coloring. The compact composition, with a sweeping line that is continued in the lower half thanks to the dog that has been kicked out and that covers the triangular space left by Venus's bent leg and Adonis's extended arm. The painting is set at dusk, with a background that prefigures the landscapes of the Baroque.

Venice Triumphant (1583). The murals that Veronese painted in the Doge's Palace after fires had destroyed it (1574 and 1577) are justifications of the Republic and allegories that sing the praises of Venice: *Venice Enthroned between Justice and Peace, Dialectics and Prosperity,* and, most of all, *Venice Triumphant,* on the ceiling of the Great Council Chamber, with Venice represented by an exuberant matronly figure who wears luxurious clothes and jewels, on a painting in oil on canvas that is about 174 feet square (228¼ × 356").

The work of Veronese is truly extensive and features the assistance of his sons Gabriele and Carletto and his brother Benedetto.

In addition to the works mentioned, other noteworthy paintings include:

Allegory of Love, in the National Gallery, London; *The Story of Esther* (c. 1555) for the ceiling of the sacristy of the Church of Saint Sebastian in Venice; *Music, Geometry, and Arithmetic* (1556), an allegory painted for the library of San Marco; *The Martyrdom of Saint George,* in the Church of the Saint in Venice; *The Martyrdom of Saint Justina* (1575) in the Saint's Church in Padua, and the *Commemoration of the Battle of Lepanto* (1575) painted for the hall of the burned down Doge's Palace.

THE ARTIST'S LIFE

1528. Born in Verona. His first apprenticeship is with his father, who was a sculptor and woodcarver. He begins to paint with an uncle, Antonio Badile, but Veronese is completely self-taught.

1552. He collaborates on various paintings for the cathedral of Mantua as part of a commission from Cardinal Ercole Gonzaga. Soon afterwards he decorates the Villa Giacomelli in Maser with frescoes.

1555. He establishes himself in Venice. He paints the *Story of Esther* and three allegories for the library of San Marco.

1562. He paints *The Marriage at Cana.*

1566. He marries the wife of his first master and has many children. Two of his sons, Gabriele and Carletto, become painters and work as their father's assistants.

1573. He paints the *Feast at the House of Levi.*

1574 and 1577. There are fires in the Doge's Palace in Venice, which he decorates with his most important murals and ceilings.

1588. He dies in Venice, twelve years after Titian and six before Tintoretto.

MANNERISM IN ROME

Roman mannerism has its natural origins in the pupils and assistants of Raphael, under whose instruction they imitated his *maniera* or style of painting. A number of artists participated in the decoration of the Vatican alongside Raphael, including Giovanni de Udine, Gianfrancesco Penni, Polidoro de Caravaggio, and, according to recent discoveries, the Spaniard Pedro Manchua. These artists worked with the sketches under the instruction of their master. However, of all the artists who collaborated with Raphael, it was Giulio Romano, to whom were entrusted the decoration of the last *stanze* or papal apartments, called the Sala di Constantino, who stands out.

Giulio Romano

Originally named Giulio Pippi, he was known as Giulio Romano (1492–1546) because he was born in Rome. He is the pioneer of the Roman tradition of mannerism, and his painting combines the concerns of the last stage of Raphael with the dynamic coloring of Michelangelo's Sistine Chapel.

In the *Constantine Stanze,* which was entrusted to him, he painted *The Battle of the Milvian Bridge* (1520–1524), which had been designed by Raphael and which was inspired by Leonardo *(The Battle of Anghiari)*, and *The Donation of Constantine*, which is similar to Raphael's *Fire in the Borgo* from the third *stanze,* a painting that Romano had colored.

In 1524 Giulio Romano moved to Mantua, where he worked in the court of the Gonzaga family, creating paintings that showed the mannerist taste for grandeur. Giulio Romano had the advantage of total liberty of creation, which he used to produce a fertile output of frescoes in the Palazzo del Te in Mantua. His frescoes in the Hall of Giants are masterpieces, producing on the walls a huge earthquake with a chaos of columns and falling arches, under which a multitude of Titans are being crushed. From the ceiling, the Gods of Olympus are contemplating the catastrophe, their forced gestures suggesting anarchic, uncontrollable movement.

The frescoes in the Hall of Psyche, in the same Palazzo del Te, are also notable. The ceiling of foreshortened nudes stands out particularly, because of its extraordinary conception, reminiscent of Raphael's decoration of the Villa Farnesina.

Mantua was the definitive residence of Giulio Romano, who also decorated the extension of the duke's palace there. He died in this city in 1546.

Giulio Romano. Vault of the Hall of Giants (Sala dei Giganti): Olympus *(1532–1534). Fresco painting. Palazzo del Te, Mantua. In his representation of Olympus, Giulio Romano depicts the troubled, perturbed expressions of the gods as they contemplate the huge earthquake that is shaking the walls of the hall. The Roman painter's frescoes manage to open up large spaces in the closed space of the hall, with the use of light and movement.*

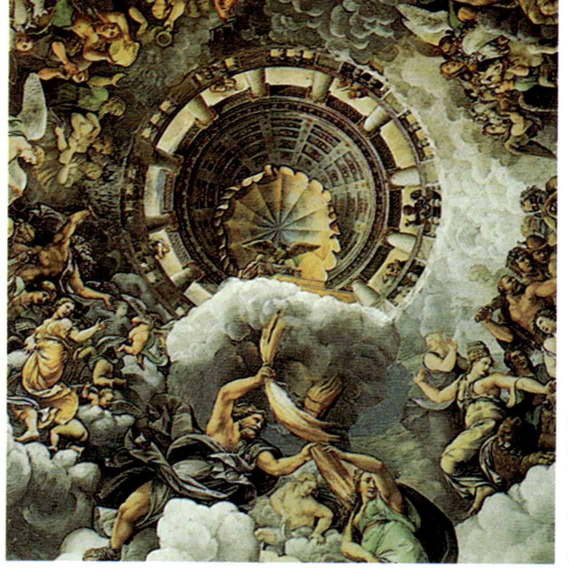

Sebastiano del Piombo

Roman mannerism had started with Giulio Romano and other pupils of Raphael in the shadow of Michelangelo. The Venetian Sebastiano del Piombo (1485–1547) also contributed to the enrichment of mannerism, a style that began with the tradition of drawing of the great Florentines who worked for Julius II.

The precursors of Sebastiano del Piombo are Giorgione, and Titian, with his colorful classicism. This classicism, a continuation of its Venetian expression, can be seen in *The Death of*

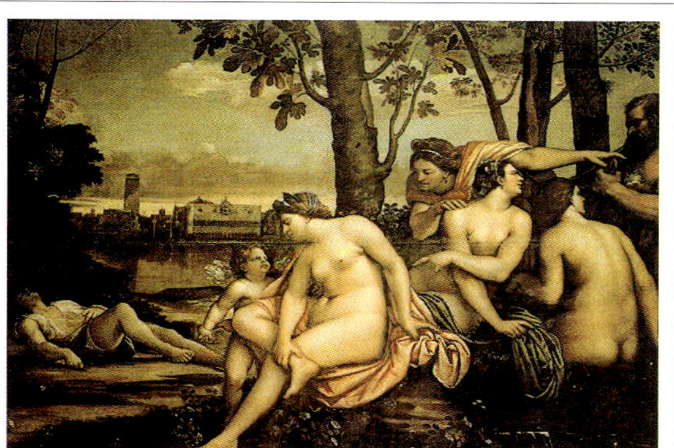

Sebastiano del Piombo. The Death of Adonis *(1512). Oil on canvas, 116 × 74⅖ ". Uffizi Gallery, Florence. Although not an outstanding painter, Sebastiano del Piombo reveals, in the nudes of this painting, a slight influence of Giorgione. In addition to the representation of the Doge's Palace in Venice, he shows his interest in the painting of Veronese and in Venetian landscapes in general. During his stay in Rome he would also gradually assimilate the influence of Michelangelo.*

Adonis of 1512, which is clearly reminiscent of Giorgione in its composition and color. The background landscape is Venetian, with the mass of the Doge's Palace reflected in the water. However the influence of Michelangelo, of whom he was a close friend, soon ceases to be evident. First in *Polyphemus* (c. 1512), a fresco in the Villa Farnesina, and more obviously in the *Pietà of Vierbo* (c. 1515), a nocturnal painting in which the light of the moon shapes the sculptural figure of Christ. *The Raising of Lazarus* (1517–1519) returns to the influence of Michelangelo and the luminosity of the Venetian painters.

As well as being a painter of religious themes (in which he shows no great originality), Sebastiano del Piombo was an excellent portraitist. He was almost the only great painter of portraits in Rome after the death of Raphael, for whom, to a certain extent, he became the substitute. The portrait of *Andrea Doria* (Palazzo Doria, Rome) and of the Pope *Clement VII* (Capodimonte Museum, Naples) are excellent examples of his portrait work. He was perhaps better known for his portraits of women. His portraits are half-body, never fully frontal, and have the gaze turned to the observer. *Portrait of a Woman* in the Uffizi Gallery, with its perfect treatment of clothing and flesh is clearly Raphaelite, so much so that some commentators have attributed it to Raphael. In his *Portrait of a Woman* in the Gemäldegalerie, known also as *Portrait of a Young Roman Woman,* and other similar works, the model shows indolence and a hint of sensuality as she sits in front of a window through which can be seen a landscape that recalls Venice.

Sodoma

To complete the commentary on the artists of Roman mannerism, one must mention Giovanni Antonio Bazzi, known as Sodoma (1477–1549). Born in Lombardy, and a citizen of Vercelli, his artistic life was essentially lived in Siena and Rome. He was a follower of the *maniera* of Roman painting, in which he collaborated, and contributed a style that can be considered the meeting point between the painting of Raphael and of Leonardo.

He was commissioned to paint the ceiling of the Stanze della Segnatura, before Raphael began it; he collaborated with Raphael on the decoration of the Villa Farnesina, with the fresco *The Marriage of Alexander and Roxanne* (1512). It has a clear Raphaelite influence, but also shows influences of Leonardo that Sodoma had brought from Lombardy. During his stay in Siena, his painting adopted mannerist characteristics without losing the influence of Leonardo (such as *sfumato,* for example). Sodoma's incipient mannerism is best represented in his *Saint Sebastian* (1522), Pitti Palace, Florence, and in *Lucretia* in the Art Gallery in Turin.

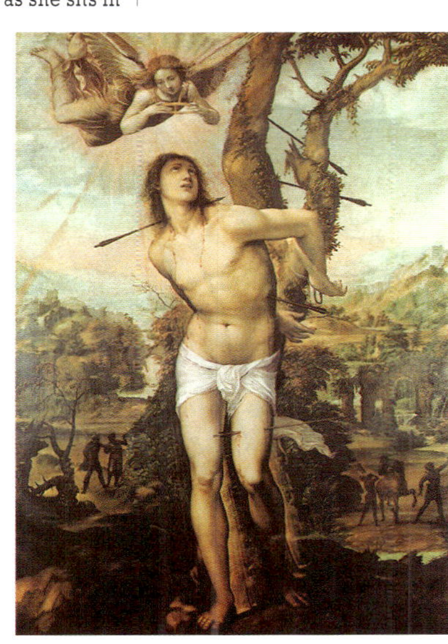

Sodoma. Saint Sebastian *(1525). Oil on canvas, 60⅝ × 81⅛". Palazzo Pitti, Florence.*

MANNERISM IN PARMA

Under the patronage of the Este family, the dukes of Ferrara and Parma, this region developed as a focus of artistic creation with painters from Ferrara such as Lorenzo Costa (1460–1535) or painters who worked there, like Francesco Raibolini, known as Il Francia (Bologna, 1450–1517). Parma developed its own form of mannerism thanks to two excellent painters, Antonio Allegri, Correggio, and Francesco Mazzola, Il Parmigianino.

The Painting of Correggio

Antonio Allegri, known as Correggio, was born in the villa of that name (1494) and was, without question, the most representative and most important painter of the school of Parma in the sixteenth century. His painting, influenced by the mannerist tendencies derived from Raphaelite classicism, also shows other influences: the softness of the painting of Costa and Francia, both from Ferrara, and the techniques of Mantegna. Although he did not visit Rome until fourteen years before his death, it seems that his assimilation of the classical style of Raphael was the result of having studied the *Sistine Virgin* (now in Dresden), which was in Piacenza, near Parma.

From Mantegna he borrowed various ideas, notable among which was to simulate transparency in the central area of a dome, dissolving with lightness, so to speak, the darkness of the architectural space. It was a technique that was used throughout mannerism, and that found its definitive expression in the lavish ceilings of the Baroque.

In his canvas paintings, both sacred and profane, Correggio gave Italian mannerism a new grace in the postures of the saints, virgins, and mythological figures, and the unmistakable ingenuity of the smiles of his children. His way of playing with light on the faces of virgins and angels gave his sacred painting an unreal, dreamlike feel, at the same time as his clothing and drapery took on an extraordinarily tactile quality.

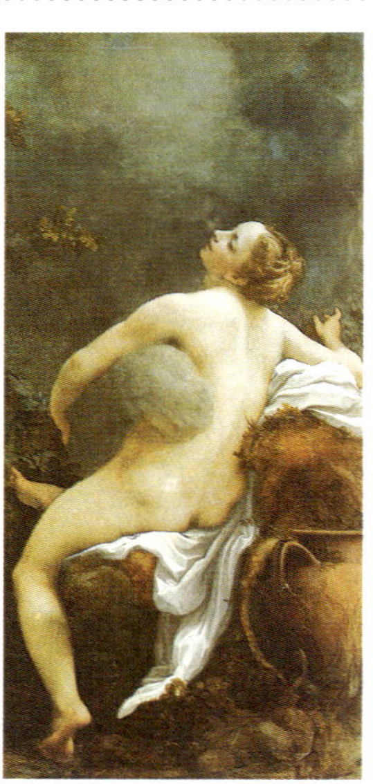

Correggio. Jupiter and Io *(c. 1530–1532). Oil on canvas, 29⅛ × 64⅛". Kunsthistorisches Museum, Vienna. This work is notable for the sensuality of the nude, who is typically mannerist. The figure of Io moves in a gentle twist, embraced by Jupiter in the shape of a cloud.*

Correggio. The Vision of Saint John the Evangelist on Patmos *(1520–1523). Fresco painting, 344½ × 370⅛". Dome of the Church of Saint John the Evangelist, Parma. Il Correggio borrowed from Mantegna's* Camera degli Esposi (Room of the Bride and Groom) *the idea of making the dome of the church transparent. Thus, on entering the church, one feels that Christ is suspended in heaven. Il Correggio dissolves the architectural space by making the opaque surfaces seem transparent.*

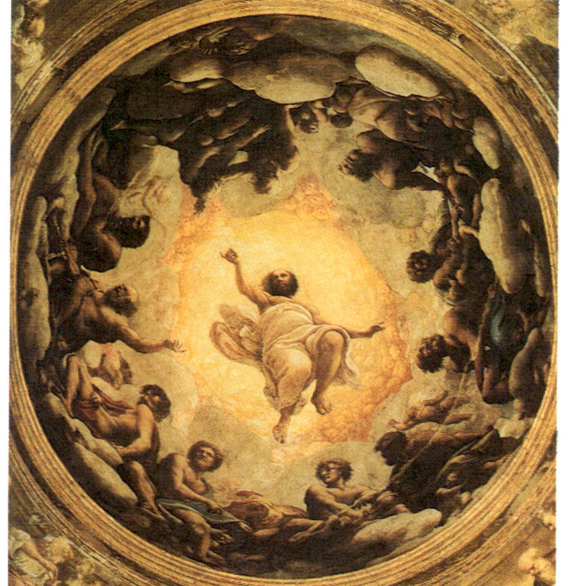

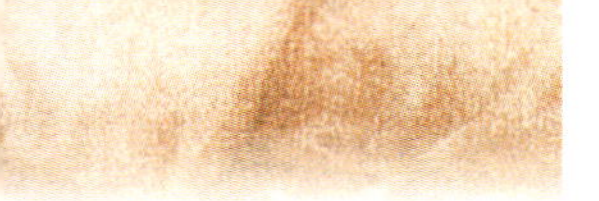

The Work of Correggio

Notable among Correggio's mural work is the dome of Saint John the Evangelist in Parma (1520–1523), a prototype of mannerist domes. A resurrected Christ is suspended in the air at the center of a circle of golden light that perforates the dome. The lower circle is in half-light, and is occupied by the imposing figures of the Apostles, in an extraordinary confusion of arms, legs, torsos, and beautiful heads, achieved with a foreshortening of impeccable skill and accentuated dynamism. The dynamism is intensified in the figures that move through the enormous area of space that Correggio created in the dome of the Cathedral of Parma (1526–1530), an open space in which, between angels and clouds, can be seen The Virgin of the Assumption.

Two of Correggio's noteworthy Madonnas are the *Madonna and Saint George* (Gemäldegalerie, Dresden) and the *Madonna and Saint Jerome* of 1527–1528 (Pinacoteca of Parma). Also in Dresden is one of his most valued religious works, *The Adoration of the Shepherds,* also known as *The Night.*

Correggio's mythological work is smoothly sensual and exquisitely depicted. Examples include *Ganymede* of 1531 and *Jupiter and Io,* 1530–1532, which features one of the greatest nudes of mannerism (Kunsthistorisches Museum, Vienna). *Danäe,* 1531–1532 (Borghese Galaria, Rome) with the theme of *Leda and the Swan,* of which there are very similar versions in Madrid and Berlin, complete his most representative work.

Little is known about his life, other than his preoccupation with the idea of glory, rather than money, despite the fact that he lived comfortably as an artist who was very dependent on the quality of his art. He died in 1534.

Parmigianino

Francesco Mazzola, known as Parmigianino, a pupil of Correggio, was the most obviously mannerist painter in Italy in the first half of the sixteenth century. His first artistic steps were taken, with the guidance of Correggio, in Parma, the city where he was born in 1505. From Parma he went to Rome (1524–1527) and also visited Florence, Bologna, and Mantua. His contact with the painting of Giulio Romano, Pontormo,and Bronzino, along with the virtuosity he acquired from Correggio, gave him a personal style. He produced superbly sinuous lines and an almost unhealthy elongation in his treatment of the female body, which was nevertheless full of grace and beauty. The somewhat grotesque bodies in some of his works seem to be disjointed.

His originality even appears in his portraits. For example, his *Count of Fontanelato* (Capodimonte Museum, Naples) has an elongated bust and appears with a still life. In his *Self-portrait in a Convex Mirror* (Kunsthistorisches Museum, Vienna) his deformed hand appears in the foreground.

Of his paintings of the Madonna, one must mention the *Virgin of the Rose* (1528–1530) in the Gemäldegalerie, Dresden and, above all, his *Madonna of the Long Neck* (c. 1535) in the Uffizi Gallery. With the artificial grace of a truly elongated body, it is the work that most emphatically proclaims his originality.

He died in 1540, at the age of just thirty-seven.

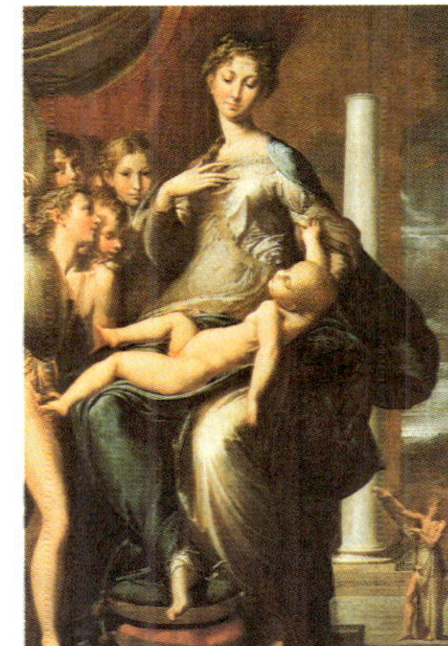

Parmigianino. Madonna of the Long Neck *(c.1535). Oil on canvas, 52³⁄₈ × 84¼". Uffizi Gallery, Florence. This Madonna contrasts with the pleasant one of Correggio. Parmigianino has painted the portrait of a distant, hermetic Madonna enclosed within her own elegance, with a face of onyx, and glasslike clothes, and strange symbols like the large columns that do not support anything, or the prophet preaching in the desert.*

Correggio. Danäe *(c. 1531–1532). Oil on canvas, 76 × 63³⁄₈". Borghese Gallery, Rome. Correggio wanted the observer to enter his paintings, so he carefully brought his figures forward toward the front plane of the painting. In this case it is the foot of Danäe who then, with foreshortening, is thrown backwards. Thus, the spectator enters the painting gradually, from the foot to the whole figure and then into the scene and finally into the landscape that opens up in the background.*

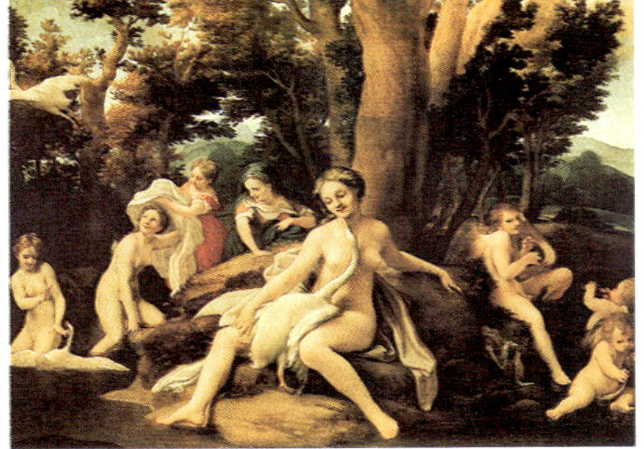

THE *QUATTROCENTO* IN SPAIN

As in the rest of fifteenth-century Europe, painting in the kingdoms that made up the territory of Spain showed an evolution from the Gothic tradition to the new Renaissance aesthetic through different areas of influence. It can be argued that the evolution in Spain was influenced by the Gothic art of Siena and by Flemish painting.

Quattrocentism in Catalonia

During the first half of the fifteenth century Catalan painting developed in local schools that were faithful to the tradition of Italian Gothic. In the second half of the century, the Flemish influence began to open up new and important developments.

Lluís Dalmau

Lluís Dalmau, who is first mentioned in the city of Valencia (1428), brought to Barcelona the style and techniques of the Van Eyck brothers. Having been sent to Flanders by Alfonso V, on his return he painted *Virgin of the Councillors* (1443–1445), which is now in the National Museum of Catalan Art. It is a bright reflection of the style of the Van Eyck brothers, both in the figures (the contract specified that they had to have "a completely individual appearance") and in the Gothic architecture, the Virgin's throne, and the background landscape.

Jaume Huguet

The great Catalan painter of the fifteenth century was Jaume Huguet (1415–1492), who was also influenced by Flemish Gothic, although with more originality than Dalmau. Huguet's figures tend to be priestly, although they display a certain majesty arising from the softly drawn folds of their clothes, the emotion of their faces, which are frequently melancholy, and the elegance of their gestures. Huguet developed an art that finds itself midway between Italian and Flemish, and prefigures the imminent birth of the Spanish Renaissance. His most important works, not including the *Altarpiece of Saint Anthony Abbot,* which was destroyed in 1909, are: the altarpieces of the *Guild of Retailers, Saint Vincent Sarriá,* and *Saint Augustine,* all of which are in the National Museum of Catalan Art. However, Huguet's incipient Renaissance tendency shows itself, above all, in the figures in his *Saint George* (c. 1460), also in the National Museum of Catalan Art in Barcelona, the central panel of a triptych whose lateral panels are in the Kaiser Friedrich Museum, Berlin. In the Cathedral of Barcelona can be found the *Altarpiece of Saint Bernard and the Guardian Angel,* whose dramatic figures, naturalist in style, stand against a gold background that seems to owe more to the imposition of tradition than the personal taste of the artist. The same is true of the *Altarpiece of the Saints Abdon and Sennen,* in the Santa Maria Church in Terrassa (Barcelona), and in the *Epiphany,* known as the *Condestable* altarpiece, in the chapel of Saint

Jaume Huguet. Altarpiece of the Saints Abdon and Sennen *(1459–1460). Tempera on canvas, 118½ × 88⅗". Church of Santa Maria, Terrassa, Barcelona.*

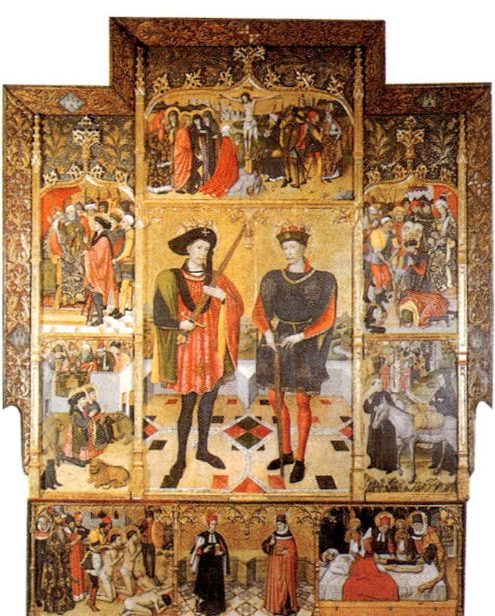

Lluís Dalmau. Virgin of the Councillors *(1443–1445). Oil on canvas, 122⅘ × 122⅖". National Museum of Catalan Art, Barcelona. This work is practically the only known painting by Lluís Dalmau, despite the fact that he introduced Flemish naturalism to Spain. He was commissioned in 1443 by the councilors of Barcelona to paint an altarpiece for the Casa de la Ciudad. Thus, in this religious scene, appear the portraits of five councillors in an entirely naturalist style.*

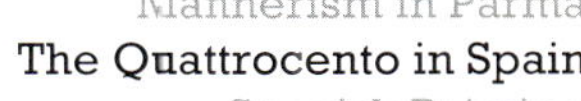

Águeda in the royal palace of Barcelona.

Jaume Huguet worked with the Vergós brothers as collaborators who, as pupils of their master's art, end the transition of Catalan Gothic toward the aesthetic of the Renaissance.

The Valencian School

Lorenzo Zaragoza and Joan Rexach

The Gothic school of the kingdom of Valencia developed through contact with the Catalan school, and particularly with Italy, acquired its own personality through a richness of color superior to that of its contemporaries in Spain, and through a more accentuated elegance in the drawing of figures. The period of Italian Gothic of the Valencian school appears toward the end of the fourteenth century in Lorenzo Zaragoza, painter to King Pedro IV, and continues up to Jaime or Jacomart Baçó, painter to King Alfonso V, who worked in the court of Naples. Stylistically, this painting was an excellent combination of elements from Italy and Flanders, which, in its figures, announces the new, more monumental style of the pre-Renaissance. Many works are attributed to him although only the *Altarpiece of Jativa* and the *Altarpiece of Cati* can be said with certainty to be his. It is possible that many of the works attributed to him were by his pupil Joan Rexach, an artist who definitively introduced geometric perspective into subject matter that shows all the conventions of Gothic painting. His *Altarpiece of Cubells,* dedicated to Saint Ursula (National Museum of Catalan Art, Barcelona) is one of his most representative works.

Aragonese Painting of the *Quattrocento*

During the period of Italian Gothic, Aragonese painting was closely tied to the influence of the Catalan schools, with the work of García Benabarre (*The Life of Saint John the Baptist,* National Museum of Catalan Art, Barcelona), who had worked with Bernat Martorell. Martín Soria, a follower of Huguet's style (*Altarpiece of Pallaruelo de Monegros*) began the naturalist tendency that marked the beginning of the Renaissance.

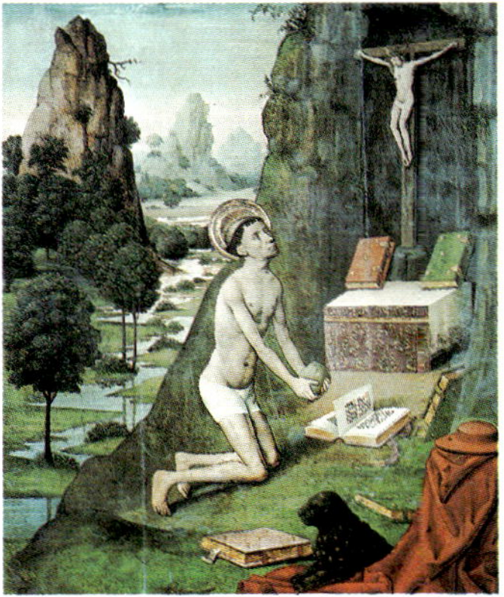

Maestro de la Seu d'Urgell. Saint Jerome Penitent *(middle of the fifteenth century). Oil on canvas, National Museum of Catalan Art, Barcelona.*

Bartolomé Bermejo

It is with Bartolomé Bermejo, traditionally assigned to the Aragonese school, that fifteenth-century Spanish painting reaches one of its peaks. Born in Cordoba, he spent his artistic life in Aragón, Valencia, and Catalonia and also possibly in Italy. His painting shows a strong individuality, not attached to any one school. What is certain is that he was heavily influenced by Flemish art, in the incorporation of the techniques of oil into his painting, and, although he still uses the traditional gold backgrounds of Gothic altarpieces, his figures are generally monumental and painted with brilliant color, luminous sparkle, and luxurious decoration. Bermejo's personal style acquires its definitive expression in the panel *Saint Domingo de Silos* (1474) in the Prado, Madrid, which is part of the *Altarpiece of Daroca,* and in the panel of *The Pietà of Canon Desplà* (1490) in the cathedral of Barcelona. In this work, Bermejo shows a dramatic tendency in the physical depiction and facial expression of the figures, who are wrapped in light from a landscape background of clear Flemish influence, which shows a preoccupation with atmospheric perspective. Through Bermejo the school of Aragon acquires its first taste for tactile qualities and for composition, visible in the treatment of clothing and landscape.

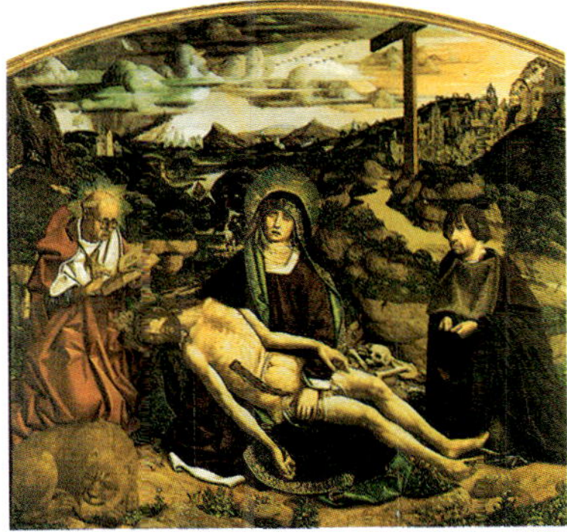

Bartolomé Bermejo. The Pietà of Canon Desplà *(1490). Oil on canvas, 69 × 73½". Barcelona Cathedral. With the intention of representing space coherently, Bartolomé Bermejo creates a work that is outstanding in its almost photographic detail, highlighting every minute aspect of nature.*

The Castilian School

While the Italian influence deeply affected Mediterranean painting in the fourteenth and fifteenth centuries, it was barely felt in Castilian painting, which was closely linked to the Flemish school. Via the Cantabrian Gateway and important fairs of the fifteenth century, Castille received works by Jan van Eyck, Van der Weyden, Hugo van der Goes, and other Flemish painters. These painters were highly appreciated by the high society of the period, including Queen Isabel of Castille herself, who assembled a large collection of Flemish work, part of which is now held in the Royal Chapel of Granada.

Jorge Inglés and the Master of Sopetrán

Nevertheless, the Flemish painters who worked in the kingdom of Castille were not first-class masters, but rather, good professionals who, like Jorge Inglés, introduced the Northern aesthetic into Castilian territory. It is known that in 1455, commissioned by the first Marquis of Santillana, Íñigo López de Mendoza, Jorge Inglés worked on an altarpiece dedicated to the *Joys of the Madonna* for the hospital of Buitrago, an immature work within the Flemish tradition. Much more skillful both in technique and form is the painting of the successor of Inglés in the house of the Marquis of Santillana, known as the master of Sopetrán because of the altarpiece he painted for the monastery of the same name. *The Altarpiece of Sopetrán* (c. 1475), now in the Prado, is of clear Flemish conception, and shows a mastery of space and portraiture that is closer to the painting of the new century.

Fernando Gallego

Fernando Gallego was a great figure in fifteenth-century painting in Castille-Leon. His origins are unknown but he is documented between 1466 and 1506. His painting is highly compositional and shows an expressionism similar to Van der Weyden, whose art he possibly became acquainted with on a hypothetical journey to Flanders. His conception of space, which is more artistic than geometrical, can be appreciated in the following works: the *Altarpieces of San Ildefonso* and of *Cardinal Mella* in the Cathedral of Zamora, the *Altarpiece of Ciudad Rodrigo (Altarpiece of Toro)* in the Prado, and especially in the *Pietà* in the Prado and the *Nativity* in the National Museum of Catalan Art. In both these oil panels, the Flemish composition and realist expressionism of the painter reach high levels of accomplishment.

Nevertheless, the most significant Renaissance work in Fernando Gallego's painting is his fresco of *The Zodiac* (1479–1493) in the University of Salamanca, which he created based on the humanist ideas that the planets and signs of the zodiac are related to the sciences and the liberal arts. In this fresco, Gallego departs from Gothic-Flemish convention to achieve a much freer style of painting. It is a new direction that was not, however, received with the acceptance of his religious painting.

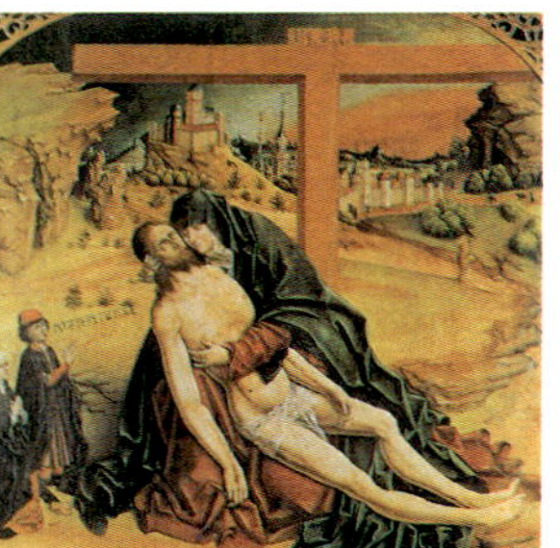

Fernando Gallego. The Pietà *(c. 1580). Oil on panel, 40⅛ × 46½". The Prado, Madrid. Fernando Gallego's use of a Flemish pictorial framework is surprising. His landscapes are typically Castilian but modeled on the characteristics of Flemish painting. The Castilian artist's way of shaping the figures is significant, making them dry, angular, and expressive.*

Pedro Berruguete

The Castilian artist who most clearly marks the transition from Gothic to Italian Renaissance painting is Pedro Berruguete, possibly born in Nava, Palencia around the middle of the fifteenth century and who died in Ávila in 1504. He worked in Italy, around 1477, specifically in the *studiolo* (library) of Federico de Montefeltro, in the palace of Urbino. Between 1483 and 1489 he worked in Toledo but there is no trace of his work there. It is in Ávila, a city he moved to in 1499, that he produced his mature work. In it, he combines the Flemish tendencies that governed Castille with a powerful descriptive realism that is more Italian-influenced, producing successful effects of perspective and light and with tones of ochre and earth, particularly characteristic of Berruguete.

His best-known Castilian works are the *Altarpiece of Saint*

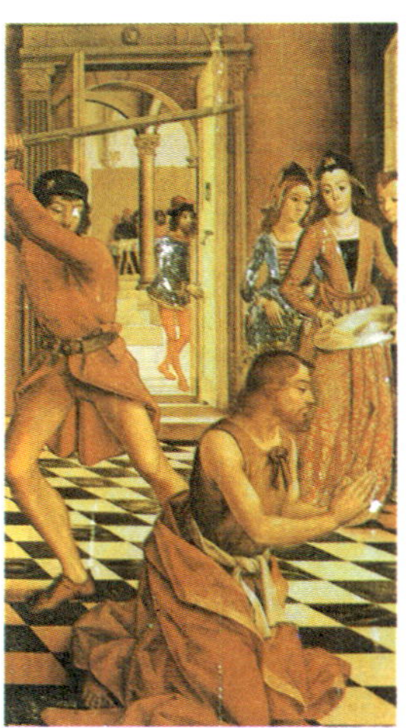

Pedro Berruguete. The Beheading of Saint John the Baptist *(c. 1482). Tempera on canvas. Colegiate Church of Santa María del Campo, Burgos. Berruguete was the artist who introduced the Italian Renaissance to Castille, which up until then had been dominated by the Flemish influence. The altarpiece of Saint John the Baptist, to which this scene belongs, is his first work in Spain following his stay in Urbino working for the Count of Montefeltro. Here his sense of Italian perspective is notable.*

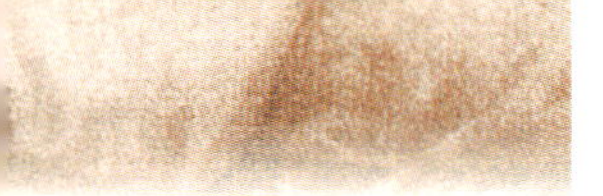

Thomas of Ávila (which has been preserved *in situ*) and that of *Saint Domingo de Guzmán,* painted for the convent of Saint Thomas of Ávila (and now in the Prado). This latter work contains an *Auto de Fe* and a *Test by Fire,* which, in its composition, perspective and technique, make it a forerunner of the imminent Renaissance.

Painting in Seville

Andalusian painting in the Gothic period saw the Italian influence greatly overshadowed by the presence of Mudéjar, so that its art only began to absorb European artistic developments through the influx of Flemish painting, with which the painters of the region were soon entirely immersed.

In Seville, on the other hand, the painting of Van der Weyden and the forms and nature of early Renaissance architecture were well known. This is shown by Alejo Fernández, who founded what can be considered the Andalusian school of painting in the fifteenth century.

In his *Saint Peter Praying before Christ at the Column* (Provincial Museum of Fine Art, Cordoba), despite its signs of the old school, its geometric perspective, and its architecture show Renaissance influences. The naked figure of Christ is that of a human being with an expression more of bereavement than of torment. This contrasts with the general tendency of other painters who, in their predilection for themes from the Passion of Christ, paint figures that are overly sentimental, and who express themselves through crying and suffering. An example of this is the *Pietà* painted by Juan Nuñez for the cathedral in Seville.

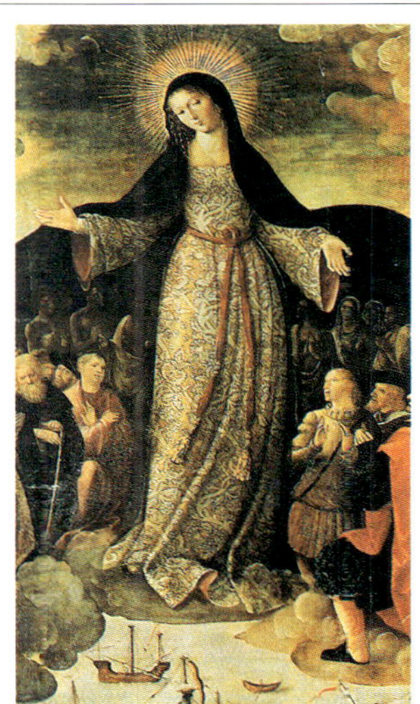

Alejo Fernández. Altarpiece of the Virgin of Seafarers *(1531–1536). Tempera on panel. Archivo de Indias, Seville. Alejo Fernández was a characteristic painter of the Spanish Renaissance, influenced by both Flemish and Italian art. On one hand there is the notable naturalism of the faces and the representation of the sky, and on the other hand there is the delightful detail and the gold that covers the clothing and halo of the Madonna. Nevertheless, this painting still represents space in a symbolic way, rather than according to the rules of perspective. Thus, the figures are placed according to their importance, rather than their position in space.*

The Portuguese Painting of Nuñez Gonçalves

The Museum of Ancient Art in Lisbon houses *The Polyptych of Saint Vincent of Fora,* which was painted in about 1470 for the Cathedral of Lisbon by the Portuguese painter Nuñez Gonçalves, who was born around 1438 and who died in 1481.

The polyptych is composed of six panels painted in oil. Gonçalves' realism matches the best Flemish painting of the time, although it has an introspective quality, rare in that period, which leads it to express the internal humanity of its figures, who are taken from the colorful society of Lisbon in the era of discovery. The adoration of the saint, patron of Lisbon, features a portrait of King Alfonso V, together with the future Joan II and the king's Uncle Henry the Sailor. An archbishop, personalities from the court, and humble monks make up a gallery of portraits. The addition of a highly developed landscape technique in the polyptych completes what is unquestionably a great example of painting from the brush of one of the most eminent painters of the fifteenth century.

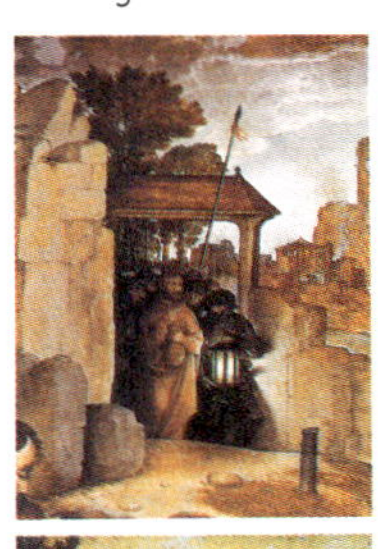

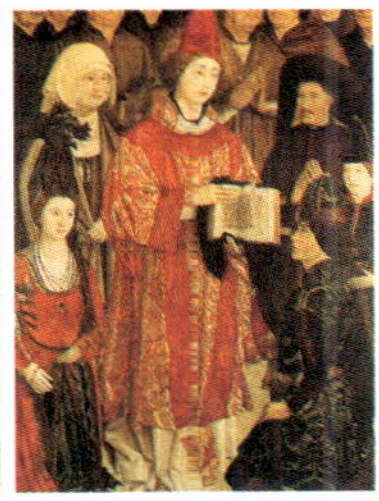

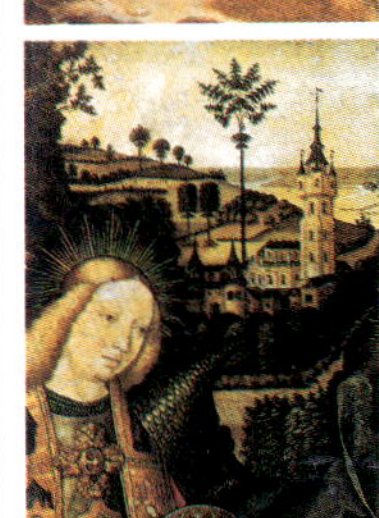

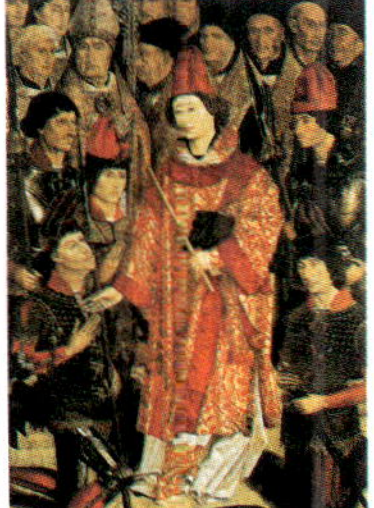

Nuñez Gonçalves. The Polyptych of Saint Vincent of Fora *(c. 1470). Oil on panel, $50\frac{3}{4} \times 81\frac{1}{2}$". Museum of Ancient Art, Lisbon. The assimilation of Flemish painting is characteristic of Nuñez Gonçalves, who was a master of detail, both in landscape and in the representation of people and their clothing.*

SPANISH PAINTING AT THE BEGINNING OF THE SIXTEENTH CENTURY

The Italian and Flemish tendencies that predominated in painting in Spain at the end of the fifteenth century evolved at the beginning of the sixteenth century into an acceptance of the style of the painting of Leonardo and the *maniera* of Raphael and Michelangelo. The contribution of Renaissance elements to the artistic output of the first years of the century is due to painters from both Northern Europe and Italy. Anye Bru (died c. 1509), who lived in Catalonia, was an artist who produced high-quality painting that was still linked to Flemish art, but with a pronounced naturalism. This can be seen in the monumental *Altarpiece for the Monastery of San Cugat del Vallés* (1507), the National Museum of Catalan Art.

Hernando de Llanos and Fernando Yáñez de la Almeida

The Italian influence of high Renaissance painting reached Spain via these two artists of Italian origin, who moved to Valencia in 1506.

Very little is known of their lives, though this does not diminish their importance. They were the first artists who, familiar with Leonardo da Vinci's advances in the art of painting, brought to Valencia their mastery of chiaroscuro and of the new trends in composition, along with a concept of spatial reality that at the beginning of the century was truly innovative. In 1507 Llanos and Yáñez received a commission to paint the door panels of the great altarpiece of Valencia. With perfect stylistic unity, the work includes a dozen magnificent compositions of the Madonna. When they finished the work in 1510, the two artists separated. Llanos stayed in Valencia before later moving to Murcia, while Yáñez went to Barcelona (1515) and later (1531) to Cuenca.

Painting of the High Renaissance. The Influence of Raphael.

The artists of the Spanish Renaissance who can be called geniuses are not painters but architects and sculptors, but the sixteenth centuryin Spain produced some very high-quality painting in the *maniera* of Raphael, emanating from centers of production in different parts of the peninsula.

Anye Bru. Martyrdom of Saint Cugat *(c. 1504–1507). Panel, 52½ × 64½". National Museum of Catalan Art, Barcelona. Although still within the conventions of medieval painting, the work of Anye Bru attempts an accentuated naturalism both in the representation of gestures and figures and in the use of perspective.*

Renaissance Painters in Valencia

Apart from the pioneering aspect of the work of Hernando de Llanos and Fernando Yáñez, it is with Vicent Macip (1475–1550) that Valencian painting provides Spain with the first clear evidence of Raphaelite mannerism. The panel *The Baptism of Christ* (1535) in the Cathedral of Valencia and the excellent panel of the *Adoration of the Shepherds* from the altarpiece of the Cathedral of Segorbe (Castellón) of 1530 show the influence of Raphael on Macip's composition and coloring. The school of Raphael appears more faithfully in the painting of Macip's son, known as Juan de Juanes, who died in 1579, especially in the *Virgin of the Mystic Marriage of the Venerable Agnesius* (c. 1560) and more

Juan de Juanes. Virgin of the Mystic Marriage of the Venerable Agnesius *(c. 1560). Oil on panel, 64½ × 30⅓". Museum of Fine Art, Valencia. In addition to the influence of Raphael, de Juanes is also influenced by Leonardo in his smooth organization of space.*

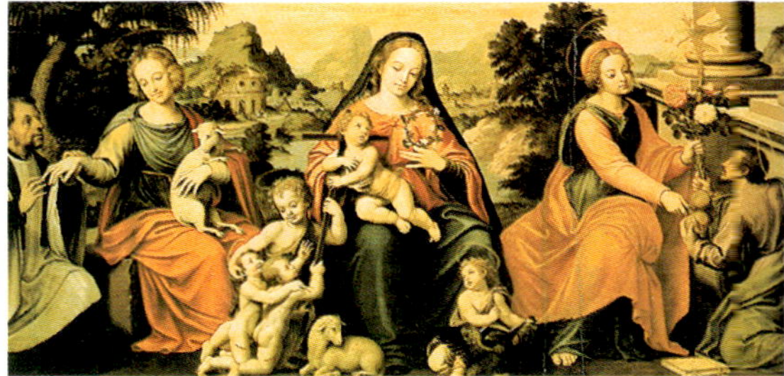

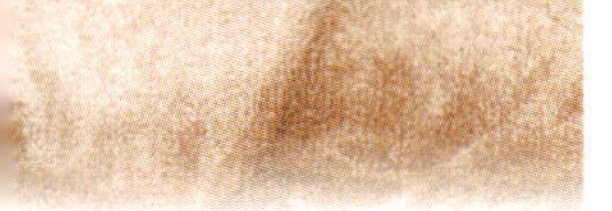

so in the *Last Supper* (c. 1570). For his representations of the Madonna, Juan de Juanes adopted the pyramidal composition and landscape backgrounds that were so characteristic of Raphael's Madonnas.

The High Renaissance in Castille

Alonso Berruguete

Castille, centered essentially on Valladolid, was part of the avant-garde in mannerism, led by Alonso Berruguete, who is better known as a sculptor (1490–1565). During his stay in Florence and Rome he had joined in the mannerist movement and in 1517, now in Spain, was attached to the court of Carlos V, as painter to the king. From 1526, based in Valladolid, he began to acquire fame as a sculptor, and to create significant paintings. The scene of *The Flight into Egypt* from his *Altarpiece for the Convent of Saint Benito* (1527–1532) is notable. Berruguete magnifies gestures and breaks up volumes with numerous light effects, using a peculiar tonal color range of grays, reds, and blues that are dissonant despite their complementary nature.

Gaspar Becerra, who was younger than Berruguete, lived between about 1520 and 1570. Just as the painting of Berruguete is very closely attached to Raphaelite mannerism, Becerra was inclined toward the school of Michelangelo. He too was a sculptor, as well as a painter of portraits and murals. He painted large frescoes for the Alcázar of Madrid, which are all now lost. His only surviving works are a few paintings with mythological themes on the ceilings of the Prado Palace in Madrid (c. 1563).

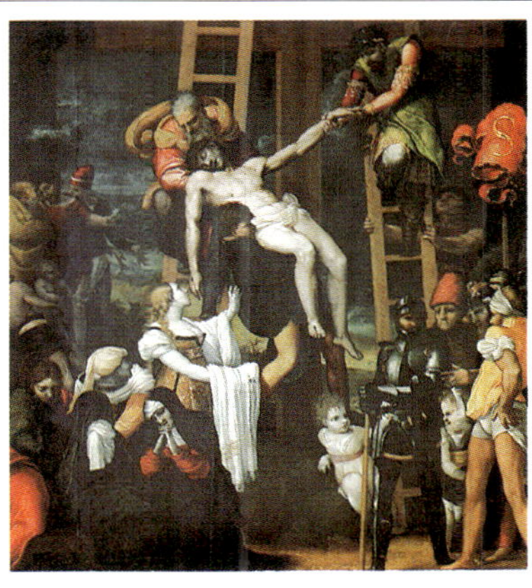

Pedro Machuca. Deposition *(1547). Oil on panel, 50⅜ × 55½". The Prado, Madrid. This is a work totally in the mannerist style, from which emanates an atmosphere of ambiguity and mystery accentuated by the nocturnal light.*

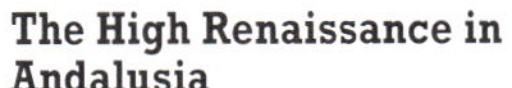

The High Renaissance in Andalusia

The Raphaelite Renaissance in Andalusia was based in Seville and Granada. Its most notable work was produced by three masters of chiaroscuro and light effects: Pedro Machuca, Pedro de Campaña, and Luis de Vargas.

Pedro Machuca (1490–1550), an architect as well as a painter, worked in the Royal Chapel of Granada (c. 1521) to paint an *Agony in the Garden,* the *Taking of Christ,* a *Descent into Limbo* and the *Descent from the Cross.* He also worked in the Cathedral of Jaen and for the Order of Santiago, in Uclés, painting a *Madonna* that is today in the Prado.

Pedro de Campaña (1503–1580). In Seville, the style of Raphael spread, thanks to the contribution of the Flemish painter De Campaña (Peter de Kempeener), a master of composition and of chiaroscuro, and skilled in effects with light. His most important works are *Deposition* (1547–1548) and the *Mariscal Altarpiece* (1555), both in the Cathedral of Seville.

Luis de Vargas (1502–1568). Born in Seville, this is the painter who best embodies the *maniera* of Raphael within the Andalusian school. Most notable among his works are the fresco of the *Last Judgment* in the Hospital de la Misericordia, Seville, and the central panel of the altarpiece of the *Allegory of the Immaculate Conception* (1561), also known as *La Gamba,* in the Cathedral of Seville.

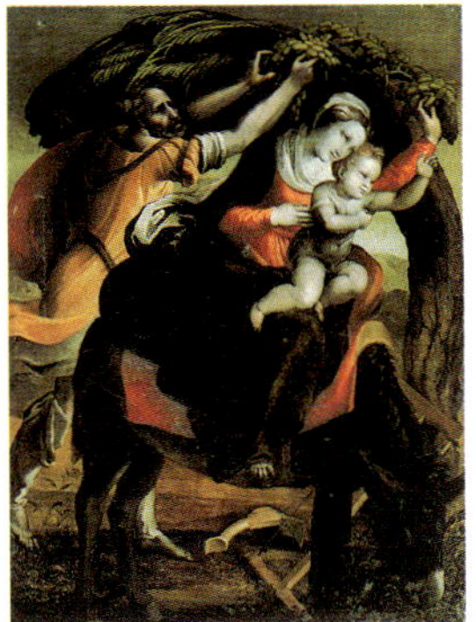

Alonso Berruguete. The Flight into Egypt *(1527–1532). Oil on panel. National Sculpture Museum, Valladolid. It is part of the Altarpiece for the Convent of Saint Benito, which consists of this painting and a* Birth of Christ. *The work is notable for its use of gold and silver tones directly borrowed from Italian mannerism.*

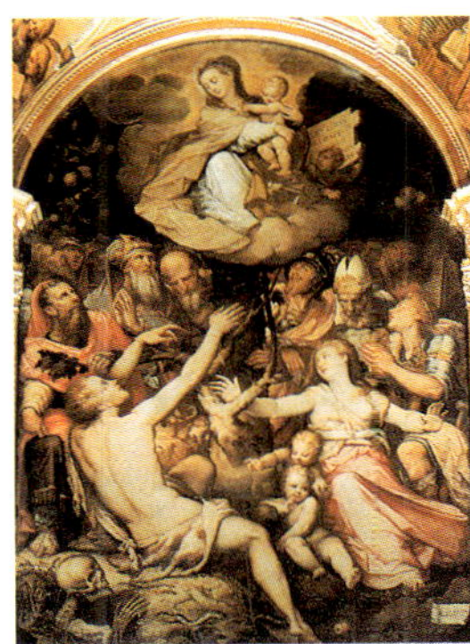

Luis de Vargas. Allegory of the Immaculate Conception *or* La Gamba *(1561). Panel, 69 × 72". The central panel of the altarpiece in* La Gamba, *Seville Cathedral.*

AN EXCEPTIONAL MANNERIST

Sixteenth-century Spanish painting produced one of the most original exponents of the art of painting ever: El Greco, who, although initially under the influence of Italian mannerism, quickly evolved toward a unique form of painting, creating a style that was born and died with its creator.

The Painting of El Greco

Although Cretan by birth, El Greco was indisputably a Spanish painter, living in Toledo, the city where he found the support that allowed him to work with absolute iconographic freedom, in a religious atmosphere with which he completely identified. It is no exaggeration to say that, removed from the atmosphere of Toledo, he would not have been able to develop his unique personality as a painter. On his way through Venice and Rome, El Greco became acquainted with the work of Michelangelo and was especially influenced by Titian and Tintoretto, borrowing from the former his Venetian coloring, and from the latter his tendency toward elongated figures and contrasting colors. However, to his Italian inheritance, El Greco added an extraordinary charge of mysticism that gave him the freedom to go beyond what was reasonable in terms of form. His color range includes blues (cold and clear), yellows (in shades that El Greco dominated with unequalled mastery), greens, and mauves. It is a range of colors far distanced from reality, and he uses them to dilute his exaggeratedly elongated, vibrant, almost flaming bodies. These bodies are evidently incorrect formally, a fact justified by compositional necessity in order to balance volumes and, above all, in order to achieve results that are free from any form of convention. El Greco's painting tends to spiritualize everything it represents, including the *View of Toledo* landscape in which, below stormy skies, the city appears with mystic connotations.

El Greco. Disrobing of Christ *(1577–1579). Oil on canvas, 68⅛ × 112¼". Toledo Cathedral. El Greco makes characteristic use of silver colors, which often swamp his paintings. His use of large areas of pure color is notable, in this case red in the center, which creates rhythm in the painting.*

El Greco affirmed that "coloring is more important than form" and said that "Michelangelo was a good man who did not know how to paint." Thus he encapsulates his views on painting.

The Work of El Greco

In his religious compositions El Greco elaborates his highly personal

El Greco. Burial of the Count of Orgaz *(1586–1588). Oil on canvas, 141¾ × 181⅛". Santo Tomé Church, Toledo. This is the most famous painting by the painter from Greece. All the characteristic properties of El Greco's art can be seen in it, though what makes it stand out is the originality of the composition of the work, full of portraits of famous people of the period. In the lower half of the painting is a gallery of important people, representing what is earthly, while in the upper half, heaven appears, sharply separated. In later years, this separation would disappear. El Greco's heaven disappears into infinity, in contrast to the limited space on earth.*

ideas about the combination of volume and space, light, and color.

Soon after arriving in Toledo, he painted the three altarpieces for the Convent of Santo Domingo El Antiguo, including *The Trinity.* The Italian influence can still be seen.

Between 1577 and 1579 he painted the impressive *Disrobing of Christ* in the sacristy of Toledo Cathedral. The figure of Christ, with his red tunic, the meekness of his hands, and his large, tear-filled eyes looking to heaven, is the best expression of the painter's mysticism.

In 1580 he painted the *Martyrdom of Saint Maurice* in the monastery of the Escorial, a painting that did not please the emperor, for whom he had already painted *The Dream of Philip II,* also in the Escorial.

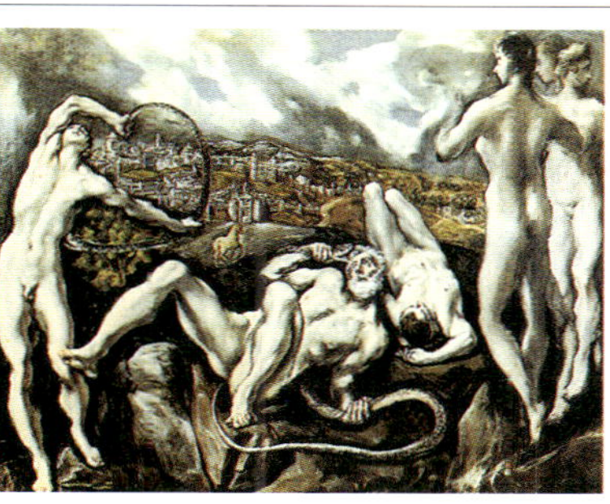

El Greco. Laocóón and his Sons *(1610–1614). Oil on canvas, 76 × 55⅞". National Gallery, Washington. This painting belongs to the final period in the artist's life, and shows El Greco giving free rein to his passion.*

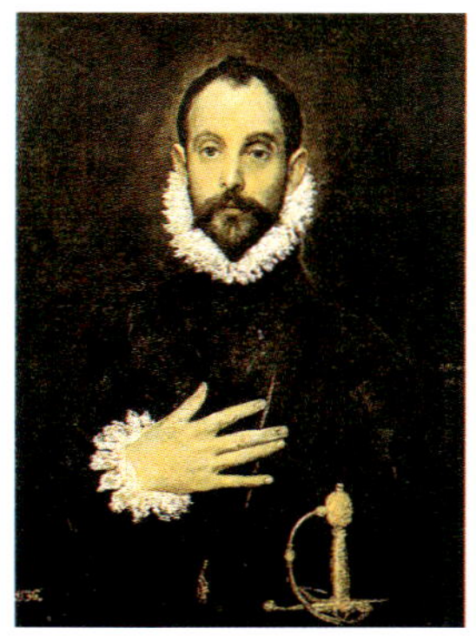

El Greco. Man with His Hand on His Breast *(1570–1580). Oil on canvas, 26 × 31⅞". The Prado, Madrid.*

Between 1586 and 1588 he painted his most famous work: *Burial of the Count of Orgaz* (in Santo Tomé Church). An impressive gallery of famous people (including the painter himself), dressed in black, their faces framed by white ruffs, separates earthly matters from the celestial world above. The obvious hardness of the upper half contrasts with the softness of the scene below, where El Greco produces unmatchable yellows.

Around 1600 he painted three of the paintings that best represent him: *The Baptism of Christ, The Resurrection,* and *The Pentecost* (the Prado), an incredible testimony to the immediacy of feeling that El Greco's brush communicated in his painting. It has been said about this painting that "everything in it has a tongue of fire."

From 1600 on, paintings such as *The Adoration of the Shepherds* (the Prado), *The Visitation* (Dumbarton Oaks, Washington), painted between 1607 and 1614 for the Hospital Tavera in Toledo, *View of Toledo* (1603–1607) in the Metropolitan Museum, New York, and *Laocóón and his Sons* (1610–1614) in the National Gallery, Washington, testify to the absolute creative liberty El Greco achieved.

Of his many portraits are the famous *Man with His Hand on His Breast* (1570–1580), the Prado, Madrid. *Cardinal Niño of Guevara* (c. 1600), Metropolitan Museum, New York, *Cardinal Juan de Tavera* (1610) in the Hospital Tavera, Toledo, *Fray Hortensio Félix de Paravicino* (1609), Museum of Fine Art, Boston.

THE ARTIST'S LIFE

1541. Born Domenico Theotokopoulos in Candia on the island of Crete. Known as El Greco.

1565. He leaves Crete under the imminent threat of Turkish invasion and goes to Venice, attracted by Titian and Tintoretto.

1570. Seeing no way forward in Venice, he moves to Rome, where he also feels uncomfortable.

1576. He arrives in Spain and travels to Madrid, with the idea of painting for the Escorial Palace.

1579. His attempts to paint for Philip II are a disaster. (His *Martyrdom of Saint Maurice* is removed from the Escorial.) He moves definitively to Toledo.

1580. By this time El Greco is already a well-known painter. He stays in the main houses of the Marquis of Villeno, and has a son with Jerónima de Cuevas, whom he does not marry. His liking for an ostentatious lifestyle is well known, although when he dies, all he leaves are 200 unfinished paintings and a library of some 150 books: Greek classics, Italian poets and humanists, architectural treatises, only one book on painting, and the Old and New Testaments.

1600. The year that marks the beginning of his final period in which he magnifies, so to speak, his stylistic characteristics.

1614. He dies in Toledo.

PAINTING IN THE FIFTEENTH CENTURY

As in the rest of Europe, French painting in the fifteenth century was nourished by the detailed realism of the Flemish school. The fifteenth century in France was a period of constant struggle that proved rather unfavorable to the flourishing of the arts. It was only in Provence, thanks to the residency of the popes in Avignon, that the artistic currents from Lombardy, Tuscany, and Catalonia flowed together and, along with the Flemish painting of the *Quattrocento,* dominated the art of the period. Following the return of the popes to Rome, Avignon became one of the most important Southern centers for the spread of Flemish realism, which evolved toward the new styles imported from Italy.

The Master of Aix-en-Provence

The work that best represents the arrival of the Flemish tradition into France, and that at the same time is one of the most notable in the whole of Europe is the triptych of the *Annunciation* (c. 1444). It is the work of an anonymous painter, though it reveals, beyond all doubt, knowledge of the painting of Jan Van Eyck. The central panel of the triptych, in the Church of the Magdalena in Aix-en-Provence, shows the scene of the Annunciation taking place inside a Gothic church. This is one of many highly conventional aspects of a painting whose detail and iconography is entirely Flemish, to such an extent that it has thrown the authority of the panel's attribution into question. Among other theories, it has been attributed to a pupil of Robert Campin.

Enguerrand Quarton

This painter, born about 1415 in the diocese of Laon, represents the fusion between Flemish painting taken from the example of the master of Aix-en-Provence and the most clearly French tradition of the Gothic school of Paris. Of the few panels that can be attributed to him with certainty, the most important are the *Madonna of Misericordia* (1452) in the Condé de Chantilly Museum, and the *Coronation of the Virgin* (1453-1455). This latter is his most ambitious work. Its artistic conception follows the tradition of detailed Flemish realism, while its iconography is that of an entirely Northern Gothic tradition.

The Master of Aix-en-Provence. Annunciation *(1444). Oil on panel, 61 × 69⅜". Church of the Magdalena, Aix-en-Provence. This work belongs to a triptych that is now divided between various European museums: The Boymans-Van Beuningen Museum, Rotterdam, and the Royal Fine Art Museums, Brussels, have the two side panels. Painted by an anonymous painter, this painting is a perfect example of the Flemish tradition in the fifteenth century. It is notable for its naturalism and the emphasis on the study of perspective as well as for its close detail.*

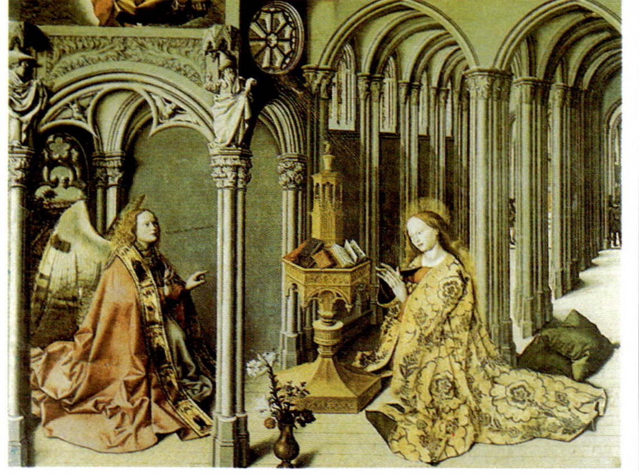

The School of Avignon. Nicolás Froment

Provençal painting owes much to the influence of Quarton, whose synthesis of French and Flemish painting took deep root in the artists of Avignon. Notable among these was Nicolás Froment (1435-1484) a Franco-Flemish painter born in the Languedoc. He painted figures, interiors, and open landscapes in the realist tradition of the Flemish school, mixed with local traditions and Italian influences. Froment was a painter for King Renato I.

The works that best define his style are the triptych of *The Raising of Lazarus* (c. 1461) in the Uffizi Gallery, and the triptych of *The Burning Bush* (1476) in the Cathedral of the Saviour, Aix-en-Provence. It is a triptych with an iconographically unusual central panel, and one that allows Froment to show his skill as a painter of imaginary landscapes and of notable effects of light and distance. In the side panels there are clear influences of Van der Weyden in the elegant realist portraits of Queen Juana de Laval and King Renato.

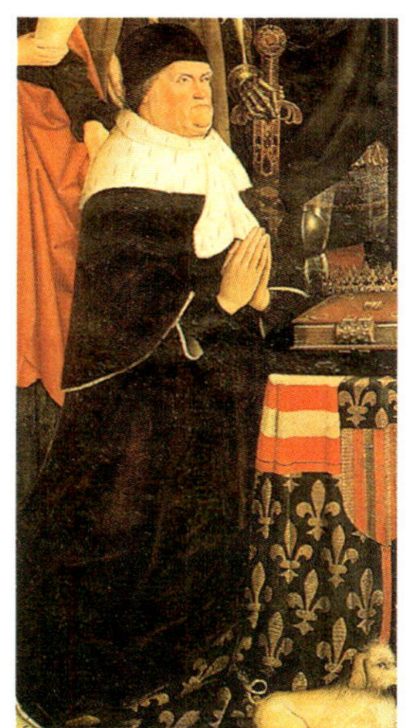

Nicolás Froment. Central Panel of the Triptych of the Burning Bush *(1476). Oil on panel, 120⅛ × 161⅜". Cathedral of the Saviour, Aix-en-Provence. Froment is a painter more suited to compositions of Flemish origin than those typical of the Florentine Renaissance. Nevertheless, in his paintings he manages to endow his figures with a volume that is almost sculptural and an expressionism that verges on caricature.*

The Courtly Painting of Jean Fouquet

France did not start to recover from the devastation arising from the Hundred Years War until the middle of the century, when painting began to regain its lost splendor under Charles VII and Louis XI.

The architect of this recovery was Jean Fouquet (1425–1477, approximately) who is considered the pioneer of humanism in French painting and who traveled to Italy between 1474 and 1477. He was a multifaceted painter who combined portraits with religious paintings and landscapes.

In his portrait of Charles VII (c. 1444) in the Louvre, Fouquet begins his monumental portraits, which are half-body and in three-quarters position, as befits an artist acquainted with Flemish painting. He is also influenced by Italian Renaissance painting as a result of his travels to Italy.

In the so-called Melun diptych (c. 1451) Jean Fouquet's Renaissance influence is clear in the left panel (Staatliche Museen, Berlin) *Etienne Chevalier* and his *Saint Stephen* (1452). It shows realistic figures in an interior with elements of Renaissance architecture. The right panel, *Madonna and Child* (1451) in the Royal Fine Art Museum, Ambères, shows truly original iconography and coloring.

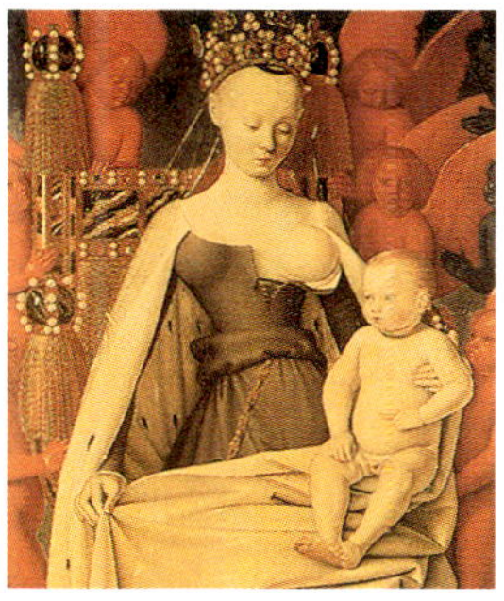

Jean Fouquet. Madonna and Child *(1451). Oil on panel, 33½ × 36⅝". Royal Fine Art Museum, Ambères. This is the right panel of the so-called Melun Diptych. The Virgin Mary is represented as a portrait of Agnès Sorel, mistress of Charles VII. Fouquet here creates a world far removed from reality, full of brilliantly and intensely colored angels in red and blue. They surround the images of the Madonna and Child, images that are fundamentally concerned with geometrical issues.*

The Master of Moulins

Moulins Cathedral, in Allier, France, houses a diptych that, for want of better documentation, has given its name to its creator: the Master of Moulins, an extraordinary painter who in the strictest tradition of Flemish naturalism incorporates idealized figures of careful and correct proportions. In addition to portraits of Charles de Bourbon and Margaret of Austria, the artist's definitive work is the already mentioned triptych of Moulins (c. 1498–1499). Its central panel depicts the Madonna and Child surrounded by angelic figures, two of whom are holding a crown. The realist tendency of the Madonna and Child is counterpointed in the stylization of the figures of the angels. The portraits on the side panels show an even greater realism, with the artist achieving truly outstanding levels of depiction, with detail in the purest tradition of Van Eyck.

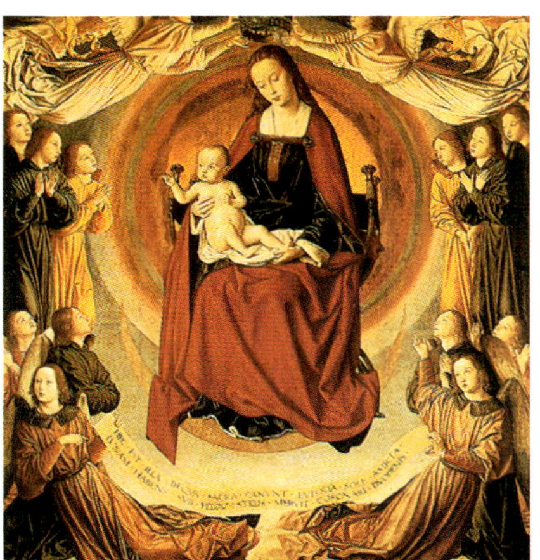

The Master of Moulins. Central Panel of the Moulins Triptych *(c. 1498–1499). Oil on panel, 111⅜ × 61⅝". Moulins Cathedral, Allier. In the painting of the Madonna and Child, a circular rainbow appears like a mystical aureola supported by the moon and bordered by a choir of angels who are crowning the Virgin. This idealized treatment contrasts with the realist representation of the side panels showing the royal family in a position to adore the Virgin.*

SIXTEENTH-CENTURY FRENCH PAINTING

Renaissance painting in the French *Cinquecento* was greatly affected by the reign of Francis I (1494-1547), whose taste for ostentation led him to direct the artistic activity of France. He entrusted it to the Italian artists for whom he did not hide his admiration, most notably Leonardo da Vinci and Titian.

Renaissance Portraiture in France

The interest in man that humanism introduced into intellectual circles of the fifteenth and sixteenth centuries doubtless reinforced the importance of portraiture as a reflection of the personality. Growing demand led to the appearance of specialists, generally of French, Dutch, and Flemish origin, who were trained in traditional styles. They maintained Flemish painting's great capacity for observing the realistic detail of their models, whom they represent in rather unimaginative poses, presumably as befitted the dignity of the person being represented.

In this period a genre of French portraiture develops, with its most important school found in the work of Jean and François Clouet.

The portraits of Jean Clouet (1485–1540) are characterized by the precision of their outlines, particularly when he works with the pictorial system of using three tones. This system has its roots firmly in Flemish art, but also shows a stylistic framework influenced by the Italian painters who worked at Fontainebleau.

Most notable of Jean Clouet's work is the famous *Portrait of Francis I* (between 1525 and 1530) in the Louvre, Paris; the portrait of the humanist *Guillaume Budé* (c. 1535) in the Metropolitan Museum, New York, and others that have been attributed to him without certainty: *Francis II as a Child* (Royal Museum, Ambères) and the *Portrait of Madame de Canaples* (National Gallery, Edinburgh). Jean Clouet's son François was also a painter.

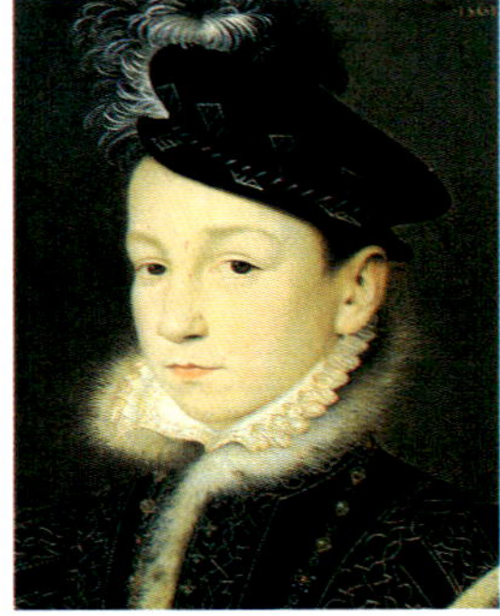

François Clouet. Charles IX *(1561). Oil on panel, $8^{1/4} \times 10$". Kunsthistorisches Museum, Vienna. The naturalism of this small portrait of the young King Charles IX is notable, corresponding to a desire for detail and elegance.*

The portraits of François Clouet, the son of Jean and a painter of four kings, evolve toward more complex frameworks. He abandoned the traditional bust and adopted the example of Bronzino, even arriving at full-length standing portraits, such as the one of *Henri II* (Uffizi Gallery) and of *Charles IX* (Kunsthistorisches Museum, Vienna). Only two of his paintings are signed: *Pierre Quthe* (1562) in the Louvre and a *Portrait of a Woman Bathing,* in the National Gallery, Washington.

The School of Fontainebleau

The most emblematic work in the French Renaissance is the decoration of the Palace of Fontainebleau, which was initiated by Francis I. As has already

Rosso Fiorentino. Gallery of Francis I *(c. 1533–1540). Fresco painting. Fontainebleau Palace, Seine-et-Marne. When the Italian painter Rosso Fiorentino arrived in France in 1530 he was already a well-known mannerist of acidic colors and harsh, precise lines. The* Gallery of Francis I *is the only part of his work in France that survives, although the Italian artist was the director of the whole series of frescoes in the palace.*

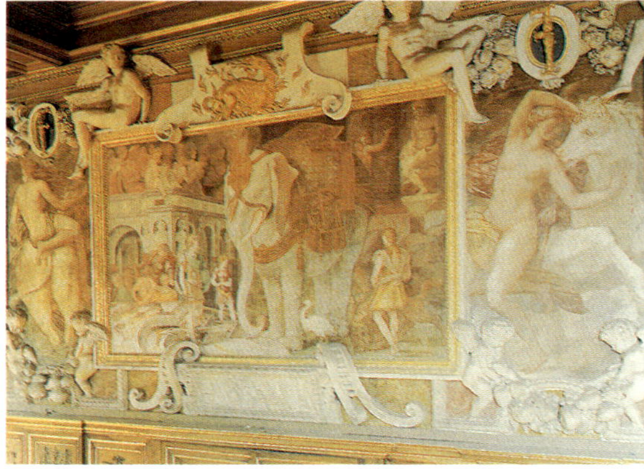

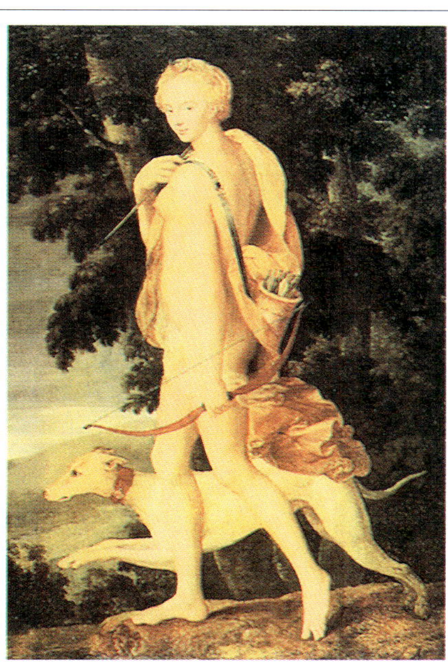

Anonymous French painter. Diana, Goddess of the Hunt *(middle of the sixteenth century). Oil on panel, 52⅜ × 75⅝". The Louvre, Paris. This is a theme, common during this period of French painting, of a female nude going to bathe, perhaps with allegorical meaning. In this case the painting is the masterful work of an unknown artist.*

been said, the real creators of the work were Italian artists: Rosso Fiorentino, Francesco Primaticcio, Nicoló Dell'Abate, and other lesser names who worked with them, such as Majorici and Pellegrini. These all had a great influence on the artists of France, who used fresco and stucco. The paintings and stucco works in the palace highlight the great predominance of the female nude, a form that the few French painters of the period also practiced.

Jean Cousin and the Anonymous Painters

Among the independent painters not attached to the royal workshops, Jean Cousin (1490–1560) is particularly important. His varied activity leans toward religious themes, although he is also attributed with one of the most disconcerting nudes of the entire Renaissance, known as *Eva Prima Pandora* in the Louvre.

Nevertheless, the most famous nudes of the French Renaissance are anonymous: *Diana, Goddess of the Hunt* (the Louvre, Paris) is a magnificent oil panel painted with a nude, life-size Diana walking with a dog. Some have seen in the painting the face and body of Diane de Poitiers.

Also of great interest is the anonymous double portrait of *The Duchess of Villiers and Her Sister Gabrielle de Estrées Bathing* (the Louvre), representing the symbolic eroticism of the Fontainebleau school. The painting seems to be an announcement by the Duchess of the imminent birth of the child of her sister, the king's lover.

The death of Primaticcio (1570) and of Nicoló Dell'Abate (1571), which led to the decline of Italian painting in the school of Fontainebleau, left the way free for less representative French painters, such as J. Goujon and Antoine Caron (1521–1599). The latter is more famous for organizing parties than for his Renaissance painting of the Fontainebleau school.

The so-called second school of Fontainebleau, moving away from the very precise decoration of the first school, begins with the work of decorating the castle under the orders of Henri IV.

French painting had to wait for the great period of Versailles, at the height of Baroque, before it would assume a more influential role within European art.

Jean Cousin. Eva Prima Pandora *(middle of the sixteenth century). Oil on panel, 59⅛ × 38½". The Louvre, Paris. This is an openly sensual work, though with an obscure symbolism. The erotic nude possibly has a moral content, given that the female figure reclines on a skull, and in the background can be seen an ancient city separated from us by a river, a typical symbol for death. Thus, the themes of the painting could refer to an allegory (vanitas) warning that the licentious past of the ancient world has no place in Catholic society.*

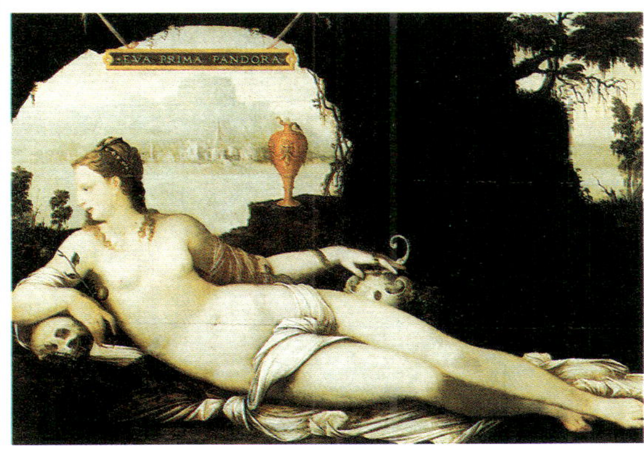

PAINTING IN TRANSITION, FIFTEENTH TO SIXTEENTH CENTURIES

The Flemish painting of the Van Eycks, Robert Campin (the Master of Flémalle), Rogier van der Weyden, and other fifteenth-century painters, all strongly rooted in the Gothic tradition, represents an artistic current that reached the highest levels of technical and stylistic perfection. Fifteenth-century Flemish painting, which influenced Gothic painting in the rest of the Mediterranean and Continental Europe, was never stylistically diluted by the Renaissance. For this reason, the Flemish and Dutch painters of the sixteenth century were reluctant to accept the new aesthetic from Italy. The Renaissance in Flanders and Holland was a late manifestation, highly adapted to a tradition steeped in gothicism.

Painters of the Transition. Quentin Metsys

Foremost among the painters of the Gothic tradition who began to show the influence of the Italian Renaissance was Quentin Metsys, a dominant figure in Flemish art at the end of the fifteenth century and the start of the sixteenth His painting maintains the fifteenth-century Flemish taste for the representation of objects, the exclusive use of oil paint, fluid and brilliant colors, and the traditional sculptural rigidity of clothing. Of his wide religious work are the triptych *Burial of Christ* (1511) from the Royal Fine Art Museum of Ambères, and the *Triptych of the Family of Saint Anne* (1509) in the Royal Fine Art Museum, Brussels. These are two monumental works representative of his Italo-Flemish sensibilities, which he translates into the realism of gesture and facial expression, and the importance of the background landscape. A follower of Leonardo and familiar

Quentin Metsys. Christ Presented to the People *(c. 1515). Oil on panel, 26¾ × 28". The Prado, Madrid. This is one of his main works.*

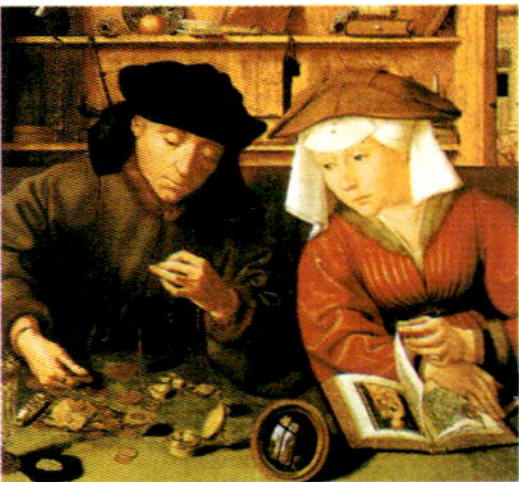

Quentin Metsys. The Banker and His Wife *(1514). Oil on panel, 28 × 26¾". The Louvre, Paris. Metsys breathed new life into Flemish art by directing it toward humanist themes and creating new formulas for the depiction of local customs. This painting shows the typical mastery of detail seen in the Flemish painters, particularly the concave mirror that reflects with perfect clarity the window in front of the scene as well as the presence of a third person.*

THE ARTIST'S LIFE

1466. Born in Lovaina. He is also known as Quentin de Smit, the Blacksmith, and the Marshal of Ambères. His father, a blacksmith by profession, dies when he is very young. The future painter follows this profession with his older brother, who is a notable smith.

1491. He forms part of the guild of Ambères.

1494. He marries Alyt van Tuyelt, with whom he has seven children.

1507. His wife dies.

1508. He remarries, to Catalina Heyns, with whom he has ten children. When the other great painter of his time, Patinir, dies, he looks after his two daughters as well. As master of the guild, he has various important painters as pupils: Ariaen (1495), Willen Muelenbroel (1501), Eduard Portugalois (1504), and Hennen Boeckmakere (1510).

1530. He dies in Ambères.

with the thinking of Erasmus of Rotterdam, Metsys pioneered a new humanist aspect in Flemish painting. This can be seen in *The Banker and His Wife* (1514) in the Louvre and in his portraits, notably his *Erasmus of Rotterdam* (Corsini Gallery, Rome), of whom he was a friend.

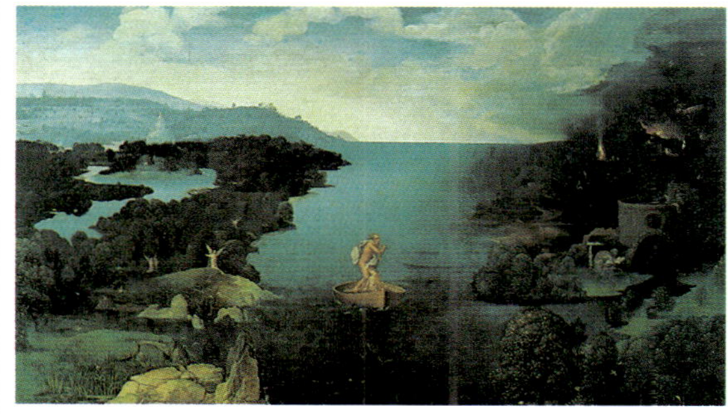

Joachim Patinir. Charon Crossing the River Styx *(c. 1515–1524). Oil on panel, 40½ × 25⅛". The Prado, Madrid. The beauty of the landscape makes one forget the subject of the painting, which shows a mixture of pagan and Christian traditions. To the left lies Paradise, with two angels who lead the saved to Jerusalem. In the center is the mythological boatman Charon, taking a soul across to Hades. Finally, to the right lies Hell, whose gates are guarded by the mythological hound Cerberus.*

Painters of the Transition. Joachim Patinir

Joachim Patinir is the second of the great Flemish painters in the period of transition. A friend and collaborator of Metsys, he was an excellent painter of landscapes, and directed his creativity toward humanism. Although his landscapes are imaginary, they are nevertheless approached rationally. Patinir's great achievement was to free landscape from its subordination to figures, and to give it a leading role in many of his religious works. His themes seem to be a pretext for planning large spaces in which the secondary figures provide atmosphere (farmers, animals) among whom he can place the figures who justify the title. In this sense Patinir was admired by Dürer and can be considered the first landscape painter in the history of art.

The Prado Museum has some of the most representative examples of Patinir's landscape work: *Rest on the Flight into Egypt, Landscape with Saint Jerome*, and *Charon Crossing the River Styx* (between 1515 and 1524), perhaps his masterpiece. In this work Charon's boat crosses the lake of the underworld between the delights of Paradise to the right, and to the left the great world of Hell. However, Charon himself, as well as the figures of the angels and devils and the fantastic architecture are incidental to the landscape, and are less important than the representation of the woods and fields, the waters of the lake, the stormy sky, and the dark region of Tartarus, guarded by Cerberus and lit only by fire.

Joachim Patinir. Rest on the Flight into Egypt *(c. 1515–1524). Oil on panel, 69¾ × 47⅝". The Prado, Madrid. Patinir was an excellent painter of landscapes. He gives them a humanist interpretation, constructing them rationally and giving them more importance than the religious subjects that he uses merely as a pretext.*

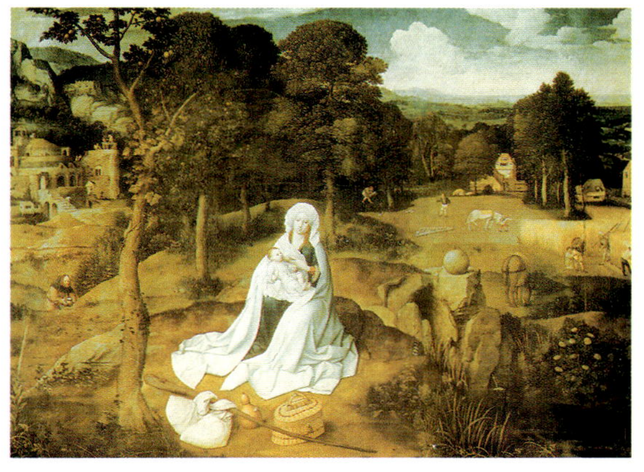

THE ARTIST'S LIFE

1480 or 1485. Born in Dinant.
1515. He enters the guild of Ambères. He marries his first wife Francisca Buyst.
1521. Francisca dies and he remarries, to Juana Noyts. One of the wedding guests is Dürer, with whom he had a close friendship arising from their many collaborations.
1519. He buys a house in Ambères.
1530. He dies in Amberes, leaving a son, Enrique, who is also a painter.

HIERONYMUS VAN AEKEN BOSCH

Within the Flemish Gothic tradition of the second half of the fifteenth century and the beginning of the sixteenth, the painter Hieronymus van Aeken Bosch is unique. He does not paint like a Flemish fifteenth-century Gothic artist, nor like a pre-Renaissance artist. He falls into the category of artists who are considered unique and very difficult to classify, having no predecessors with whom to compare them, and leaving no followers after them.

Bosch's Painting

The work of the artist best known as Hieronymus Bosch (in Spanish, El Bosco) combines elements taken from popular art of the Middle Ages (although he does not in any way follow the Gothic tradition). These he places within a fantastical picturesque world of illusory landscapes that show his complete mastery of perspective. He fills this world with creations of the most passionate surrealism, strange people, demons that could be either terrible or comic, and other monstrous beings that seem to have been taken from the world of gargoyles of Gothic cathedrals. All his work is rooted in a caricatured vision of humanity that, under a pretext of religiosity, mysticism, or allegory, he places equally in scenes full of terror or others full of humor.

It is true that, like Patinir, Hieronymus Bosch is a painter of fantastical landscapes, but the difference is that he takes his imagination to extremes that would not be reached again before the painting of the twenthieth century. His landscapes are designed to be part of a world of nightmares, dreams, grotesqueness, and irony.

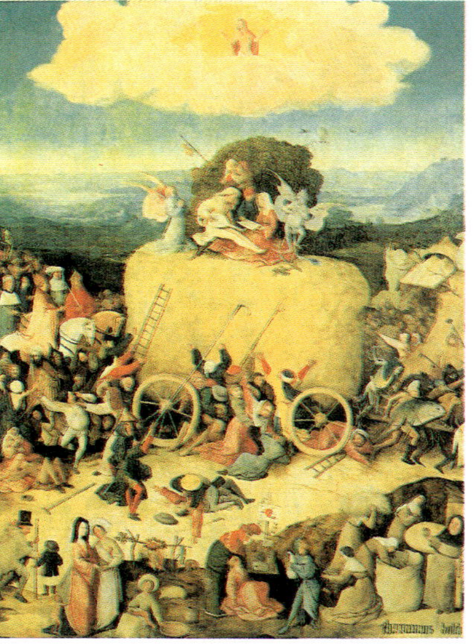

Hieronymus Bosch. The Hay Wagon. *Oil on panel, doors 17¾ × 53¼", central panel 39⅜ × 53¼". The Prado, Madrid. On the left cover panel of the triptych is a representation of Adam and Eve, The Temptation and the Banishment from Paradise, origin of all the problems that ravage humanity. In the central panel the hay wagon is shown, a scene inspired by a Flemish proverb: "The world is a hay wagon from which everyone takes what they can." On the right cover panel is a representation of hell, with the punishments of humanity's sins. In summary, it is a great moralizing and satirical work.*

The Work of Hieronymus Bosch

Little is known about the life of Hieronymus Bosch, including the dates of his work and the people for whom he worked.

The *Seven Deadly Sins* in the Prado is one of his first paintings in which he synthesizes the ethical-religious discourse that would dominate his work, the idea of human stupidity in failing to listen to divine exhortation.

The *Adoration of the Magi* (the Prado, Madrid). Madness, or at least extravagance, is one of the underlying themes in Bosch's painting, even in those works, such as this magnificent triptych, that seem to approach more

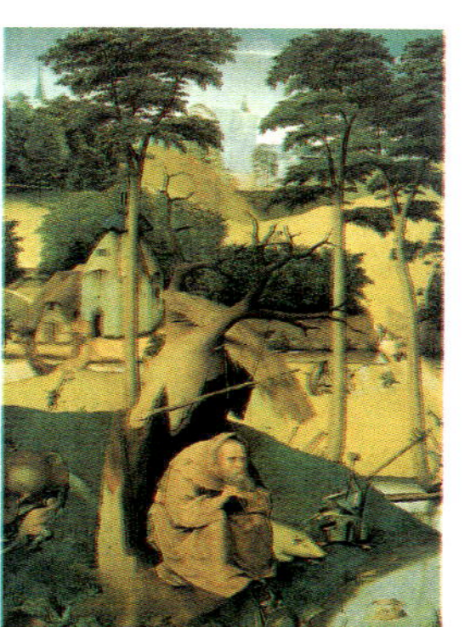

Hieronymus Bosch. The Temptations of Saint Anthony *(c. 1510). Oil on panel 20⅛ × 27⅝". The Prado, Madrid. This is one of Bosch's masterpieces, and an example of work from his late period. His technique is richer in color and chiaroscuro, and so the figures appear more monumental and individual. On the other hand, the landscape is more naturalistic and extends back deeply. This is one of Bosch's clearer works, although this does not mean it is without elements that are difficult to interpret.*

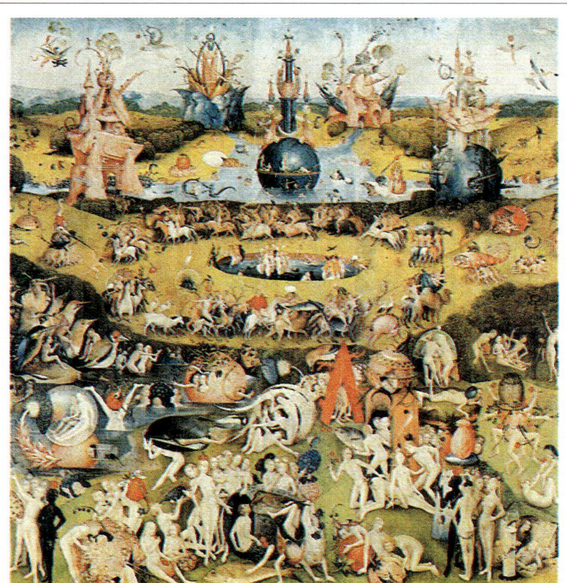

Hieronymus Bosch. The Garden of Earthly Delights *(early sixteenth century). Oil on panel, 76⅞ × 85⅝". The Prado, Madrid. This is one of the last works by the artist of Flemish origin. His iconography is enigmatic, although this is one of the works in which Bosch develops his characteristic language. Very close to twentieth-century surrealism, the painter gives his imagination free rein.*

orthodox methods. Not only the originality of this composition is surprising, but also the presence of the half-naked, anachronistic figure in the background.

The Ship of Fools (the Louvre) concerns the idea of humankind's madness, according to the satire of the German Sebastian Brant (1457–1521) in which members of society of the period (noblemen, judges, peasants, servants) embark on a boat to sail to Narregonia, the kingdom of madness.

Stone Operation or *Cure of Folly* (c. 1490), a satire against false science and its admirers, with a highly notable background landscape.

The Hay Wagon (the Prado, Madrid, with a copy in the Monastery of the Escorial) is an allegory related to a Flemish proverb, according to which the world is like a haystack (an environment in which all evil things can hide) from which men, even through terrible metamorphoses, try to take what they can.

The Garden of Earthly Delights (the Prado, Madrid), painted between 1485 and 1505, is without question one of his best conserved works. It is a triptych on the theme of Creation, the world, and hell, seen through Bosch's typically strange allegories. Closed, it represents the creation of the plant world. Any possible explanation, apart from always being open to debate, would require rivers of ink. A document from the Monastery of the Escorial dated July 8, 1593, calls the triptych "a painting of a worldly variety, marked with various *nonsense* by Bosch, which is called the Madroño painting." Nonsense refers to the fact that grotesque, naked figures writhe and squirm, while naked women bathe with birds on their heads, and very strange animals dedicate themselves to carnal pleasures (some couples are shut in a kind of glass egg), and mad figures throw themselves headfirst into the open mouths of fish-shaped creatures, while others crawl inside broken egg shells from which legs and arms emerge. The strawberries, mistaken for tree strawberries or madroños, which some of the figures carry on their backs, gave the painting the name "The Madroño Painting." This is said to be the symbol of sinful pleasure that, once experienced, can only lead to boredom: "The vainglory and brief gesture of the strawberry or madroño, with its little smell that is barely noticeable once it is gone."

Almost overlooked by these portentous stories is the attractiveness of his landscapes, which show the way toward a new pictorial rationalism. Bosch is notable for landscapes like: *Saint John the Evangelist on Patmos* (Gemäldegalerie, Dresden), *The Temptation of Saint Anthony,* in the Museum of Lisbon, and the triptych of *The Epiphany* (the Prado).

Bosch was born in Hertogenbusch (Bois-le-Duc) in Bramante (today a part of Holland), between 1460 and 1464, and died in the same city in 1516, leaving about 40 works, all of a high artistic and conceptual quality.

Hieronymus Bosch. The Ship of Fools. *Oil on panel, doors 17¾ × 53¼, central panel 39⅜ × 53¼". The Louvre, Paris.*

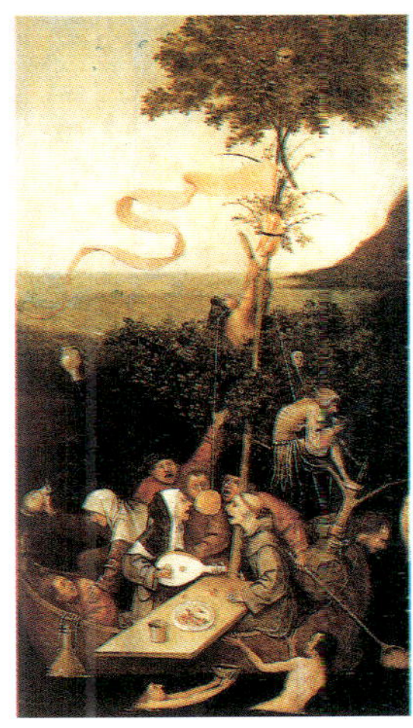

PIETER BRUEGEL THE ELDER

In the sixteenth century, Dutch painting saw a new school of painting flourish under the painter Pieter Bruegel, considered by many to be the founder of a genre that deals with popular custom and local tradition, depicting domestic scenes and rural activity.

The Painting of Pieter Bruegel the Elder

Although it is not immediately evident, the painting of this sixteenth-century artist is related to that of Hieronymus Bosch. However, where Bosch uses extravagant symbolism, in Bruegel this is translated into parables and anecdotes loaded with feeling. These are the logical evolution of a tradition-based painting that is, without a doubt, one of the most interesting manifestations of painting in the period of the Renaissance, although it is not closely related to the Italian aesthetic of the time. Like Bosch, Bruegel was a noted landscape painter, an innovative artist who created authentic land and seascapes in which he mixed the reality of the landscapes of his own country with elements of fantasy and views he had recorded during his visit to Italy.

Taken overall, Bruegel's painting is a chronicle of rural life. He paints parables that transform into art the way of life and traditions of the people of his country, with their customs, the extraordinary vitality they show in their celebrations, their way of relating to one another and their work. A good observer and painter of perspective, his paintings show a confident realism that verges on the grotesque, an element that gives his paintings a certain charge of drama.

Bruegel the Elder. Hunters in the Snow *(1565). Oil on panel, $63\frac{3}{4} \times 46$". Kunsthistorisches Museum, Vienna. The painting of Bruegel the Elder stands apart from the Italian models not just in technique but also in theme, as can be seen in this snow-covered landscape.*

Technically, the paintings of Bruegel the Elder show a very direct way of drawing and are well constructed in terms of perspective and foreshortening. As far as chromaticism is concerned, Bruegel shows an extraordinary instinct for coloring, which is clean, contrasting, and harmonious.

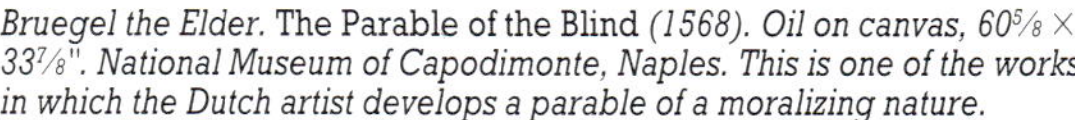

Bruegel the Elder. The Parable of the Blind *(1568). Oil on canvas, $60\frac{5}{8} \times 33\frac{7}{8}$". National Museum of Capodimonte, Naples. This is one of the works in which the Dutch artist develops a parable of a moralizing nature.*

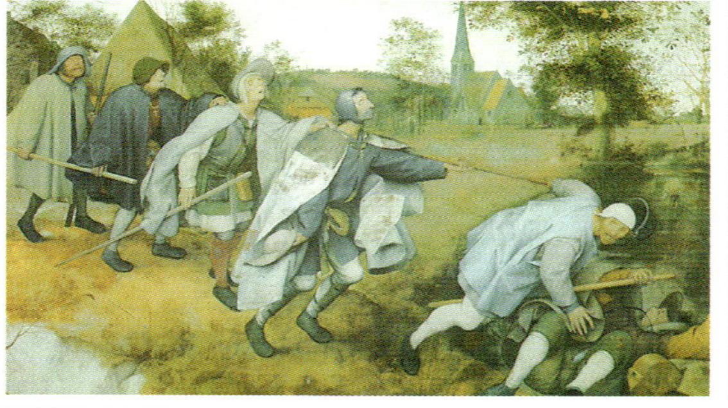

The Work of Bruegel the Elder

Bruegel left few works, fewer still if one considers his most original creations, the ones that show him as an innovative artist whose essential theme is nature, and the absolute integration of nature with human life.

Bruegel produced dramatic paintings with religious themes that were influenced by the work of Hieronymus Bosch, of whom he was a great copyist.

The Fall of the Rebel Angels (Royal Fine Art Museum, Brussels) shows a vision of hell

toward which the rebel angels are falling, transformed into grotesque, repellent monsters in a painting that stands alongside the most feverish inventions of Hieronymus Bosch.

The Triumph of Death (the Prado), c. 1560, is a painting with a clearly rhetorical intention. Very close to metaphysical painting and the Surrealism of the twentieth century, it shows a landscape that disappears into the horizon with a nightmare scene in which a motley multitude of spectral beings instigate scenes of death.

There is a particularly interesting collection of Bruegel's work in the Museum of Vienna (Kunsthistorisches Museum), beginning with his well-known *Tower of Babel* of 1563 and the *Massacre of the Innocents* of 1566. These paintings transfer biblical stories to locations from the painter's surroundings, complete with anecdotes and popular touches, and showing the green or snow-covered valleys, the people, and the traditional houses.

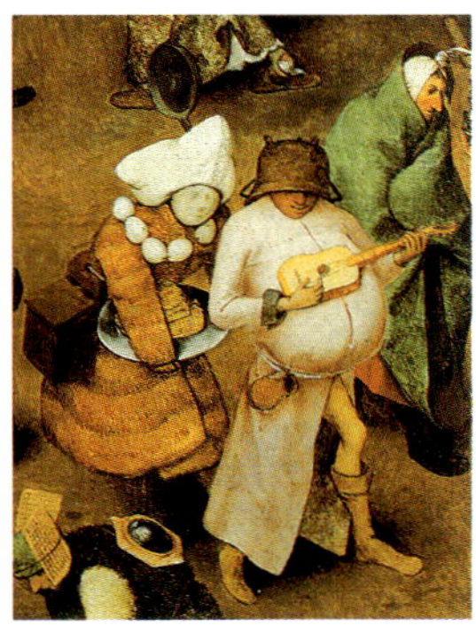

Bruegel the Elder. The Fight between Carnival and Lent *(1599), detail. Oil on panel, 46⅜ × 64¾". Kunsthistorisches Museum, Vienna. In addition to the symbolic aspects of the painting, which has strongly religious content, one can see Bruegel's liking for popular themes.*

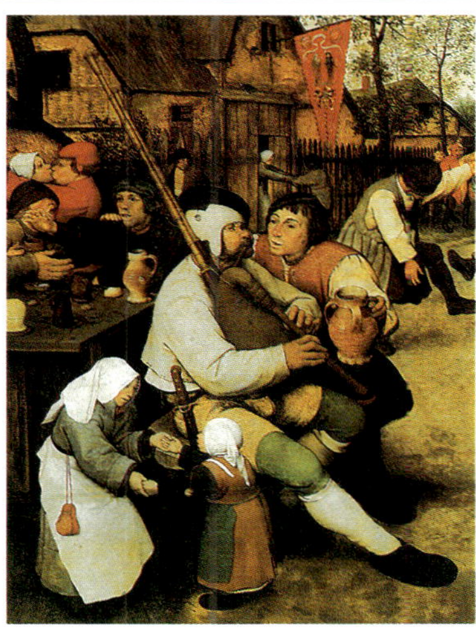

Bruegel the Elder. Peasant Dance *(1568). Oil on panel, 65 × 96½". Kunsthistorisches Museum, Vienna. Bruegel the Elder was very interested in the rural world and was an exceptional observer of the activities of his contemporaries, reflected in work that is a chronicle of its time.*

The Visit of the Holy Family to Bethlehem (Royal Fine Art Museum of Belgium) is another of his best-known paintings, in the same vein as the previous two.

The Bruegel of rural, country scenes is best represented in the following paintings, in the Kunsthistorisches Museum:

Peasant Dance (c. 1568). This painting of an open-air celebration in front of the humble houses of a Dutch village draws the viewer, for one marvelous instant, into a festive gathering in which peasants throw themselves into a spirited scene of dancing, drinking, and making love. The faces of the people, despite their realism, prove to be somewhat caricatured. The grotesque aspect of life is one of the most attractive social elements of Bruegel's work.

Return of the Hunters (1565). In a winter landscape entirely dominated by the white and greenish blues of snow and ice, three hunters come down a mountainside with their dogs, supposedly on their way home, in the valley, where the frozen water has formed skating rinks full of happy skaters. It is a marvelous study in atmosphere and perspective.

In the final stage of his life Bruegel adopted a critical attitude toward society, which shows itself in his representations of certain parables:

The Misanthrope, signed and dated in 1568, whose satirical intentions are difficult to interpret, and *The Parable of the Blind,* also of 1568, both in the National Museum of Capodimonte, Naples. This parable shows a pathos and richness of facial detail that is truly moving. It illustrates the parable of the Gospel of Saint Matthew (15,14) "...if the blind lead the blind they will both fall into the same ditch."

THE ARTIST'S LIFE

c. 1520–1525. Born to a family of Dutch origin (Hertogenbosch). It is not known where.

1545. In about this year he was a pupil of Pieter Koeck van Aelst and of Hieronymus Cock. For him he painted some reproductions of Bosch.

1551. He is admitted into the guild of Ambères.

1552–1553. He visits Italy. Magnificent paintings and sketches survive from this trip, especially of Alpine landscapes.

1563. Having returned from Italy, he moves from Ambères to Brussels.

1569. He dies in Brussels.

ALBRECHT DÜRER

Dürer is the most important representative of the Renaissance in Germany, and one of the most prestigious non-Italian artists of the fifteenth and sixteenth centuries. He is a complete humanist who brings to painting an interest in nature and in the science of drawing. In this respect Dürer represents in the Germanic world what Leonardo did in the Italian.

The Painting of Dürer

Dürer was an extremely talented draftsman, an artist who, with charcoal, chalk, a quill, an engraver's chisel, or a paintbrush could reproduce the most insignificant of details and give them the same artistic quality that he conferred on all his compositions. He achieved a perfect synthesis between the thematic and decorative richness of Gothic art and the dynamism and naturalism of Italian painting.

Although it has been said that German artists are better suited to lyricism, German poets and musicians have also been great admirers of Italian art, almost certainly because in it they find the clarity, order, and simplicity not found in Northern European traditions. More than any other German artist, Dürer represents the universality and objectivity of the new language of Renaissance classicism, although he was still able to remain within the medieval world in order to maintain its inherent wealth of fantasy and lyricism.

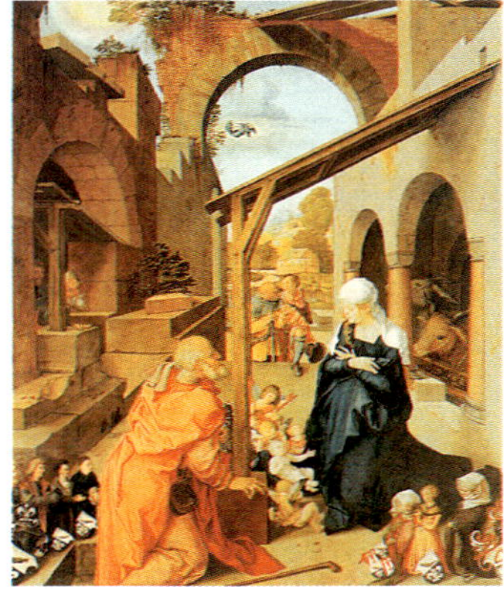

Dürer. Birth of Christ *(1503–1504). Oil on panel, 49⅝ × 61". Paumgartner Altar. Alte Pinakothek, Munich. This painting is dominated by a taste that lies between classicism and romanticism, between veneration for the classical past in the arches and architectural elements and nostalgia for this past, which is in ruins. It shows a combination of these references and a compositional structure of geometrical elements that form a trajectory through the arcades and columns.*

In form and coloration, Dürer's painting reveals his early training influenced by the Flemish and Germanic traditions, to which is added the Italian influence of Bellini, Pollaiolo, and Mantegna.

Dürer's Work

Dürer's work is multifaceted: His artistic legacy consists of about seventy oil paintings done on canvas or wood, about a thousand drawings and watercolors, a hundred or so copperplate engravings, and some two hundred woodcuts.

A good part of this work is dedicated to religious themes, mostly from the New Testament.

Dürer. Adoration of the Trinity *(1511). Oil on panel, 48⅝ × 53¼". Kunsthistorisches Museum, Vienna. Compared with the* Birth of Christ, *the geometry is no longer provided by architectural elements that dominate the space, but by the figures themselves in the painting.*

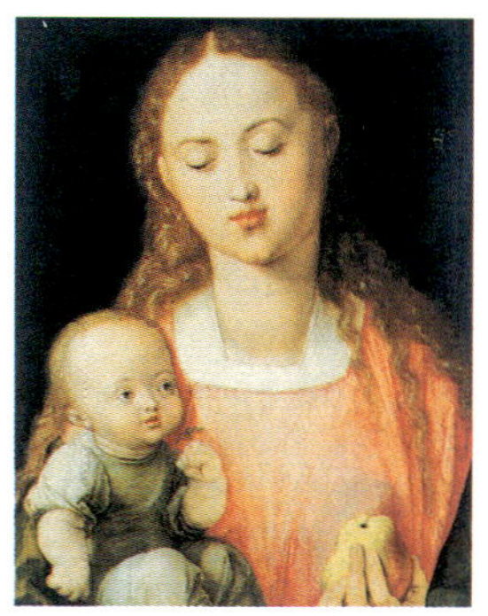

Dürer. Virgin of the Pear *(1526). Oil on panel, 12½ × 16⅞". Uffizi Gallery, Florence. This is an example of the rich iconography with which Dürer understands the motives for his painting and for his mastery of portraiture.*

When he paints or engraves themes from the Old Testament, it seems that he does so in order to study the human nude. In his engraving of *Adam and Eve* of 1504 (Gabinete de Estampas, Berlin), he applies, for the first time, the classical proportions of the human body (specifically the canon of eight heads of Vitrubio), while maintaining the stillness that gives the figures *contrapposto.* Three years later, in 1507, he created the first life-size nudes in German painting: *Adam and Eve*, (the Prado) are two nudes with the attributes to identify them with the characters in the Bible. The *contrapposto* that is still visible in Adam disappears in Eve, and is replaced by movement. The anatomy loses hardness and the bodies acquire the suggestive sensuality of the Venetian Renaissance.

If Adam and Eve were the pretexts that allowed Dürer to investigate the problems of the human form, themes from the New Testament were the pretext for the study of composition and space. In *Adoration of the Magi* (1504) in the Uffizi Gallery, and the *Birth of Christ,* painted between 1498 and 1504 for the Paumgarter Altar (today in the Alte Pinakothek, Munich), the study of space is strictly a problem of geometric perspective. In contrast, in his mature works, such as *Adoration of the Trinity* of 1511 (Kunsthistorisches Museum, Vienna), the definition of space becomes a matter of composition, that is resolved by the distribution of the figures.

The theme of The Passion in paintings and engravings was very dear to Dürer, as was the theme of the Madonna and Child. Examples include *Adoration of the Child* (1496–1497) for the altar of Dresden, *Madonna and Child with Pear* (Kunsthistorisches Museum, Vienna), which is very clearly in the German iconographic tradition, and another *Virgin of the Pear* (1526) in the Uffizi Gallery. Combining the German tradition and the greater naturalism of the Italian tradition, Dürer was able to focus the theme so that it approaches portraiture.

From his final period are the panels of *Saint John and Saint Peter* and *Saint Paul and Saint Mark* (Alte Pinakothek, Munich).

Dürer's *Self-portrait with Gloves* in the Prado (1502) and *Self-portrait with Fur-lined Coat* in the Alte Pinakothek, Munich (1500) explore most deeply the painter's own character. His *Portrait of a Young Woman* of 1505 (Kunsthistorisches Museum, Vienna), *Jacob Muffel* of 1526, and his *Hieronymus Holzschuher* (Gemäldegalerie, Dresden) show the prodigious detail with which Dürer painted his models.

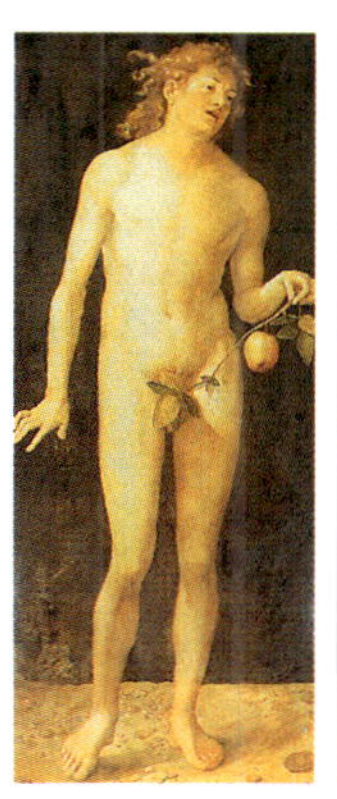

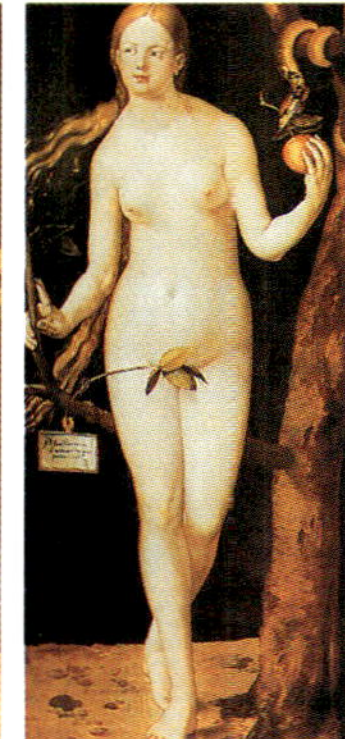

Dürer. Adam and Eve *(1507). Oil on panel, 32⅝ × 82¼". The Prado, Madrid. For Dürer, the treatment of themes from the Old Testament is no more than a pretext for carrying out a work. In this case, Adam and Eve are a pretext for Dürer to devote himself to the subject of the nude.*

THE ARTIST'S LIFE

1471. Born in Nuremberg, the son of a goldsmith.

1486–1490. He is an apprentice with his father and the sculptor Michael Wolgemut.

1490. He finishes his apprenticeship and travels to various German cities.

1494. He returns to Nuremberg and marries Ines Frey. Soon afterwards he travels to Italy.

1496. He sets up his workshop in Nuremberg, where he travels intensely as a painter and engraver, becoming well known and popular throughout Europe.

1505. He travels to Italy for the second time.

1512. He is hired by the Emperor Maximillian I to paint his portrait and produce a collection of engravings.

1519–1520. Following the death of Maximillian, he travels to the low countries and meets the new Emperor, Charles V. He is received by the foremost Flemish painters of the time.

1525. Back in Nuremberg, he spends the final years of his life dedicating himself to writing his technical treatises.

1528. He dies in Nuremberg.

OTHER REPRESENTATIVES OF THE GERMAN RENAISSANCE

The figure of Albrecht Dürer overshadows the work of the other German painters. Nevertheless, they have their own place in the history of art as artists of strong character who lived through the transition from the fifteenth to the sixteenth century, while the Italian Renaissance was conquering the art of Europe. Above all, German artists expressed the Germanic spirituality that had its aesthetic roots in Flemish Gothic.

Matthias Grünewald

Little is known of the life of this painter who was possibly born in Würzburg c. 1480 and died in Halle in 1528. Grünewald is considered the most genuine of the German artists known for the expression of great pathos. In his Crucifixions, he expresses the tragedy of the humiliation of Christ. The Christ in his *Crucifixion* (1500-1502) in the Art Museum of Basel, dies, overcome by pain and grief, with his begging hands, his breast swollen with spasms, and his feet deformed by the weight of his broken body. In this and other crucifixions, the tragedy is echoed in the shadowy landscape that surrounds it, a landscape not related to rationalism but rather with sources of knowledge of a supernatural or magical nature.

Cranach the Elder

Lucas Cranach was named after the village of Kranach, where he was born in 1472. He became a painter in the service of the Dukes of Saxony, in Wüttemberg, where he became a friend of Martin Luther, whose portrait he painted in 1529, now in the Uffizi Gallery. In the field of portraits, Cranach expressed himself with balanced realism, very different from the feeling, between idealism and expressionism, of some of his religious works, such as *Flight into Egypt* (1504) in the Gemäldegalerie, Dresden, and the panel *Paradise* (1530), in the Kunsthistorisches Museum, Vienna.

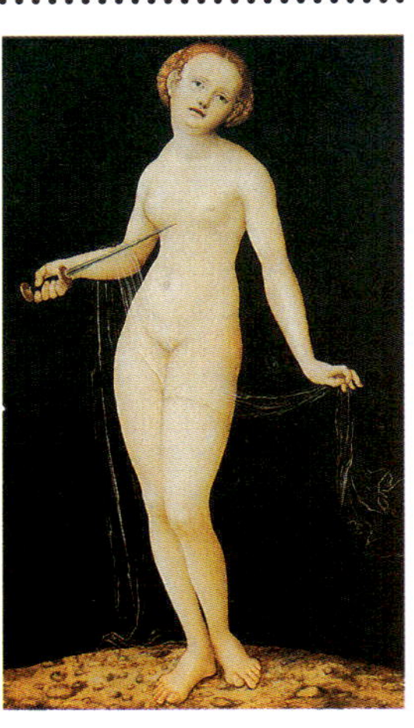

Cranach the Elder. Lucretia *(1532). Oil on panel, 9⅝ × 14¾". Gallery of the Academy, Vienna. Humanism and the Reformation liberated the female body from its medieval ostracism. Following the teaching of Luther, the nudes of Cranach emphasize the decisive importance of women in married life, and are very different from the Christian models of the adoration of the Virgin and the most sensual models of the Mediterranean.*

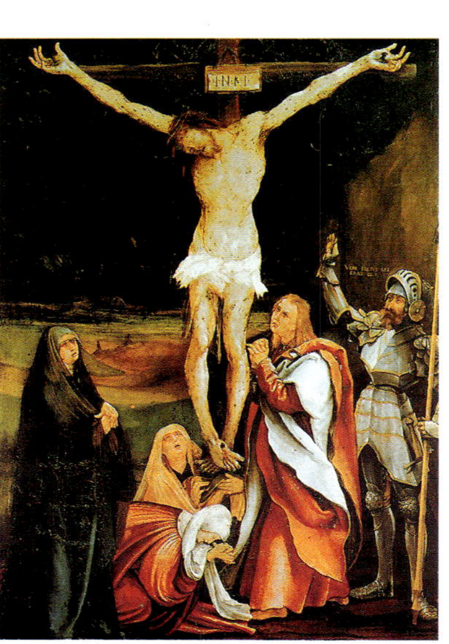

Grünewald. Crucifixion. *Oil on panel, 20⅝ × 28¾". Art Museum of Basel. Grünewald's art is characterized by mystical rapture and dramatic realism, in which the serenity of Dürer is replaced by tragic tension. Because of his deformed figures and the shadowy nature of his themes, the work of this German painter does not really fit into the Renaissance, but rather corresponds to the loss of security typical of mannerism.*

Despite its drama, such as in the *Great Crucifixion* of 1503 in the Pinakothek, Munich, for example, Cranach's religious painting shows a sentimentality that is more poetic than pathetic. It was perhaps this feeling for lyrical naturalism that led Cranach to cultivate the female nude, which he interpreted with an entirely Germanic personality. His female bodies do not share the morbidity of the Mediterranean nude. *Lucretia* of 1532 (Gallery of the Academy, Vienna), with her slim waist, rounded stomach, adolescent's face, and long legs,

represents the sixteenth-century Germanic ideal of the female figure.

Around 1530, Lucas Cranach painted his final works: *The Hunt* of 1529 and *Judith with the Head of Holofernes* (both in the Kunsthistorisches Museum, Vienna). His coloring as a great painter still stands out. He died in Wüttemberg in 1553, having ceased painting because of business and public obligations.

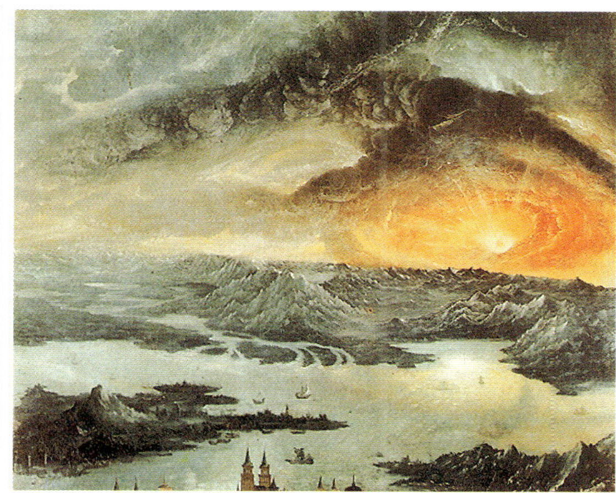

Altdorfer. Battle of Alexander *(1528). Oil on panel, 62⅛ × 47¼". Alte Pinakothek, Munich. In Altdorfer's paintings the subject becomes a simple excuse to develop the artist's true interest: landscape. His is a turbulent landscape, an expression of feelings that initiates the movement in Germany and its importance during the Romantic period.*

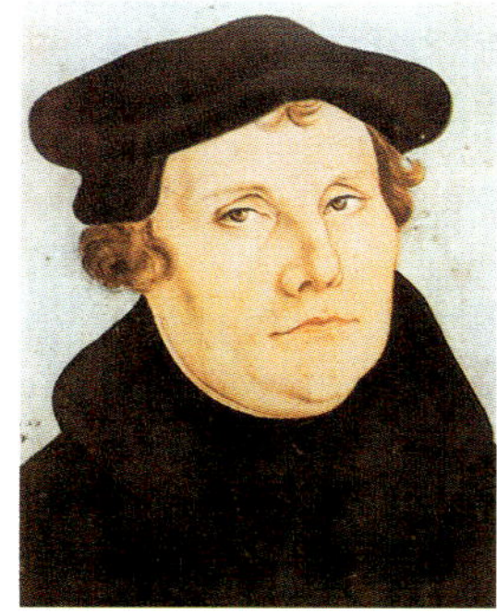

Cranach the Elder. Luther *(1529). Oil on panel, 9 × 14¾". Uffizi Gallery, Florence.*

Albrecht Altdorfer

Albrecht Altdorfer, born c. 1480, was a municipal architect in the city of Regensburg from 1526 until his death in 1538. However, it was not architecture that brought him his fame but rather his painting, which was completely divorced from Flemish and Italian influences. It has been said, rightly, that Altdorfer's painting emphasizes emotion over action. In his work, the thematic motifs are always secondary to nature, which is depicted with unusual fantasy and grandeur, with its woods and trees, its threatening skies, and its dawns and sunsets, all of which reveal the state of mind of the figures in the painting. The themes are no more than anecdotes that get lost in the grandeur of nature as occurs in *Saint George and the Dragon* (1510) in the Alte Pinakothek, Munich. Similarly, in *Susana Bathing,* of 1526 (also in the Alte Pinakothek) the theme remains physically camouflaged. Altdorfer's main interest was the creation of a landscape transformed into an architecture of dreams and caprices.

The use of landscape as a pictorial entity amplifies its importance to a degree up to now inconceivable. In *Danube Landscape with Castle Worth near Regensburg,* for example, in the Alte Pinakothek, Munich, he paints purely with the object of representing a landscape. Similarly, in *Battle of Alexander* (1528) in the same museum, he depicts a sensational panorama in which he combines the masses moving around the battlefield with a landscape representation of Creation, when the waters separate and the sun appears on the horizon to reveal the grandeur of the Earth.

While Altdorfer's main theme was landscape, from 1525 his painting dealt with the human figure in themes that allowed him to investigate the expression of human passions, as in *Lot and his Daughters* (1537) in the Alte Pinakothek, Munich.

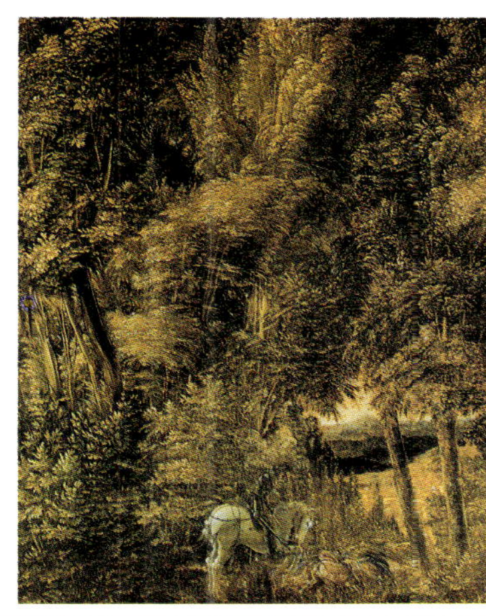

Altdorfer. Saint George and the Dragon *(1510). Oil on panel, 8⅝ × 11¾". Alte Pinakothek, Munich.*

HANS HOLBEIN THE YOUNGER

This important artist brings to a close our succinct description of the painting of the Renaissance, a flowering in culture that greatly ennobled humankind, despite the upheavals in Europe during the fifteenth and sixteenth centuries.

The Painting of Hans Holbein the Younger

Holbein was a German painter who definitively abandoned the Gothicism that was still visible in the work of Albrecht Dürer and Grünewald. Instead, his aim was to express himself with absolute realism, guided by humanism that he cultivated with passion and conviction, doubtless influenced by his friendship with Erasmus of Rotterdam.

The humanism of his painting is profoundly German, and through it he expresses the human condition, both in his religious paintings and in his portraits. He was an exponent of sincere, and at times dramatic, naturalism to which he adds, with the passing of time, a growing symbolism. Occasionally, his understanding of Italian art manifests itself in the architectural elements of his paintings.

As a portrait painter, Hans Holbein the Younger paints his models with objectivity and extreme detail. Holbein does not show their success through grace or the sublime, but rather through balance, serenity, and the psychological and symbolic aspects of the painting.

Hans Holbein the Younger. Erasmus of Rotterdam *(1523) Tempera on panel, 13 × 16⅞". The Louvre, Paris. This is one of the four portraits Holbein painted of the Dutch thinker. The two men were great friends, which can be seen in the understanding each had of their humanistic contribution to their particular fields.*

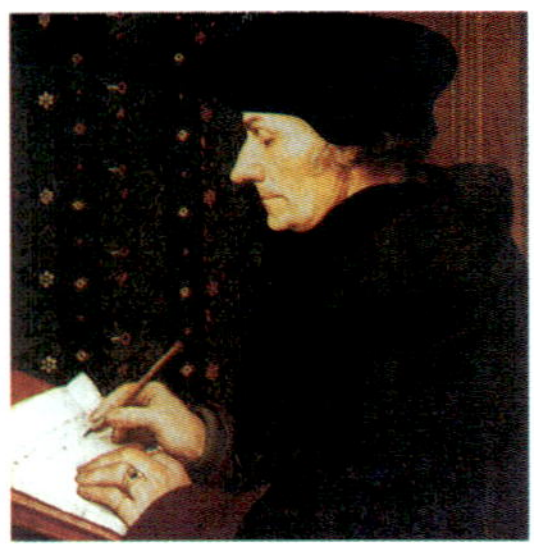

The Work of Holbein the Younger

From his first period, one must mention the decorative work he created for the house of the burgomaster Hertenstein in Lucerne (c. 1517), which was sadly destroyed in 1825.

Although not yet completely artistically mature, his first period in Basel was intense and productive. Apart from his portraits, Holbein produced one of the best examples of dramatic naturalism in *Christ in the Tomb* (1521–1522) in the Offentliche Kunstammlung, Basel. It is an entirely humanist version of the entombed body of Christ. With this painting, Holbein expresses a human, rather than idealized, divine quality of Christ.

As an engraver, he was highly valued by the publishers of Basel, thanks to his illustrations for *In Praise of Folly* by Erasmus. As a humanist who painted the greatest humanists of his time (Erasmus and Thomas More), Hans Holbein the Younger left his most outstanding work in the art of portraiture.

In his portrait of *Jacob Meyer and his wife Dorotea Kannengiesser* (1516) in the Offentliche Kunstammlung, Basel, one of the first works he painted in the Swiss city, Italianate architecture frames the figures.

His *Erasmus of Rotterdam* of 1523 in the Louvre, shows, beyond question, one of the moments in which Holbein was able to express best and most deeply the affable irony and enormous internal strength of this great humanist. Ten years later, in approximately 1532, another representation (*Erasmus of Rotterdam,* Offentliche Kunstammlung, Basel) reveals the same character, perhaps accentuated by Erasmus' ironic facial expression.

Holbein the Younger, the Greatest Painter of the English Renaissance

Painting in sixteenth-century England only reached a notable level with the work of the German painter Holbein, first between 1526 and 1528 and later between 1532 and his death in 1543. Protected by Sir Thomas More and as a painter in the court of Henry VIII, Holbein's

Hans Holbein the Younger. Christ in the Tomb *(1521–1522). Tempera on panel, 78¾ × 12". Offentliche Kunstammlung, Basel. Hans Holbein was the German painter who understood the I talian Renaissance most deeply. In this painting, the artist portrays a human Christ with humanist drama, which in some way is a Northern European response to Mantegna's* Dead Christ.

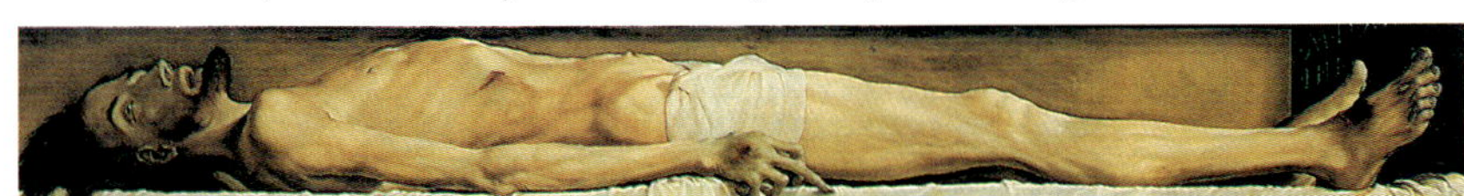

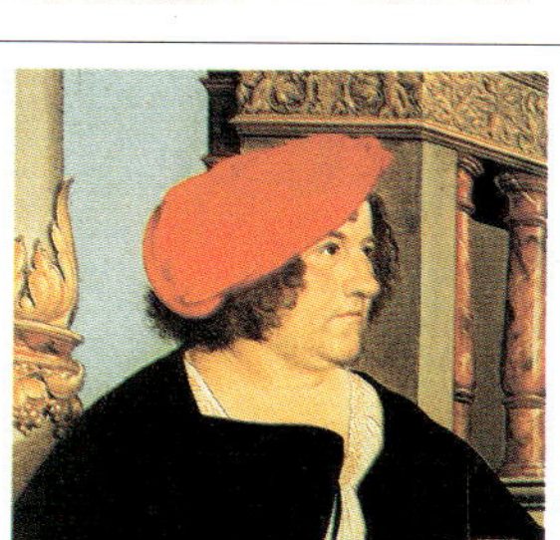
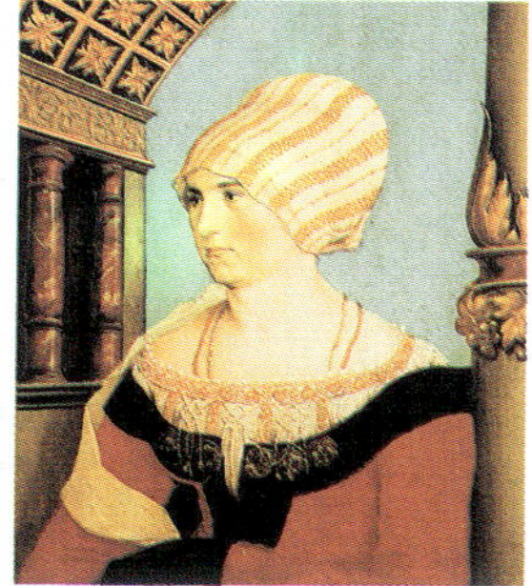

Hans Holbein the Younger. Jacob Meyer and his wife Dorotea Kannengiesser *(1516). Tempera on panel, 12⅛ × 15⅛". Offentliche Kunstammlung, Basel. Painted after his return from England, it is part of a series of portraits of wealthy merchants that made Hans Holbein famous.*

portrait work was extensive and of the highest quality, from his *Portrait of Lady Guildford* of 1527 to what is considered his masterpiece, *The Ambassadors* of 1533, in the National Gallery. It is a double, full-length portrait of Jean de Dinteville, ambassador of Francis I, and the archbishop of Lavour. The humanist investigates the themes of love and death, by means of symbolism of objects and a distorted skull that emerges between the two figures.

As a painter for Henry VIII, he painted portraits of the king that express the grandeur of power. *Henry VIII,* in the Thyssen-Bornemisza Collection, is perhaps the most representative.

His portrait of *Nicholas Kratzer* (c. 1528) in the Louvre, Hans Holbein emphasizes the symbolism of objects, instilling them with sensitivity and minute detail. The mental concentration that can be seen in the face of the astronomer is linked to the objects he has in his hands.

Portrait of the Merchant Georg Gisze (1532) in the Gemäldegalerie, Dresden, is one of the most outstanding of Holbein's works, not for the portrait itself, but for everything that surrounds it: wall hangings, furniture, and objects, from which it is possible to reproduce the atmosphere of the merchant's life.

Jane Seymour, the third wife of Henry VIII, *John Chambers* (Kunsthistorisches Museum, Vienna) and many others show how the drama of German Renaissance painting loses its strength in the English work of the most important German painter since Dürer.

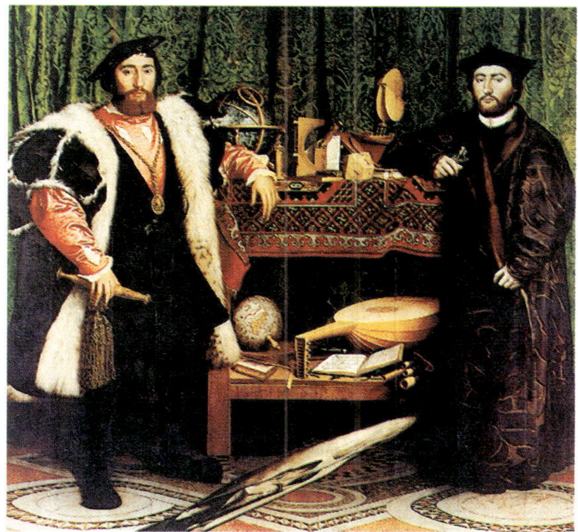

Hans Holbein the Younger. The Ambassadors *(1533). Tempera on panel, 42⅞ × 81⅛". National Gallery, London. This is one of the best-known works by the German artist, in which he gives free rein to an entire universe of symbolic elements and attributes. The mathematical, physical, and cartographic instruments on the top shelf refer to the new sciences that were discovering truths about the world. On the lower shelf, the books are a symbol of spiritual nourishment. However, the broken string on the lute symbolizes the futility of life.*

THE ARTIST'S LIFE

1497. Born in Augsburg.
1515. He moves to Basel and works as an engraver.
1517. He travels to Lucerne to decorate the house of the burgomaster Hertenstein.
1519. He returns to Basel, gets married, and establishes a workshop.
1523. He meets Erasmus of Rotterdam and paints the first of four portraits of him.
1526–1528. Because of the puritanism of the Reformation, Holbein moves to England.
1532. After going back to Basel, he establishes himself definitively in England.
1536. He is named court painter of Henry VIII.
1543. He dies in London, victim of the plague.

Original title of the book in Spanish: *El Renacimiento*

Published by Parramón ediciones, S.A., Barcelona, Spain.
Author: Parramón's Editorial Team
Illustrators: Parramón's Editorial Team

All inquiries should be addressed to:
Barron's Educational Series, Inc.
250 Wireless Boulevard
Hauppauge, New York 11788
http://www.barronseduc.com

International Standard Book No. 0-7641-5103-7

Library of Congress Catalog Card No. 98-74721

Printed in Spain

9 8 7 6 5 4 3 2 1

Front cover:
Michelangelo. *The Last Judgment* (detail).
Sandro Botticelli. *The Birth of Venus* (detail).
Leonardo da Vinci. *La Gioconda (Mona Lisa)* (detail).

Back cover:
Sandro Botticelli. *The Birth of Venus* (detail)
Bronzino. *Lucretia Panciatichi.*
Michelangelo. *The Oracle of Delphi* (detail).

Note: The titles that appear at the top of the odd-numbered pages correspond to:

The previous chapter
The current chapter
The following chapter